You Can't Make Me!

This book is dedicated to the millions of teachers and parents who are heroes in their children's lives and to the children, themselves, who deal every day with a world that isn't always ready for the beauty and challenges they present.

You Can't Make Me!

From Chaos to Cooperation in the Elementary Classroom

Sylvia Rockwell

CORWIN PRESS
A SAGE Publications Company
Thousand Oaks, CA 91320

KH

For information:

Corwin Press
A Sage Publications Company
2455 Teller Road
Thousand Oaks, California 91320
www.corwinpress.com

Sage Publications Ltd.
1 Oliver's Yard
55 City Road
London EC1Y 1SP
United Kingdom

Sage Publications India Pvt. Ltd.
B-42, Panchsheel Enclave
Post Box 4109
New Delhi 110 017 India

Printed in the United States of America

Library of Congress Cataloging-in-Publication Data

Rockwell, Sylvia.
You can't make me!: From chaos to cooperation in the elementary classroom/Sylvia Rockwell.
      p. cm.
Includes bibliographical references and index.
ISBN 1-4129-1661-5 or 9781412916615 (cloth)
ISBN 1-4129-1662-3 (pbk.)
   1. Problem children—Education (Elementary) 2. Problem children—Behavior modification. 3. Classroom management. I. Title.
LC4801.R62 2007
372.139'3—dc22

                                        2006009842

This book is printed on acid-free paper.

06 07 08 09 10   9 8 7 6 5 4 3 2 1

Acquisitions Editor:	Kathleen McLane
Editorial Assistant:	Jordan Barbakow
Typesetter:	C&M Digitals (P) Ltd.
Indexer:	Pam VanHuss
Cover Designer:	Lisa Miller

2/7/08

Contents

List of Figures

Preface

Teaching children to behave—to act responsibly—takes a tremendous amount of time and energy. There are no magic potions or solutions. Some children by temperament are easier to manage than others. All children, however, have the right to be taught. The good news is that most behaviors are learned. If we, the educators and parents, do not like the behaviors children present, it is our responsibility to teach new, more satisfactory behaviors.

Years ago, when I was still a student in high school, I saw a movie about Helen Keller. In one scene, Helen's teacher, Anne Sullivan, asked the parents to leave the dining room so she could teach Helen to sit in her chair, use a spoon, wipe her face with a napkin, and keep her hands in her own plate. Helen's well-meaning and loving parents had allowed her to run around the table grabbing from whatever plate or bowl was available. They did not believe she could be taught because of her blindness and deafness. Anne understood that unless Helen was taught to behave in socially acceptable ways, her quality of life would be horrific. As she grew older and larger physically, she would be institutionalized. Helen fought like a wet cat initially, but she did, in fact, learn to eat at the table like a young lady. As we well know, Helen eventually learned to read, write, and speak. Instead of living out her days in a dreary residential hospital, she traveled, inspired many, and led an incredibly productive life.

I have chosen to dedicate my professional life to children who need desperately to learn how to behave. The children with whom I have worked have typically had average or higher levels of intelligence and do not suffer from severe, multiple disabilities such as deafness and blindness. Some of these children have been abused, sexually molested, or severely neglected. Some have been abandoned by their parents. Some have psychiatric disorders. Some are considered to be socially maladjusted. Some have been in general education classrooms. Others have been diagnosed with disabilities. What all of them have in common, however, is the ability to learn. I might have to structure those learning experiences and the environment in which they occur more rigidly for some than for others. The process might be much lengthier for some than for others. The number of additional people necessary to implement an effective plan might vary. The one constant across all settings and all children is the self-righting potential each individual possesses. Corrective teaching facilitates and strengthens that self-righting potential. The spirit and intent of this book is to foster the self-righting potential within the lives of students who others may believe to be beyond hope and help. Some of the information and anecdotes are more applicable to general education elementary-level classrooms. Other information and anecdotes are more applicable to special education elementary-level classrooms. General guiding principles are applicable in both settings. I have chosen to address the full continuum of educational settings in this book because of the emphasis on inclusionary practices and the need for all educators to understand children who exhibit challenging behaviors.

Although the stories shared in this book are true, critical identifying information about the children has been changed to protect who they are now as well as who they will grow to be in the future.

Acknowledgments

While a person may decide on her own to fail, no one succeeds at anything entirely on her own. I have been blessed with a wonderful family—John, my husband; Kala, Donnie, and Jesse, my children; Brad and Kasey, my grandchildren; and a loving, supportive extended family. Their presence is a constant source of inspiration.

In addition, many friends, contributed to this work—Beth and Ernie served as readers during the development of the manuscript and provided invaluable feedback; Gwen, Susan, and Kathleen asked thought-provoking and motivating questions; and Michele, Fran, and Linda shared the laughter and the tears behind the stories of the very real children described in these pages.

In addition, Corwin Press gratefully acknowledges the contributions of the following reviewers:

Alyssa M. Carter, Director of Special Education
    Kuna Joint School District No. 3, Kuna, Idaho

Mary Guerrette, Director of Special Education
    Maine School Administrative District No. 1 (M.S.A.D.),
    Presque Isle, Maine

Philip S. Greengus, Special Education Instructor
    Echo Glen School, Snoqualmie, Washington

Rachel M. Babson, MSW, Behavior Specialist
    Issaquah School District, Issaquah, Washington

Rosemary Richards, Special Education Teacher
    Pryor, Oklahoma

Thomas E. Bell, M.Ed., LPC, Associate Director, Licensed Professional Counselor
    Oklahoma State Department of Education, Oklahoma City,
    Oklahoma

About the Author

 **Sylvia Rockwell** has more than 25 years of experience in the field of education. She began her career in elementary education classrooms. Over the years, she has taught in a variety of public school settings, which include segregated day schools for students with severe emotional and behavioral disorders, self-contained classrooms in general education settings, resource rooms, and inclusion classrooms. In addition, Rockwell worked for three years in a residential wilderness therapeutic educational program for youth with emotional and behavioral disorders. She currently serves as Assistant Professor of Education at Saint Leo University in Florida.

1

Foundations and Frameworks

Chapter Overview

■ INTRODUCTION

What would you do with a 6-year-old who greets you on the first day of school with, "Shut up you four-eyed, snot sucking, cracker—." While this particular behavior might be unusual in your classroom or school, defiance of authority is all too common in schools today. Depending on the demographics of a given school, 10% to 20% of the students can be expected to have emotional and behavioral disorders (EBD) requiring treatment (Brandenburg, Friedman, & Silver, 1990; Kauffman, 2001; U.S. Department of Health and Human Services, 2001). School systems formally serve about 1% of the student population in special education programs for youth with EBD (Kauffman, 2001; U.S. Department of Health and Human Services, 2001). A gap clearly exists between the numbers of students who need assistance and those who receive it. *You Can't Make Me! From Conflict to Cooperation in the Classroom* offers some insight into the limitations of a one-size-fits-all approach to discipline planning while assisting readers in developing a working framework from which to make research-based decisions about implementing the most effective interventions, given (a) the needs of specific targeted students, (b) the needs of a larger classroom group, (c) the setting, (d) the demands of the task, (e) short-term desired outcomes, and (f) long-term desired outcomes. Multiple perspectives on addressing emotional and behavior problems are integrated to maximize the potential for correctly identifying the child's or group's needs and selecting interventions that have the highest likelihood of successfully addressing those needs. The foundational principles that follow establish the groundwork for all other chapters. Teaching students to behave requires an understanding of cause and effect across the developmental domains. Discipline is not something that can be applied externally like an ointment on a wound. Those most in need of our interventions will not respond readily to a behavioral contract, a sticker for being "good," or the time-out chair. *You Can't Make Me!* is designed to bring together the best of what is known about youth who misbehave. This book is designed to address the needs of educators in general as well as those in special education settings. Some information and anecdotes are more applicable to general education classrooms. Other recommendations and anecdotes are more applicable to the needs of students identified as needing special education services. The guiding principles are applicable to the needs of all children with challenging behaviors, regardless of their status as general or special education students. Figure 1.1 illustrates the organization and scope of information included in this text.

■ FOUNDATIONAL PRINCIPLES

Educators and parents carry a heavy burden. They are expected to control children—to *make* them behave. Teachers and parents are praised for having well-behaved, compliant children. Those who have active, difficult to manage children are often considered less able, less worthy, less skilled, and less knowledgeable. Over the 25 years that I have worked with children who have EBD, more than one administrator has asked, "Why do you do what you do?" Their assumption is that nice people; good people; able, worthy people would want to work with the talented and gifted

Figure 1.1   The, *You Can't Make Me!* Model for Facilitating Cooperation

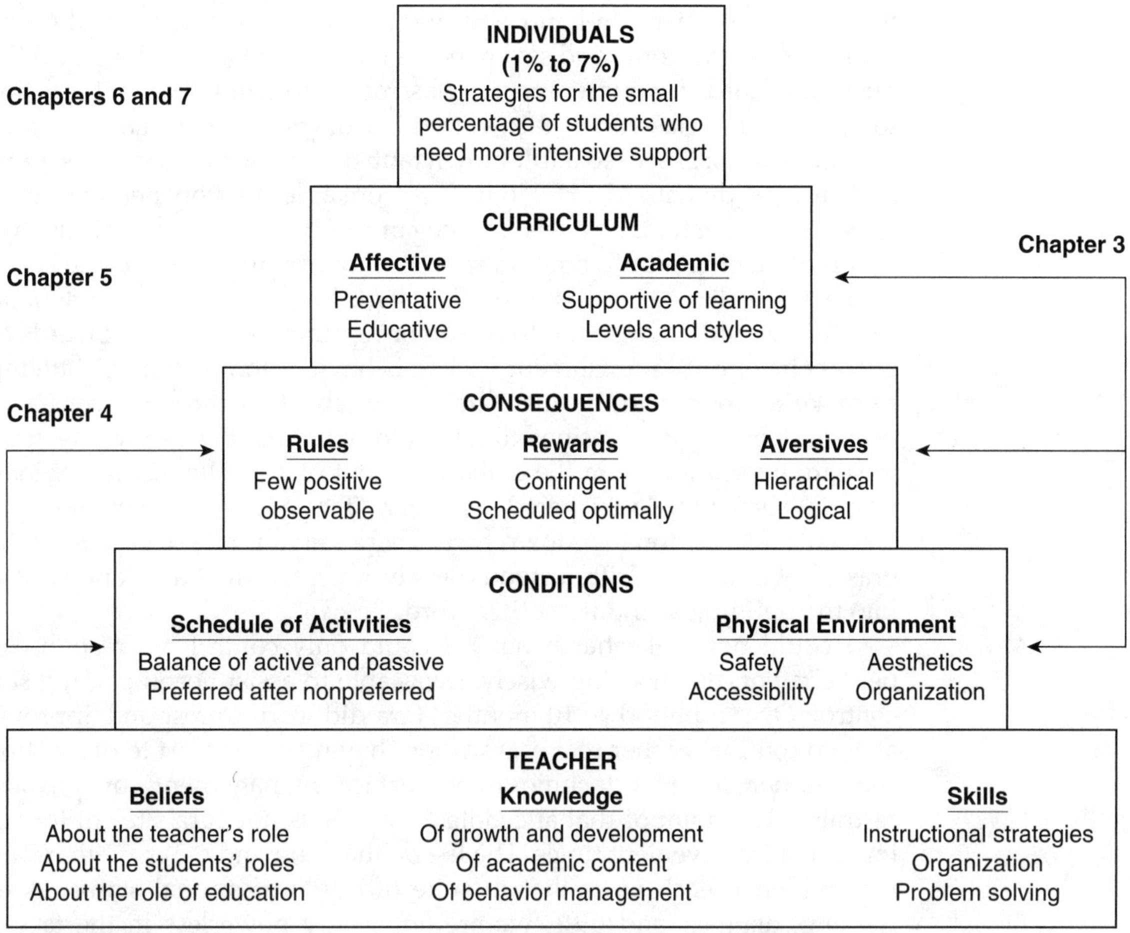

Chapters 6 and 7

INDIVIDUALS
(1% to 7%)
Strategies for the small
percentage of students who
need more intensive support

CURRICULUM

Chapter 5

Affective	Academic
Preventative	Supportive of learning
Educative	Levels and styles

Chapter 3

CONSEQUENCES

Chapter 4

Rules	Rewards	Aversives
Few positive	Contingent	Hierarchical
observable	Scheduled optimally	Logical

CONDITIONS

Schedule of Activities	Physical Environment	
Balance of active and passive	Safety	Aesthetics
Preferred after nonpreferred	Accessibility	Organization

TEACHER

Beliefs	Knowledge	Skills
About the teacher's role	Of growth and development	Instructional strategies
About the students' roles	Of academic content	Organization
About the role of education	Of behavior management	Problem solving

Note: Chapters 1, 2, and 8 address the *teacher* section of the pyramid

children—those who behave. I have many complex answers to their simple question. The first is that I find it rewarding to do a tough job well. The second is that I know beyond a shadow of a doubt that when one of my students achieves a full year's academic growth or more in one year that I had a large hand in his or her success. Some students achieve in spite of us. Those with learning and behavior problems achieve only with appropriate levels of support and carefully scaffolded guidance. A third reason is that the toughest kids keep me honest with myself and the universe. They have a way of stripping us of our feigned self-importance and know-it-all mind-sets. A former student named Tara, introduced below, was among the children who taught me my first lesson of behavior management.

Foundational Principle 1: The only person I can control is myself (Glasser, 1998)

Tara was an 8-year-old girl with a healthy set of lungs and vast quantities of misdirected energy. Her response to any request she believed to be unfair was to fall to the ground, scream, kick, and flail about like a beached whale. One beautiful, sunny day I took her and the rest of the class of students with EBD outside to enjoy a butterfly garden, which the middle school students had built for our enjoyment. Tara skipped down the mulch path hand-in-hand with her buddy, George, a child of 6 with fetal alcohol syndrome and severe behavior problems. They loved finding bugs and lizards for our temporary classroom terrarium. When it was time to return to the classroom, Tara voiced her displeasure with a few grunts and foot stomps. I sensed a full-blown tantrum on the horizon and sent the audience inside with Ms. Hill, our classroom aide. Tara opened her mouth to begin her customary wails and began to crumple at my feet just as a group of visiting administrators from the county office turned the corner of the sidewalk near our spot on the lawn. I knew from past experience that Tara would not respond to reason or reprimands. Neither rewards for good behavior nor punishment for bad behavior would abort her attempt to make a scene. Simply put, Tara had established through words and behaviors on many occasions that I could not make her behave. Wanting to spare myself and Tara the embarrassment of a public display of inappropriate behavior, I whispered in her ear, "Tara, Sweetie, I know how you hate ants. Please don't sit down here. There's an ant pile over there in the grass." With that said, Tara stood quickly, accepted my hand, and walked into the building without another word.

I could not make her behave. I could only control my response to her behavior. By choosing wisely, I was able to assist her in gaining self-control. Over a period of 10 months, Tara did learn to respond appropriately to routine teacher requests without having staff resort to distraction, some other indirect technique of surface management, or physical restraint. The point of that anecdote, however, is not Tara's talent for acting-out at inconvenient times. The lesson that Tara and others with behavior problems teach us is that in spite of our professional status, skills, training, degrees, and gifts, we are hopelessly powerless in the face of another's noncompliance. Tara has more energy than the adults in her life, fewer time constraints than the staff, and the law on her side as a minor with a disability. She will win any battle that pits ugly behavior against ugly behavior. Adults just can't out-ugly the Taras of this world. The first and most important foundational understanding in the management of student behavior is the battle cry of many students with challenging behaviors, *"You can't make me!"* Our job, therefore, is not to force students into compliance but to teach them self-control, self-reliance, and responsible self-determination. The only person I can control is myself.

Foundational Principle 2: Behavior is purposeful
(Alberto & Troutman, 1990, 2002; Glasser, 1998)

Think about something you liked to do as a child. Did you enjoy those activities enough as a child that you still do them when you can, even if you have modified them to meet your present level of functioning? Did you enjoy those activities enough as a child that you taught your own children or children you love to engage in them? After all of these years, what brings you back to those activities? What need or needs do those activities fulfill for you?

When I ask folks to share their thoughts on these questions during workshops, I am often told that people enjoyed riding a bike, visiting with extended family or grandparents, and playing outside with friends. They report that they still enjoy some or all of the activities listed and encourage the children in their lives to participate as well. As they explore the needs satisfied by the activities discussed, they mention a feeling of freedom, belonging, love, and fun, as well as basic needs such as food and rest.

Consider these questions as a follow-up to the pleasant memories. What activities did you dislike as a child? With the exception of life-sustaining chores that are required of responsible adults such as yourself, do you participate in the activities you disliked as a child now that you have a choice? What did you do when adults in your life attempted to make you participate in those activities?

Workshop participants often mention household chores such as washing dishes or ironing clothes, practicing a musical instrument, or going to bed at a specified time. They laugh openly as they share ways that they used to try to trick their parents into thinking they had done the required task or to avoid being compliant in some other way. Whining, crying, pretending to be too sick or too tired, hiding a flashlight under the blankets, and suddenly needing to go to the bathroom are the most frequently reported avoidance tactics. Some folks report hating their chores so much that they have purchased labor-saving devices or hired others to do the work they were once required to do.

Now, think about the ways students with behavior problems attempt to avoid following directions in your class or at your school. Are their behaviors radically different from yours or those of your friends?

Behaviorists have determined through multiple research studies that behavior serves a function. People behave in ways that they have learned will allow them to escape or to gain access to attention, tangible items, and activities. Unraveling the behavioral sequences, environmental contributors, and particular needs of a specific group or individual can be time consuming and mind boggling. In the end, however, a successful resolution is always worth the time and effort.

Students with challenging behaviors engage in noncompliant behaviors more frequently and with more passion than other children, but they are often not terribly different in terms of methods or motives. Our children with challenging behaviors are attempting either to fulfill a need or want or to avoid something they believe to be unpleasant. Their behavior, however misdirected, is their best attempt at that moment to communicate a want or need. Sometimes their behaviors are so contradictory on the surface that we have trouble understanding what it is that they are trying to tell us. Jeremy's story in the next section illustrates the purposefulness of behavior, the complexity of the behavioral message, and the power of success.

Foundational Principle 3: Reinforcement increases the likelihood that a behavior will be repeated; people are attracted to objects, activities, and others who are reinforcing (Alberto & Troutman, 1990, 2002; Glasser, 1998)

Jeremy bounded into the classroom as if propelled by invisible jets. He talked nonstop and ran from one desk to the next, slapping table tops, kicking chair legs, and snatching other students' work from their hands. Greased lightning would have been easier to contain. My associate and

I looked at each other in momentary stunned silence. Most of the students in this fourth-grade class were academically capable and quick to use their fists to settle a disagreement. Jeremy had a borderline IQ, a history of physical abuse and neglect, few social skills, and the attention span of a gnat. For his protection, we had to find a way to engage him academically and behaviorally. His classmates were not going to tolerate his talents for disruption.

During lunch, I read his files. According to the child study team, Jeremy hated to read, write, complete math worksheets, or engage in anything remotely educational. Previous attempts to establish contracts, reinforcement schedules, and aversive consequences for noncompliance had failed. His chronological age was 9. I roughly estimated his mental age at about 6. His expressive language skills and academic levels were more typical of a 3- to 4-year-old. Socially and emotionally, he appeared to be even younger. Children like Jeremy had always intrigued me. As I watched him fight his way through the day, I wondered what had happened to the precious baby boy he once had been. How can a teacher address the infantile needs of a 9-year-old for touch, protective boundaries, mirroring, and attention? Ms. Haines, the associate, and I decided to attempt to meet Jeremy's needs for attention and touch in an age-appropriate manner by rubbing his back, touching his shoulder, shaking his hand, rubbing his head, and engaging him in a high five every 3 minutes throughout the day. As long as one of us got to him within a 3-minute time period, Jeremy remained in his desk and completed simple academic tasks. His fine motor skills were very poor. Because of this, we modified assignments and engaged him in a variety of activities designed to strengthen motor control while simultaneously addressing academic skills such as sound-letter correspondence, place value, and word recognition. Attention to Jeremy's developmental ages across various domains made it easier to design successful interventions.

Within the second week of our reinforcement program, Jeremy was able to remain in his seat and on task with 5-minute intervals between physical touch. By the end of his first month with us, he was able to work for 20 minutes at a time. He made adequate academic progress that year, but the most striking changes in him were behavioral. He was able to play simple games with peers, participate in group lessons, and contribute positively to the class. Getting a reluctant student to read, write, or stop hitting others requires careful attention to what reinforces that child. People are not successful because they do more. People do more because they are successful (Katz, 1997).

Foundational Principle 4: Punishment decreases the likelihood that a behavior will be repeated; people avoid activities, objects, and other people they believe to be punishing (Alberto & Troutman, 1990, 2002; Glasser, 1998)

Behaviorists have known for many decades that punishment delivered immediately and with sufficient intensity stops a behavior from occurring. Punishment does not, however, teach a replacement behavior. In the movie *The Truman Show,* the main character, Truman, wants to get off the island where he lives to find a woman he loves. He was taught to be afraid of the water when he was a boy by being caught in a storm and being made to believe that he was partially responsible for his father's death. In spite of his great fear, he finds a sailboat and sets off on his journey. The director of the Truman television show does not want Truman to escape. He has the special effects technician increase the intensity of the storm. Winds whip the boat. Lightning strikes close to the boat. Truman hangs on to the mast and screams, "Is that the best you can do? You're going to have to kill me!" Truman continues even after two attempts are made to frighten him into returning to the island by nearly drowning him. He needs to get to the woman he loves. Death is an acceptable price to pay for trying. As I watched that movie for the first time, I thought about all the children who had told me over the years that they would persist in their disruptive, non-compliant behavior to the death if pushed by adults to go that far.

The more youth with behavior problems test our patience and good-will, the more willing we often become to strike back—to attempt to make them behave with force and punishment. Many of them become immune to adult threats even before they are old enough to attend school. Of what consequence is a time-out room to a child who has had both legs broken at the age of three by a stepparent? How punishing can the school be to a child who has been raped repeatedly by a family member? For children who are called degrading names and slapped across the head and face, our contrived punishments are a joke. It is no wonder that they laugh at us. The most difficult foundational principle for many folks to understand is the first one about having control only over our own actions. The second most difficult foundational principle for many folks is this one: Punishment is too often a weak and meaningless exercise of power in artificially contrived school settings.

Punishment does not teach a new behavior, inspire compliance, or encourage the student to engage with us. For our most challenging students, punishment should be a last resort simply because we have so little with which to bargain in the beginning. We must have something positive to offer them before the removal of that positive, reinforcing object, person, or activity will be meaningful. In addition to the limitations of punishment given students' life experiences beyond the school, punishment does not teach a desired behavior. When their behaviors present a safety risk to themselves and/or others, we have a responsibility to remove aggressive, disruptive students from a situation until they regain control. That should not be confused with punishment. Too often adults think they are punishing children when, in fact, they are rewarding the children by allowing them to avoid a task they dislike or giving them the attention they crave during the time away from class.

Foundational Principle 5: All people have the same basic needs (Glasser, 1998)

In the 1960s, Maslow proposed a theory of motivation that included levels of need. He believed that one level of need must be satisfied before people would be motivated to move to the next level of need. The medical community still uses Maslow's (1962) hierarchy as an informal assessment of patients' well-being in hospital settings. Glasser (1998) identifies five basic human needs. While survival is a necessary prerequisite to achieving the other needs, he proposes a model that is aligned with a classroom setting in terms of need fulfillment. The other four needs that Glasser proposes are (1) love, (2) power, (3) freedom, and (4) fun. Driekurs, Grumwald, and Pepper (1982) identify motivations for misbehavior as (a) a need for power, (b) a need for revenge, (c) a need for fun, and (d) a need for assistance or attention satisfied through feigned helplessness. Behaviorists such as Alberto and Troutman (1990, 2002) identify motivation for behavior in terms of actions that assist the student in gaining or avoiding objects, attention, sensory stimulation, or activities. Time and energy could be spent arguing the merits of a strict behavioral approach that ignores the cognitive and emotional components of motivation and behavior. The fact remains, however, that regardless of the model from which an educator identifies motivations for behavior, students who exhibit more than their share of behavior problems are working to meet the same needs as students who have learned to comply with classroom, school, and social rules. Tara tended to fall on the ground and scream when she wanted to continue an activity she preferred. Glasser (1998) would describe Tara's quality world or cognitive picture of a good day as containing only a limited number of tasks and people in the beginning. He would probably suggest that changing Tara's behavior should include opportunities for her to broaden her interests, relationships with others, and skills across different domains. Alberto and Troutman (1990, 2002) would probably focus on Tara's skill deficits in communicating her needs and her performance deficits in making successful transitions. Tara would be taught to express her needs verbally and would be reinforced when she successfully communicated and transitioned from one activity to another. The point of this foundational principle is that students with behavioral challenges are more like others than different from others. Correctly identifying a student's need or a group's need is essential to selecting the most effective intervention.

The events and behaviors exhibited by the following class of students illustrate the power of need identification in addressing problem behaviors. Ms. Lambert came to me one day to discuss unexpected changes in her class. For the first nine weeks of school, the students had been well behaved and exceptionally productive compared to other classes she had had in the past. Over a 3-week period of time, however, their behavior problems had increased. The principal called her in to discuss the number of office referrals she had written. In addition, progress reports would be sent home in another week and a half. She dreaded the parents' reactions when they saw the decline in achievement. As we talked, it became apparent that the class was reaching a peak of noncompliant, off-task behavior right before lunch. I asked her if anything had changed with regard to her schedule. She reported that because of overcrowding in the cafeteria and at physical education (PE), her class was now attending lunch 45 minutes later than usual and was going to PE during the first hour of school. We knew that many of the students were not eating a proper breakfast and hypothesized that the late lunch combined with an early PE was leaving them feeling hungry. At my suggestion, she sent a note to parents requesting that the students bring a healthy snack to school. When the students returned from PE, they were allowed to eat their snacks while the teacher read a story. Behavior problems decreased immediately and dramatically.

Work production increased immediately and dramatically. Neither Ms. Lambert nor I had ever been quite as successful at pinpointing and resolving a problem before this time, but we were thrilled with the results. Too often teachers begin by establishing a complex behavior management system with tokens, hierarchies of punishment, and other strategies when the problem is more basic and more easily addressed once the students' needs are identified.

Foundational Principle 6: Each person has his or her own belief about how to meet a particular need (Glasser, 1998)

Our ideas of how to best meet our needs have developed over the course of our lifetimes. Before we were able to make our own decisions, our families introduced us to some options. As we grew, we rejected some of those early choices and added new ones. A child's prior experiences, areas of strength or skill deficits, and temperament will interact to create his or her personal beliefs about how to best meet his or her needs. When children are very young and dependent on the environment, they will tend to react to more immediate events. As the children gain in cognitive ability, they will bring more of their own agenda to the present experience. People, activities, objects, and types of sensory stimulation that have pleased them in the past will be sought in the present and the future. People, activities, objects, and types of sensory stimulation that have been unpleasant for them in the past will tend to be avoided in the present and the future. Children who have experienced failure and rejection during their early experiences with school are at great risk for developing negative beliefs about (a) their own abilities to learn, (b) the value of attempting to make friends and participate in school-related activities, (c) the trustworthiness of the adult authority figures in school environments, and (d) their abilities to positively impact the overwhelming odds they perceive to exist in the classroom. One of the biggest hurdles I face when I work with children who have experienced ongoing school failure is convincing them that school can be a pleasant place to be. The second biggest hurdle is convincing them that they are capable of achieving.

People sometimes think that children are not affected by their thoughts and beliefs because of the immediacy of their response to the environment. Seligman (1995) reports that children as young as seven develop thinking patterns clearly oriented toward learned helplessness or learned optimism. One little 9-year-old I worked with several years ago exhibited frequent acts of physical aggression. He would throw furniture, hit, kick, scratch, bite, and destroy instructional materials when he became angry. Early in our year of working together, he told me that he could not help being violent. He explained that his Daddy was in prison for hurting people. When Carson became angry and aggressive at home, family members told him he was just like his Dad. One day after a particularly nasty tantrum, I talked with Carson about his choices. He had been making tremendous progress academically. He was beginning to believe that he could achieve school success in reading, writing, and math. As I held his hands, his little body shook with the last sniffles and tears of his outburst. I asked him what he was thinking. Tears rolled down both beautiful cheeks as he slowly choked out, "I'm afraid."

"Carson, what frightens you?"

"I'm afraid that I will go to prison like my Daddy. I want to be good, but I'm afraid that I can't be."

My response was clear, firm, and direct. "Carson, look at me." His gaze slowly moved from the carpet to meet mine. "You decide who you will be. You know that you are smart. You know you have made great progress already in your school work." Carson nodded affirmatively. "Remember this, young man, if you remember nothing else. You decide who you will be—not your Daddy—not your Mom—not your Grandma. All of us, including your Daddy, want you to be successful. We care about you and want to help you. *But,* you decide who you will be."

Carson still had problems with violent behavior from time to time after our talk. His ability to self-manage increased, however. By the end of the following school year, he had attained grade-level achievement across subject areas and had learned to talk to a trusted adult when he was angry instead of taking his anger out on the environment. The last news I had of Carson was that he played football for his high school team and earned a scholarship to college. Before Carson received corrective experiences, he believed that school was a place to fail and to fight. He believed that he had little chance of being successful. He could not read or spell. His Dad was in prison. His family told him that he was headed to prison like his Dad. What reason did he have to work hard, manage the inevitable frustration of the learning process, and trust adults who were too stupid to understand that he was already doomed to a life of crime? The context of a problem includes the setting, events in the setting that occur before and after a problem, people involved in the setting, and the thoughts of the person who is targeted for intervention. Foundational Principle 7 addresses three basic assumptions from which successful people operate.

Foundational Principle 7: People who have had their needs met reliably through socially accepted means operate from three basic assumptions (Janoff-Bulman, 1993): (1) We live in a benevolent and just world, (2) life has meaning, and (3) we are worthy

Marian Wright Edelman (1992) describes her early years as being supportive of her growing belief in her ability to achieve and contribute to her community. In spite of factors in her life that might be perceived by others as creating a level of risk for her and her siblings, she persevered. She learned by example and through direct interaction with significant adults that while the world was not entirely safe or just, there were reasons to believe that benevolence and justice were qualities worth championing. She learned that life has great meaning and that an understanding of that meaning was a call to action. She also learned that she was worthy—indeed, that all people are worthy. Her early experiences with people who reliably met her needs fostered a deep and abiding faith that has continued to propel her into action on behalf of others who are less fortunate. In her own words, she describes how this process unfolded for her.

I was 14 years old the night my Daddy died. He had holes in his shoes but two children out of college, one in college, another in divinity school, and a vision he was able to convey to me as he lay dying in an ambulance that I, a young Black girl, could be and do anything; that race and gender are shadows; and that character, self-discipline, determination, attitude, and service are the substance of life. I have always believed that I could help change the world because I have been lucky to have adults around me who did—in small and large ways. Most people were of simple grace who understood what Walter Percy wrote: You can get all A's and still flunk life. Giving up and "burnout" were not part of the language of my elders. You got up every morning and did what you had to do and you got up every time you fell down and tried as many times as you had to get it done right. They had grit. (Edelman, 1992, pp. 7–8)

It is clear from Edelman's brief description of her early years that protective and supportive structures surrounded her from her first beginnings. She reports feeling loved and challenged through multiple experiences with family, friends, and community members. While she faced many hardships and obstacles, her earliest beliefs about herself reflected those of the adults who surrounded her with high expectations, an unwavering sense of hope for her and for the world at large, and an honest appraisal of what it would take to succeed. Her sense of personal and interpersonal responsibility as an adult was built on those childhood messages, experiences, and beliefs. Many students who exhibit problem behaviors have not had such protective, predictable, supportive care. Trauma and repeated exposure to threat or failure can erode a child's belief in self and others. Understanding the cognitive components that underlie overt behavior is important in designing effective interventions.

Foundational Principle 8: Trauma and long-term exposure to shame-producing events shatter those assumptions (Janoff-Bulman, 1993; Katz, 1997; Seligman, 1995; Terr, 1990); chronic and long-term exposure to failure can erode a person's belief in those assumptions as well (Katz, 1997; Seligman, 1995)[1]

As students grow, they add more experiences to the life stories they construct (Singer & Salovey, 1993; Wood, 1996). If the majority of their experiences have been unproductive, they carry a set of beliefs with them that actively work against more direct efforts to teach social skills and manage surface behavior (Kendall, 1991; Seligman, 1995; Wood, 1996). In contrast to Edelman's story and as an illustration of the power of children's beliefs in the maintenance of their behaviors, an experience with a group of fourth- and fifth-grade boys with EBD is offered.

All of the boys in this class lived with parents who either were addicted to drugs or engaged in illegal activities. The boys often told me about shootings at night in their neighborhoods. According to them, all of the children who lived in their area went inside at dusk to play games or watch television. They remained flat on the floor each evening to escape bullets that might hit them from drive-by shootings. One child was 5 years old when he watched his mother die after his stepfather had chopped off the woman's arms. It took several hours for the police to talk the man into releasing the children. Another boy in the class had witnessed a violent attack by his mother on his father's pregnant girlfriend. The mother came home to find the father having sexual relations with the girlfriend in the master bedroom. The mother went to the kitchen, returned with a butcher knife, and stabbed the pregnant woman in the abdomen. The baby died.

I repeatedly attempted to discuss the benefits of maintaining a nonviolent classroom with this group. I told them that fighting was not a responsible way to handle anger and conflicts, but they had plenty to tell me about the subject! They told me about their lack of trust, their need to defend not only their honor, but also their very existence. They challenged me to live just one day in their shoes. They were only 10 and 11 years old. In spite of my determination to run a safe and trustworthy program, they persisted in seeing danger and reasons for aggression at every turn. They cursed, threw furniture, smashed windows and other school property, and resorted to a group brawl on the lawn in front of the classroom on more than one occasion. They were so determined to prove to me that might is right.

While I could not totally change those beliefs in the short period of one school year, we did eventually establish a peaceful classroom. The boys learned to be responsible within the four protected walls of our environment. We cooked, read, wrote books, built model towns, sang, and talked. Our book and model town were placed on display in the school office. Our treats were shared with staff and other classes. We established a community of mutual respect, trust, and care that allowed those young men to be responsible with me and with each other. To accomplish that, multiple experiences over a period of months were developed to satisfy their needs for safety, trust, nurturing, protective and supportive boundaries, achievement, choices, and service to others.

Neither a behavior-management system nor a series of social skills lessons alone would have been enough. The students needed to be heard, and I needed to know what they were thinking. I could not even imagine living in such a terrifying environment. Even if they embellished some of the details and were less than accurate at times about all that they reported, their beliefs about themselves and others came through in our discussions. By listening to their stories, I gained a better understanding of how to meet their needs in ways that would make sense to them. They needed the same things that we all need—to feel safe, valued, strong, capable, and worthy. When past experiences have not led to socially acceptable methods for meeting those needs, however, teaching personal and interpersonal responsibility is a tremendous challenge.

I'd like to pretend that I began the year in that classroom with a clearly defined plan. The reality is I did not. The students' propensity to interpret every action as a threat was as wearing as it was disturbing. This group of children required diligently enforced controls on all acts of aggression within a structure that protected their needs to see themselves as strong and independent. I drew large boxes on the floor around their desks with chalk. Time-out was immediately enforced for any movement that extended out of their assigned areas. Academic work was carefully structured for success.

Anytime a student said, "I can't do this," I replied, "I will never ask you to do anything that can't be done. Tell me what you know. We'll go from there together." Daily routines included negotiable and nonnegotiable items. A sense of power and control can be enhanced through opportunities to make choices and give suggestions. In spite of their limited abilities in the beginning to make responsible choices and provide appropriate input, carefully structured academic and affective lessons were offered that elicited such responses.

Independent work was often assigned with a group project in mind. In the beginning, working together was impossible. Working alone to contribute to a class product allowed the students the safety and sense of accomplishment they needed while encouraging them to take pride in group membership. As projects took shape, they were shared with the larger community of the school. Students received positive feedback from other teachers, administrators, and peers. Family members were encouraged to visit as well. Being strong, capable, and worthy extended beyond the ability to fight. Power, control, and achievement were possible through school-appropriate behaviors. The group was finally able to function peacefully. I no longer drew boxes on the floor around their desks. They did not give up their belief that the world beyond the classroom was a threatening place. They still believed in violence. However, new choices were added to their repertoire and practiced daily, although it must be said that the new did not by any stretch of the imagination erase the old.

When one of the students was asked at the end of the school year what he had liked about the class, he said that the teacher did not want to talk about what he could not do—only what he could do. Students with behavioral challenges are often too aware of what they cannot do. Empowering them to become responsible members of a class, school, and community requires a balancing of their needs for attachment versus independence, autonomy versus external control, and initiative versus destruction or apathy.

Foundational Principle 9: Human beings work to maintain a sense of control (Terr, 1990)

The group of students described in the previous section used violence as their primary method for maintaining control of any situation they disliked or distrusted. Other students quietly refuse to comply with routine expectations, curse, run away, or are truant. As early as the age of 18 months to 2 years, children will exercise control over eating, drinking, and elimination. The drive to be independent is a double-edged sword. Educators and parents want children to self-manage, self-regulate, and self-evaluate as long as the children decide to comply. If children decide to follow their own agenda—one that is at odds with the adults in their lives—power struggles begin. Foundational Principle 1 states that the only person one can control is oneself (Glasser, 1998). Our need to feel as if we have some control over our lives is essential to our mental health (Glasser, 1998; Janoff-Bulman, 1993; Seligman, 1995; Terr, 1990). Adults tend to attempt to take control away from students who refuse to comply. This increases the students' levels of tension, which intensifies their commitment to noncompliant behavior. The power struggle cycles (Wood & Long, 1991) and spins out of control unless someone with an understanding of the process intercedes. Jordan's story, revealed in the next section, clearly illustrates his need to remain in control and how a sense of shame intensified his motivation to act in undesirable ways. In any given situation, the adult has a choice—to model respect for the individual and self or to model the emotion acted out in the child's behavior. A student walks into the room, throws his backpack on the floor, and screams, "Shut-up, you son-of-a-b___!" when the teacher asks him to pick up the backpack. The teacher can scream, "You can't talk to me that way! I won't have it" and write a discipline referral; or the teacher can quietly walk closer to the student and say, "I see that this is a tough morning for you. I'm sorry that you are not happy. Please tell me how you feel without screaming and using inappropriate language." The first teacher response models the level of disrespect and anger the child exhibited. The child has little to lose at this point and will probably escalate. Because the law, professional ethics, and good sense place a limit on how far the teacher can escalate, the student will win in his own mind if the teacher continues down this path. The second response will probably be unexpected. The element of surprise alone might be enough to get the student's attention the first time a teacher tries it. The advantage to the second teacher response is that it allows the student to save face, remain in control, and make a decision. The student is not backed into a corner where he will feel that lashing out is his only choice. Jordan provides an even more complicated scenario related to control with an added level of shame that many students with behavior problems feel, even though they rarely reveal it openly.

Foundational Principle 10: Shame comes from public exposure of one's own vulnerability; human beings work to avoid shame (Terr, 1990, p. 113)

Jordan had a medical problem. His bowels leaked feces—especially when he became anxious. Four operations failed to correct the inherited condition that caused his chronic *incoprecis.* Jordan was understandably distressed by this disorder. Until a successful intervention was conducted at school, other kids wouldn't play with him. They marked his seat with foul names and refused to sit near him. If one of his classmates was asked to sit in a chair that Jordan had used, the whole group erupted with taunts. To make matters even worse, Jordan refused to change his clothes when he had an accident. The stench in the classroom was unbearable and only invited further ridicule from his peers. He was 9 years old. The teacher could not make him change clothes. He was too big and too old for a female teacher to wrestle him to the ground, strip, sanitize, and dress. Over the feigned gagging, screams of laughter, and ugly names that Jordan's peers called out could be heard Jordan's shrill and insistent refrain, "I'm not changing my clothes, and *you can't make me!*"

Jordan had been offered rewards for changing his clothes and endured punishments for refusing to change his clothes. His mother was beside herself with embarrassment and had all but given up on trying to help him. School officials were fearful of the health issues related to human waste products and were tired of the ongoing, daily battles Jordan created with his refusal to take responsibility for his actions. Jordan attended a public school and was assigned to a self-contained class for students with

EBD. His academic achievement had suffered slightly due to hospitalizations and frequent refusals to follow directions when in school, but he was capable of learning.

I watched Jordan's daily battles from afar the year he was in second grade. When he was assigned to me for his third-grade year, I talked with him and his mother. I found out that when Jordan was fully grown the doctors would be able to operate again. The success rate with adults who have his condition is higher than 90 percent. His physical problems would be over in 8 to 10 years. Unless we were successful soon; however, his social, emotional, and behavioral problems would be out of control by then. With Mom's knowledge and permission, I decided to move beyond (a) attempting to keep Jordan calm to help him avoid an accident, (b) rewarding him for changing his clothes when he had an accident, and (c) punishing him for refusing to change his clothes when he had an accident. I asked Jordan what he was thinking when he refused to change his clothes. He told me that he was afraid that the other students would tease him more. He said that if he changed his clothes, they would know he had had an accident. I couldn't convince him that the smell was proof enough of an accident. On a hunch, I asked him if he was mad at the kids for making fun of him. He began to cry and shook his head in affirmation.

"Jordan, could it be that you are trying to punish them?"

"What do you mean?" he asked through sniffles and tears.

"Well, you know that it stinks when you have an accident. I was just wondering if you were mad at the kids for teasing you. Making them suffer with you might be a way of punishing them."

"Yeah, I do get mad. So what if they have to smell it!"

"What if they didn't tease you any more? Would you still want to punish them?"

Jordan began to cry again. "I just want somebody to like me. I can't help it if I have this problem. It isn't fair. It just isn't fair."

"I agree, Sweetie. It isn't fair. Would you be willing to talk with the class?"

"NO WAY! They'll just tease me even more."

"I don't think they will. I think if they understood everything, they might act differently. Besides, it's worth a try. What if I stood behind you while you talked and made sure that no one teased you? Would you be willing to tell the students about your operations and all the medical reasons for your problem?"

"I guess so."

"When you finish telling them, I'll want them to talk with you about how they feel. I won't let anyone be mean to you, though. OK?"

"OK."

Later that day, I placed the students' chairs in a semicircle. Jordan sat in the center with me behind him. I explained the ground rules for the class meeting before Jordan started.

1. Only talk about yourself—your thoughts, your feelings.

2. No name calling.

3. No teasing.

4. Anyone who violated a ground rule would be removed from the group immediately.

Jordan told his medical story. The students were amazed. They had no idea that he had suffered so much pain. They asked insightful and sensitive questions about his experiences in the hospital and wanted to know if the doctors would ever be able to help him. He was quite knowledgeable. With quiet confidence and surprising competence, he answered all of their questions. When he was finished, I asked his classmates to talk with him about how they feel when he refuses to change his clothes.

"No offense, man, but it really stinks." said Jose.

"Yeah, we're sorry about your medical condition. We didn't know. We thought you were just being mean to us." added Marcus.

"Why do you do that, Jordan?" asked Janine.

"I was afraid you'd tease me even more if I changed my clothes."

The discussion continued. The class offered to be friends with Jordan and stop teasing him in return for his cooperation when accidents occurred. At the end of the group meeting, several students spontaneously hugged Jordan; others asked him to sit at their table during lunch. Within a short period of time, Jordan was taking responsibility for more than his medical condition. He was mainstreamed back into a general education classroom and never returned to full-time placement in special education classes again.

Jordan's story illustrates the power of understanding the purpose of a particular behavior. Jordan wanted friends, was angry that his peers made fun of him for something he could not entirely control, and felt deeply ashamed of his inability to control his bowel movements. His peers were angry with Jordan, because they thought he could control the medical problem. Jordan was punishing his classmates for their mean comments and simultaneously attempting to avoid the shame and embarrassment that he felt. Jordan's classmates were punishing Jordan for soiling his pants. Once they communicated their thoughts and feelings, they were able to develop a plan that worked well for all of them. Behavioral strategies designed to reward and punish the class and Jordan were doomed to fail. Third graders are not going to forgive another third grader for soiling his pants and refusing to change them, no matter how big the punishment or reward might be. Jordan wanted and needed friends. He felt that he had no way of making friends, given his medical condition. No reward or punishment offered by the school could overcome his anger, loneliness, shame, and despair. Thoughts and emotions become increasingly powerful factors in the behavior of students as they become older and more able to plan ahead, self-evaluate, and assess the people with whom they interact. Beliefs and attributions may not be directly observable but are important factors in addressing the behavioral and emotional needs of older, higher functioning students.

Foundational Principle 11: The four components of behavior are (1) overt, observable actions, (2) thoughts, (3) emotions, and (4) physiological reactions (Glasser, 1998); interventions need to address all four components of behavior

A former student named Sammy illustrates the importance of understanding the physiological, behavioral, ecological, and cognitive factors that contribute to overt behavior. Sammy was a 7-year-old who had just been released from a community-based psychiatric facility in another community. A social worker stopped by my classroom the day before his arrival to give me a brief description of his case. He was placed in the custody of his grandparents at the age of 6 months due to severe neglect. His mother had abused drugs while pregnant with him. He did not smile for several months and had frequent, violent, and unprovoked tantrums. The grandparents sought professional help when he began at the age of 4 to verbalize his intent to kill animals and people. The incident that prompted his referral to the psychiatric facility was Sammy's attempt to kill his grandparents while they slept by setting the house on fire. He scored in the gifted range on individually administered intelligence tests, so his inability to act responsibly was not a function of poor cognitive skills.

On that first Tuesday morning, he greeted me politely and participated calmly and appropriately in class activities for the first 2 hours. Then without warning or noticeable provocation, he began violently banging his head on a brick wall, scraping his face with his fingernails, and smashing any materials within his reach. His screams were ear-splitting. I sent my aide to another room with the rest of the class and attempted to calm him.

Some of Sammy's problems were related to temperament and other biological factors, and some were learned behaviors. He had frightened people often enough in the past to know that certain behaviors sometimes achieved a useful purpose—people demanded less from him and gave him more of what he wanted. In addition to learned and biologically controlled responses, Sammy exhibited advanced cognitive abilities. While this was helpful in redirecting Sammy's energy to more productive, achievement-oriented academic goals, it also worked against him in establishing peer relationships in other situations.

Sammy received counseling to help him understand and manage his thoughts, beliefs about himself and others, and emotions. Physiological reactions were targeted through a combination of medication and instruction in anger management. His overt behavior was addressed through classroom strategies. The environment of a self-contained classroom provided him with the structure and safety he needed through clearly defined limits, immediate consequences, predictable and balanced scheduling of activities, social skills instruction, and academic tasks modified for his level of cognitive functioning.

As he required less external support, expectations for his participation in problem-solving sessions and cooperative learning activities increased. Sammy began to ask permission to visit the media center and general education classrooms unattended. He made friends with peers in other classes and was a welcome member of the school community. His grandparents reported that he was also making excellent progress at home, in counseling, and in community-based youth programs. Collaborative, developmentally sensitive, and individually modified interventions helped Sammy gain new skills and reframe his beliefs about himself and those around him. School, friends, family, and neighborhood experiences became increasingly reinforcing. Sammy was well on his way to developing the personal and interpersonal skills necessary for living a healthy, productive life.

Foundational Principle 12: What we do *to, for,* and *with* youth has powerful, long-term effects

I am struck regularly by the mechanistic approach we use to help youth self-right. We too often observe, take data, analyze data, hypothesize about the child's needs or wants, design interventions, implement interventions, and make further decisions about programming without even consulting the child. We try to "fix" the child, the classroom group, and the family without looking at more than the surface variables. The more we do things *to* children and *for* children, the less responsibility they take for their actions. We have a responsibility to take care of our young people. That, of course, will include providing them with food and shelter and directly teaching them the academic and behavioral lessons our society expects them to learn. What we must never forget, however, is that while we are doing *to* them and *for* them, they are learning about who we think they are and who they expect they will become. The unspoken messages sent during our attempts to control and to protect are as powerful as the direct lessons we teach.

Children learn best when we do things *with* them—when we model the behaviors we want them to emulate, when we provide them with carefully scaffolded opportunities to make age-appropriate decisions, when we do not shelter them from the natural and logical consequences of their choices but believe in them even when they experience a momentary setback. Teaching is more than the sum of its parts.

Carson believed that he was doomed to a life of crime because of what his mother and other family members told him. He did have a difficult temperament as a baby and a quick temper as a young boy. His future, however, was not predetermined by his genes, his socioeconomic status, his race, or his gender. He had within him the abilities, even at his young age, to self-select the people he would emulate, self-regulate his actions to a degree, and self-evaluate the appropriateness of those actions. One of our most important roles for youth like Carson is to be a positively distorted mirror that reflects back to them not who they are at the moment but who they can be. Carson learned through interactions with many people that he had choices. He could give up on himself and give in to the aggressive impulses he felt, or he could learn to manage his temper and succeed. With support at home, in the community, and at school, he did indeed succeed.

This last foundational principle is critical because we too often forget to do things *with* the most challenging children. We are tired and frustrated. We just want the disruptive behavior to stop, so we focus on that. As long as we focus on the "bad" behavior, the students will also put their energies there. Engaging them with us in academic success, affective education, the arts, physical education, and the rich array of productive options available helps them to redirect their energies, emulate more positive models, and begin to see themselves as worthy of more than they had ever dreamed.

Theoretical models for understanding emotional and behavioral problems follow. Each approach defines the components of diagnosis and treatment differently. While some researchers subscribe to a narrowly defined definition or theoretical model, practitioners benefit from understanding and integrating research from the behavioral, ecological, biophysical, and cognitive-behavioral approaches.

THEORETICAL APPROACHES TO BEHAVIOR MANAGEMENT ◼

Proponents of each theoretical approach define EBD, assess the disorders, and design interventions differently. An overview of the behavioral, biophysical, ecological, and cognitive approaches to understanding and treating EBD is provided below.

The Behavioral Approach

Major Assumptions:

1. Behavior is learned.

2. Behavior is a function of the environment.

Assessment:

1. Collect data on the frequency, intensity, and duration of observable, definable overt behaviors.

2. Analyze the data collected on the antecedents, behavior(s), and consequences within and across contexts.

3. Develop a hypothesis about the function of the behavior, given the data collected.

Interventions:

1. Reinforcement contingent on exhibiting a targeted behavior.

2. Teach a replacement behavior.

3. Change a component of the context.

4. Punishment as a last resort.

The behavioral approach gained widespread popular appeal through the work of B. F. Skinner. Over time, researchers have refined the early behavioral work on conditioned responses and developed a process for identifying and addressing behavior problems called Positive Behavior Support. Proponents subscribe to the following research-based assumptions (Scott & Nelson, 1999; Sugai et al., 2000):

1. Behavior is meaningful and is an attempt to communicate a want or need.

2. People behave in certain ways to get or avoid attention, sensory input (music, touch, movement, etc.), and/or tangible items (food, toys, etc.).

3. Behavior is contextual. The purpose and meaning of a behavior is related at least in part to the setting in which the behavior occurs.

4. To intervene successfully, the purpose or function of the behavior must be understood and addressed in the intervention plan.

5. Skill deficits indicate a need to teach new replacement skills.

6. Performance deficits indicate a need for increasing reinforcement when the behavior is exhibited.

7. Environmental contributors to the problem behavior should be assessed and addressed in the intervention plan.

8. To decrease an undesirable behavior or increase a desirable behavior, the following components should be included in the Positive Behavior Support Plan process: (a) an analysis of current behaviors with regard to time, frequency, and place; (b) a hypothesis of the purpose or function of the behavior; (c) environmental supports; (d) educative interventions; (e) reinforcement; and (f) aversive consequences on a limited basis and as a last resort.

The Biophysical Approach

Major Assumptions:

1. Behavior is affected by biologically determined conditions.

2. A heritable predisposition to mental illness can be affected by environmental conditions.

3. Mental illness is a disease process that is not the patient's fault.

4. Mental illness is a disease process that is the patient's responsibility.

Assessment:

1. Medical tests

2. Physician or psychiatric evaluation

Interventions:

1. Medication

2. Diet

3. Exercise

4. Sleep and wake cycle regulation

Proponents of the biophysical approach to understanding and treating children with emotional and behavioral problems emphasize the neurological and underlying biological difference among youth who exhibit troubling learning and behavior problems. Many children have no detectable biological conditions known to contribute to problem behavior. Only children with severe and profound conditions exhibit a clear relationship between biological conditions and behavior problems (Harris, 1995). Children with ADHD, bipolar disorder, obsessive compulsive disorder, and other disorders known to have a biological origin, however, do often benefit from taking medications (Forness & Kavale, 2001).

Understanding normal growth and development with regard to impulse control, fine and gross motor control, and social-emotional milestones is helpful in determining differences among students with and without behavior problems. Sometimes people think that everything a child does is a symptom of a disorder. It is helpful to know that many children of a particular age who do not have an emotional or behavioral problem have difficulty with a specific skill.

The Ecological Approach

Major Assumptions:

1. The problem does not necessarily originate with the child.

2. The environment is a critical variable in determining the cause of a problem.

3. Changing a variable in the environment can have unforeseen consequences and effects on behavior.

Assessment:

1. A review of relevant cognitive, biophysical, and social information about the child

2. Collection of data that includes an assessment of the environment; the nature of the task; information about the frequency, intensity, and/or duration of the behavior(s) of concern; and information about the circumstances under which the behavior is unlikely to occur

3. An analysis of the interaction of the child and the environment

Interventions:

Interventions may include one or more of the following:

1. Change the environment.

2. Change the response to the child.

3. Provide biophysical support (medications, food, rest, fluids).

The emphasis on the interaction of the child and his or her environment is a key component of the ecological approach (Nelson, 1984). Behaviorists have increasingly integrated an analysis of the context in their assessment and intervention processes (Scott & Nelson, 1999; Sugai et al., 2000).

The Cognitive-Behavioral Approach

Major Assumptions:

1. Thoughts, emotions, and behavior affect each other.

2. Emotions and behaviors can be modified by addressing thoughts.

3. The situation is not the problem. The thoughts about a situation affect the emotions and behaviors.

4. The targeted person has an active role to play in the diagnosis and treatment of the problem.

Assessment:

1. Self-report checklists and surveys

2. Interviews

3. Observations of student's statements in targeted situations

Interventions:

1. Skill instruction that includes attention to self-talk

2. Modeling of effective or corrective self-talk

3. Role-play with attention to self-talk—making the self-talk audible during the practicing of the desired skill

4. Teaching students to recognize physiological reactions and moderate them

5. Teaching students to refute inaccurate self-talk

6. Teaching students to collect data to confirm or refute beliefs

Proponents of cognitive-behavioral approaches work with the student to determine the beliefs and thoughts that interfere with academic and behavioral progress (Bernard, 1990; DiGuiseppe & Bernard, 1990; Seligman, 1995). Social-cognitive theory is based on the assumption that overt behavior is a result of reciprocal interactions among the environment (physical, social), personal factors (thoughts, emotions, perceptions, biological reactions and conditions), and the individual's behavior. Albert Bandura (1977, 1978, 1986) refers to the causal connections among the three factors as triarchic reciprocality. Social-cognitive theory reconceptualizes the analysis of the direction, interaction, and effects of behavior. Researchers use the tools of natural science (a) to investigate human abilities to use symbols for communication, anticipate future events, learn from vicarious experiences, evaluate, self-regulate, and be reflectively self-conscious; (b) to determine the reciprocal effects of person variables, environment, and behavior; and (c) to develop interventions that are most likely to be effective, given an analysis of the variables listed above.

■ **A RATIONALE FOR INTEGRATING THE THEORETICAL APPROACHES**

As children mature, their cognitive and behavioral repertoires tend to increase. They begin to *self-select* preferred people, places, and things with which to interact; *evaluate* people (including themselves), places, and things; and *self-regulate* their overt responses to internal as well as external factors. As children develop into preteens and adolescents, the differences in their immediate, contextual experiences alone will often be insufficient in generating a hypothesis for a targeted behavioral problem. Failure to generate an accurate hypothesis weakens the probability that the intervention(s) selected will be effective (Oneill et al., 1997). The analysis of cognitive components that interact with other social-cognitive factors related to the targeted behavior(s) is often the missing link in functional behavioral assessment for older, higher functioning students (Nichols, 1998). Positive behavior support uses empirically validated processes to analyze the interaction of behavioral and ecological components (Carr et al., 1999).

Children develop at different rates across domains. They might fall into the 98th percentile in height and the 50th percentile in weight; they might exhibit early language skills and attain fine motor control later than their peers. An understanding of developmental processes and the biophysical contributors to maximizing a child's biological predispositions across domains is important in the diagnosis and treatment of learning and behavior problems. The biophysical approach to understanding children's needs offers a model of expected norms for each age that acts as a scope and sequence for educators to follow. As students grow and develop, they learn about themselves, the environment, and how to access the people, items, attention, and sensory stimulation that they need or want. The behavioral approach offers a rich research foundation for determining the function of a behavior, the sequence of events and conditions that tend to elicit a particular behavior, the type of deficit—skill or performance—that the student exhibits, and ways to intervene effectively once critical variables have been identified. Ecological theorists include biophysical and behavioral data in the analysis and treatment of challenging behaviors with an emphasis on the interaction of variables. Sometimes the setting variables such as scheduling of activities, orderliness of supplies, light, and temperature affect behavior more dramatically than a teacher might suspect on first inspection of a problem. Individual as well as group variables contribute to the overall setting and often offer insight into intervention design when more direct behavioral approaches have less than desired results. The cognitive-behavioral approach is included because of the benefit of understanding how a child's thinking affects emotions and behavior. Children are not passive recipients of our interventions. As they move through the elementary school years, their abilities to think logically improve. They begin to anticipate our actions, plan ahead, and use our interventions against us through various manipulative maneuvers. A failure on our part to understand the increasing impact of cognitive development and self-talk on overt behavior can be detrimental to the success of our interventions.

The Individuals With Disabilities Education Act (2004) requires extensive prereferral processes and stringent assessment procedures when addressing the needs of students with challenging behaviors. School districts must now collect data, analyze the patterns and functions of the observed behaviors that are suggested by the data, and develop behavior intervention plans that address the hypothesized function of the behavior. The research on functional behavior assessment was largely conducted on students with developmental disabilities such as mental retardation and autism. While the technology is well documented and highly effective in controlled settings, little research has been conducted on its application to higher functioning youth who do not have developmental disabilities; less easily managed and controlled group-oriented classroom settings; and behaviors that occur with low rates of frequency (one or fewer times per day). Sasso, Conroy, Stichter, and Fox (2001) are among the researchers who have begun to address the limitations of a strict reliance on the behavioral approach alone. Some of the research on cognitive-behavioral techniques (CBT) for higher functioning students (students who function within the average to above-average intelligence ranges) is outlined below as a rationale for including cognitive-behavioral interventions with children who have learning and behavior problems.

1. Programs that rely exclusively on externally controlled contingencies fail to maintain student motivation and can impair learning (DiGangi & Magg, 1992; Nelson, Smith, Young, & Dodd, 1991).

2. First and third graders who receive CBT exhibit higher rates of classroom-appropriate behavior than students who received externally controlled contingencies without CBT (Manning, 1988).

3. Students at the elementary level respond favorably to CBT (Fantuzzo, Rohrbeck, & Azar, 1987; Smith, Siegel, O'Conner, & Thomas, 1994).

4. Children with behavioral disorders respond favorably to the implementation of CBT (Ager & Cole, 1991).

5. Delinquent students exhibit higher rates of social adjustment after the implementation of CBT (Larson & Gerber, 1987).

6. Preschool and grade school children can self-instruct to inhibit impulsivity and aggression (Pressley, 1979).

7. CBT has application for behavioral challenges as well as academic achievement (Dixon, 1985; Paris & Oka, 1986; Yell, 1993).

8. Low-achieving students benefit from training in self-monitoring because they make poor use of time and don't know what they don't know (Malone & Mastropieri, 1992; Schunk & Rice, 1992).

9. Low-achieving students benefit from attribution training and achieve less academically when taught strategies without addressing the cognitive components of learned helplessness (Schunk & Rice, 1992).

10. Low achievers attempt to avoid feelings of failure by engaging in one or more of the following behaviors: (a) withdrawing, (b) feigning interest, (c) shifting blame to an external agent, (d) selectively forgetting, (e) procrastinating, (f) cheating, and (g) lowering expectations of self (Paris, Wasik, & Turner, 1991).

Their achievement scores increase when interventions directly related to feelings of failure are implemented (Schunk & Rice, 1992).

■ CONCLUSION

Mental health issues are poorly understood in school settings. Children and parents are too often blamed for conditions that are beyond their control. Parents and students, in return, blame the schools for not providing appropriate levels of support. We can stop the blame game. We can marshal the energy and interventions necessary for effective treatment through (a) understanding the nature and needs of our most challenging youth, (b) accessing a rich foundation of knowledge about how children grow and learn, (c) constructing a framework from which to make professional decisions, and (d) engaging all concerned in taking responsibility for the resolution. A child's problems are no one's fault. Blame is an unproductive waste of precious time and energy. Children's problems are their, their parents', their teachers', their school administrators' and support personnel's, and their community's *responsibility.*

In the chapters that follow, cognitive and social-emotional development through the elementary school years will be explored. Group development, the conflict cycle, and components of effective classroomwide behavior management will be illustrated through school-based examples, anecdotes, and a review of relevant research. Special case interventions are offered in Chapter 7 for youth with the most challenging disorders. Chapter 8 addresses the research on resilience. Far more children grow beyond their present challenges than teachers realize. Researchers have followed hundreds of children from early childhood through their mid 30s. The good news is that what we do matters! Information about how to identify resilient traits in a student and nurture those traits is described along with information on how to nurture educator resilience. Our youth need for us to have "true grit"—in the spirit of Marian Wright Edelman (1992), to get up every morning, to do what we have to do, to get up every time we fall down, and to try as many times as needed to get the job done right. It is through our eyes that our children see themselves and in our eyes that they see their futures. They deserve to see hope!

NOTE ■

1. The anecdote from Foundational Principle #8, was reprinted with the consent of the Council for Children With Behavioral Disorders and the Council for Exceptional Children. From Rockwell, S., Cuccio, S., Kirtley, B., & Smith, G. (1998), *Developing Personal and Interpersonal Responsibility in Children and Youth With Emotional/Behavioral Disorders.* Reston, VA: Council for Exceptional Children.

2

Typical and Atypical Development

<table>
<tr><td colspan="2">Chapter Overview</td></tr>
<tr>
<td>

</td>
<td>

</td>
</tr>
</table>

INTRODUCTION ■

Many parents take great pride in comparing their baby's development to the milestone charts that pediatricians provide at an infant's first well-baby checkup. Little Julie might be in the 50th percentile for weight and the 30th percentile for length. The doctor may inquire about feeding schedules and whether or not the baby is being given cereal in her milk. These growth charts are useful to doctors and parents in documenting patterns over time, in identifying potential abnormalities early, and in addressing the infant's nutritional needs. Height and weight are expected to increase at a predictable rate and to be correlated with chronological age. Milestones in motor skills, language development, cognition, social-behavioral functioning, and academic achievement are also expected to proceed with increasing complexity and sophistication. When an individual's development across all domains (i.e., cognitive, linguistic, motor) falls within an acceptable range of mastery, the individual is considered to be normal. When an individual's development in one or more domains lags significantly behind age or grade-level norms, the individual is identified as having a disability, disorder, or handicapping condition. When an individual's development in one or more domains exceeds age or grade-level norms, the individual is identified as gifted and talented. Norms have been determined by observing a large subsection of children at different ages and documenting the skills typically mastered at each age (Wallace, Larsen, & Elksnin, 1992). When the first special education services were mandated by the Education for All Handicapped Children Act (PL 94–142) in 1975, many people assumed that typically developing children were the responsibility of general educators and that atypically developing children were the responsibility of *special* educators. Political attitudes have shifted since 1975. Increased political and legal pressure to include children with a range of atypical developmental needs in the general education environment continues. To make the issues even more complex, researchers have discovered through advanced medical technologies that development is not as stage specific or linear as once thought. A wide variation of strengths and needs across developmental domains (i.e., linguistic, social, cognitive) may, in fact, be normal. An understanding of typical and atypical development is within the realm of both general and special education professionals. This chapter briefly explores typical and atypical development with attention to shifts in assessment analysis and intervention development.

■ TYPICAL DEVELOPMENT

So what is normal or typical? Piaget (1970), Erikson (1950), Gesell and Ilg (1946), and other researchers have compiled an extensive list of motor, verbal/linguistic, social-emotional, and cognitive skills typical of children and youth. Figures 2.1, 2.2, and 2.3 contain information about typical milestones from birth to age 12.

During the early years of development, a wider variation of behaviors falls within normal limits (Crain, 2000). Neurological development itself begins with functions necessary for survival. Muscle control begins with the upper body in terms of movement and support of the head and coordination of the arms and fingers, proceeding to voluntary control of the trunk and lower extremities. This typical progression of neurological development is easily observed in the motor skill milestones that infants and toddlers exhibit—turning the head to gaze at a moving object at 3 to 4 months, reaching for a toy and grasping it at 6 months, standing while holding on to furniture or walking alone at 12 months, and walking up two to three stairs at 24 months. Social-emotional, cognitive, and verbal/linguistic skills are also developing during these preschool years. Patterns of skill development across domains tend to occur at specific ages. At the age of about 6 months, a baby learns to roll over, sit up, pass toys from the right hand to the left hand, and put toys in the mouth. Social-emotional learning at this age is evidenced by withdrawing from strangers and cooing, crying, or holding arms

(Text continues on page 33)

Figure 2.1   Developmental Milestones

	Motor Skills	Social-Behavioral (Erikson, 1950)	Verbal/Linguistic	Cognitive (Piaget, 1970)
3 to 4 months	Turns head Follows a moving object or person Waves arms at a toy dangled overhead Lifts head when lying on stomach	Trust versus mistrust (birth to 12 months) Smiles at self in mirror Smiles at a familiar person Welcomes a familiar person by wiggling body and waving arms	Repeats sounds when a person imitates a sound the baby has made Laughs at peekaboo games Makes cooing and gurgling sounds	Sensori-motor stage (birth to 2 years) Derives pleasure and information about the world through the senses
6 months	Reaches and grasps toys May sit unassisted Holds head steady when supported in a sitting position	Begins to understand that crying brings a reaction from others Shows discomfort around strangers	Makes sounds like da, ga, ka, and ba Holds out arms when wanting to be held Communicates with cries, laughter, etc.	Puts objects in mouth
12 months	Sits well without support May walk without assistance Grasps small objects with thumb and index finger Turns pages in a book if the pages are very stiff (cardboard consistency)	Autonomy versus shame (12 months to 2 years) Shows anxiety at being separated from parents Shows affection to familiar people Expresses emotions: pleasure, anger, excitement, happiness, and sadness	Understands simple commands Points for desired items Says two or three words such as *mama* and *dada* Looks for or hands over a known object when asked	Begins to understand that actions make things happen (i.e., pushing a ball makes it roll)
24 months	Walks up and down a few stairs Stacks three to seven blocks Scribbles Drinks from a cup with minimal spilling Brings spoon to mouth but turns spoon over Walks, climbs, runs, and kicks a ball	Asserts independence Easily frustrated Tantrums Forms strong attachment to parents Initiative versus guilt (2 years to 6 years)	Refers to self as *I* or *me* Speaks 20 to 50 words Understands more words than is able to use Points to body parts when named Correctly identifies a picture of a known object when asked	Preoperational (2 years to 7 years) Pretends when playing with toys
3 years	Washes hands alone Dresses with help Catches a large ball Rides a tricycle Rolls, pounds, and squeezes clay	Begins to be able to take turns Tends to be physically aggressive Begins to show empathy May cling or whine	Uses sentences of three to five words Uses 50 to 500 words Answers simple questions Can follow a two-part direction	Matches six basic colors Can categorize and sort common objects (i.e., clothing and toys) Acts out simple stories
4 years	Can button large buttons Can put a coat on a hanger Draws people with three or more major body parts Copies simple shapes Can use the toilet without help	Likes to act out adult roles and help adults during routine tasks (i.e., shopping, cleaning, laundry) Begins to accept that some items,	Can follow three unrelated instructions Understands *over, under,* and *between* Uses names of things and action words	Can compare simple concepts such as hot versus cold and heavy versus light Recites rhymes or sings songs from memory Sorts objects by color

(Continued)

Figure 2.1 (Continued)

	Motor Skills	Social-Behavioral (Erikson, 1950)	Verbal/Linguistic	Cognitive (Piaget, 1970)
4 years	Moves in time to rhythm or music	activities, and/or topics are off limits without overreacting emotionally Enjoys new experiences such as zoos, museums, sporting events, etc.	Can talk about the past and future using the correct tense	
5 years	Large muscle coordination of major interest to the child: jumping, running, and throwing are favorite activities Frequent colds Hypersensitive to small injuries	Cooperative May lie or steal Exaggerates May boss others Likes to make people laugh Plays cooperatively in small groups without constant supervision Comforts playmates Understands nonverbal cues of pleasure in others	Follows directions using words like *through, away from,* and *toward* Can count to 20 Joins in a conversation Tells stories and jokes Answers "why" and "what would happen if" questions	Enjoys rote learning Understands the concepts of same and opposite Acts out a story using props, puppets, and/or toys Intuitive thinker Concepts are not well integrated Attention span increases Initiates organizing by planning and following through during play
6 years	May seem to be more messy, fidgety, and chatty Small muscle skills and hand-eye coordination still developing	Industry versus inferiority (6 years to 12 years) Oppositional Brash Cheats Plays best in groups of two May overreact to losing Wants to be the best Motivation easily thwarted Warm and enthused when getting what is desired, quickly angered and/or teary if denied desired items or activities	Most aspects of grammar are mastered by the age of 5 or 6.	Able to use mental imagery to begin the integration of ideas Thinking process susceptible to shutting down if feeling unsuccessful Interested in learning to read Primary focus of attention is on mastery of motor skills
7 years	Small muscle skills advance to increase enjoyment in puzzles, drawing, marbles, coloring, and putting simple models together Tires easily Headaches, leg aches, and muscle discomfort reported	Can be confrontive and aggressive Jealous of siblings Small setbacks may result in work paralysis Easily distracted and forgetful Nightmares and other signs of distress such as sucking fingers, chewing nails, or nervous tics are common	Sentences that use the passive tense are difficult for children to understand before the age of 7	Concrete operations (7 years to 11 years) Begins to understand causality and continuity in time, objects, and numbers May begin to understand reversibility in the conservation of matter and liquid

	Motor Skills	Social-Behavioral (Erikson, 1950)	Verbal/Linguistic	Cognitive (Piaget, 1970)
		Nonverbal cues of anger and pain are recognized in others May wish to do good work for an internal sense of responsibility In terms of misbehavior, intention is not relevant; wrong is wrong and right is right Getting caught and not getting caught are of paramount concern		
8 years	Small muscle skills consolidate Reading and writing are easier due to maturation of hand-eye coordination May enjoy gender-specific physical activities Sports and outside play are especially alluring	Shows off Opinionated More interested in reality than fantasy Tendency to overdramatize failure Underneath a confident façade is a tendency to be easily hurt A best friend becomes important Moral reasoning is black and white; good is good, bad is bad Tattling and issues of fairness are common	Subtle grammatical nuances continue to develop through age 10 Complex vocabulary and subtle, contextual cues for the application of vocabulary develop through adulthood as exposure to increasingly complex concepts occurs	Thinking may be more logical Movement toward a less egocentric understanding of the world Begins to be able to keep an end goal in mind while working toward successive approximations Review as a method for more deeply understanding and more efficiently being able to use a concept or skill appreciated or welcomed
9 years	The child begins to look more mature Physically active Increased interest in the workings of the body	Resents bossiness in others Awareness of others heightens Nonverbal cues of fear and surprise are recognized in others Tattling as a way to look superior is less likely Telling the truth is likely unless a lie will assist in avoiding a punishment Group loyalty may form	Continual development of concepts; vocabulary; and subtle, complex grammar	Concrete operations still common and appropriate Maps, graphs, and other representational models begin to make sense Causal relationships can be taught with concrete examples The child begins to understand that he or she is not the center of the universe

(Continued)

Figure 2.1 (Continued)

	Motor Skills	Social-Behavioral (Erikson, 1950)	Verbal/Linguistic	Cognitive (Piaget, 1970)
		Jobs and responsibilities may be accepted, but acted upon with a degree of procrastination Understands right and wrong Responds well to praise		
10 years	Gross and fine motor skills become consolidated Girls may enter puberty	Hot-tempered Competitive Clubs, secret codes, and items that represent group membership are important A second-person perspective and appeals to act out of a sense of respect hold appeal Fairness tends to be evaluated in terms of the best deal for self Payback for wrongs becomes valued Natural and logical consequences understood Open to and able to make good use of deal making, family or classroom meetings, and democratic processes	Continual development of concepts; vocabulary; and subtle, complex grammar Conversations clearly exhibit a flow of information More able to express ideas and insights	Generally engaged in concrete thinking processes, but begins to exhibit abilities to apply intuitive logic Begins to think about how he or she thinks (metacognition) Individual learning styles (strengths, needs, and preference) become evident
11 years	Many girls enter puberty Girls are usually taller Children who have not begun to develop (grow taller or look more mature) may feel anxious Some children begin to experiment with sex, smoking, alcohol, and/or drugs	Self-centered Peers become more important than adults May act out to gain peer approval Hero worship is common Questions about God and worship may become more important Ambivalence and mercurial changes in thinking, feeling, and behaving are common Hates and loves are felt and expressed intensely and are quickly forgotten	Continual development of concepts; vocabulary; and subtle, complex grammar	Formal operations (11 years to adult) Problem solving may become more logical Benefits from cooperative learning tasks that integrate increasing abilities to conceptualize, problem-solve, think logically, and share ideas

	Motor Skills	Social-Behavioral (Erikson, 1950)	Verbal/Linguistic	Cognitive (Piaget, 1970)
		Black and white thinking about moral choices is still evident: either/or thinker Acts more self-assured than feels Wants to appear good, but still be considered "cool" by peers		
12 years	Skeletal growth elongates Large and small muscle coordination becomes enhanced and brings pleasure Secondary sexual characteristics may emerge Able to work for an extended period of time on a project	Exhibits sudden bursts of "goodness" Struggles with independence and dependence Adults are viewed as old and out of touch Preoccupation with and oversensitivity toward self Mood swings are rare Bossy—especially toward siblings Tends to quote authorities (teacher, coach, band instructor, etc.)	Continual development of concepts; vocabulary; and subtle, complex grammar	Sense of humor may emerge Begins to talk about abstract ideas Arranges thoughts with some logic and understanding of ideas—moves beyond rote memorization May think of self as an authority on one or more topics

out to elicit a response from caregivers. Babbling signals the beginning of expressive language development. A rudimentary cognitive understanding of cause and effect begins to emerge with games like "peekaboo" and the tendency to turn the head to look for toys that have been dropped. Given the parallel acquisition of skills across motor, social-emotional, cognitive, and linguistic domains during infancy and early childhood in typically developing individuals, it is logical to assume that milestones requiring increasingly complex skills would continue in a complementary fashion during middle childhood and adolescence. For the majority of children and youth, this concept of parallel, complementary development across domains at increasing levels of complexity is useful. In general, development progresses (a) from simple to complex (Crain, 2000; Gesell & Ilg, 1946; Piaget, 1970), (b) from concrete to abstract (Crain, 2000; Gesell & Ilg, 1946; Piaget, 1977), and (c) within predictable sequences (Ellsworth, 1996; Gesell & Ilg, 1946; Levine, 2002; Piaget, 1977). Rates of skill mastery are not as predictable (Ellsworth, 1996; Levine, 2002). Domains of development do, however, function interdependently (Ellsworth, 1996; Levine, 2002). While all individuals exhibit unique strengths and weaknesses, development in an area of strength is usually sufficient to compensate for an area of relative weakness. As individuals move into late adolescence and stages of adult development, an expectation that individuals demonstrate parallel levels of mastery across all domains becomes less essential as greater specialization in an area of strength is valued (Levine, 2002). Those with a talent for mathematical reasoning enter professions such as engineering, accounting, and physics that use their unique strengths. Those who excel in performing arts enter musical or theatrical

Figure 2.2   Erikson's Theory (1950) of Psychosocial Development

Infancy: Trust Versus Mistrust

If parents respond predictably to the infant's needs for food, warmth, protection, and attention, the infant begins to trust and to take pleasure in responding to others. The world feels safe and inviting. If basic needs are not met, the infant begins to learn that others do not necessarily bring comfort. The world feels threatening and lonely.

Toddler: Autonomy Versus Doubt and Shame

During the toddler years, the child begins to explore the environment. If boundaries established during this time are safe and still allow for exploration, the child learns to take joy in doing some things on his/her own. If the boundaries are too restrictive or permissive, the child learns to feel doubt about his/her abilities to manage the world and shame over his/her limitations.

Early Childhood: Initiative Versus Guilt

During early childhood, children begin to want to be like the adults in their lives. They enjoy helping with chores and pretending to be an adult by playing dress-up. If they are successful in learning to complete some of the self-help tasks that are expected of them, such as using the toilet, sleeping through the night dry, and dressing themselves, they learn to feel confident about their abilities to take initiative. If they are often unsuccessful, or are harshly punished for failing to master tasks quickly enough to satisfy the adults in their lives, they learn to feel very guilty.

Elementary Years: Industry Versus Inferiority

The major tasks expected of youth during the elementary school years are to learn to read, write, and compute. Youth at these ages begin to enjoy being part of clubs and sports teams with other young people. If they experience success in some of the areas that are important to them and to valued adults in their lives (i.e., parents, teachers, clergy, and coaches), they learn to see themselves as capable and take pride in their industrious efforts. If they experience too much failure—particularly in areas that valued adults feel are important, they learn to feel inferior—not good enough.

Important Note: Before the age of 10, children do not typically understand the differences between good/bad behavior and ability/inability to perform. If they are unable to read, play a sport important to the family, or accomplish some other task they know their parents value, they will think that they are *bad*. It is extremely important that youth experience high rates of success.

Figure 2.3   Piaget's Theory of Cognitive Development

Sensori-Motor (birth to 2 years)	*Preoperational* (2 years to 7 years)	*Concrete Operations* (7 years to 11 years)	*Formal Operations* (11 years to adult)
The child gains information about the environment from senses and from movement The two important milestones attained during this period include: • Objects do not cease to exist when they are hidden • A movement from reflex actions to goal-directed activity	The child gradually develops language skills and the ability to think symbolically Actions and concepts are developed logically, but can only be understood from one perspective Other's points of view are difficult to comprehend	The child is able to solve problems in a logical manner through the use of real life, hands-on experience Laws of conservation and the ability to sequence as well as classify develop during this period The child is also able to understand reversibility	The youth or adult is able to solve problems abstractly and in a logical manner The scientific method is clearly understood and is applied informally in real world problem solving Concerns about social issues and identity develop as well

careers. Adults are expected to be competent across a wide range of concepts and skills, but they are not expected to maintain mastery in all domains simultaneously. School-age children are not so fortunate.

Schools are focused on a narrow range of developmental skills. If they have been exposed to optimal learning experiences prior to entering school and if their neurological development is sufficient to keep pace with grade-level demands, children enjoy the challenges they encounter in the classroom. If they have not been exposed to adequate opportunities to develop language skills, social skills, and foundational concepts and if their neurological development in one or more areas is insufficient to the demands of a classroom setting, children encounter frustration and failure at an age when they are ill equipped to understand or cope with those demands.

ATYPICAL DEVELOPMENT ■

Developmental theories, lists of age-related milestones, and state-mandated grade-level expectations lead the uninitiated to believe that development proceeds in a linear fashion that is best represented by an inclined plane or rungs on an upright ladder. Ellsworth (1996) and Levine (2002) point out, however, that within a particular individual, development can often proceed unevenly across cognitive, social-emotional, motor, and linguistic domains. In the area of reading achievement, for example, norms for any given age reflect expected levels of achievement for about 68% of the children (Ellsworth, 1996). This means that the other 32% are working above or below the expected level of mastery. If one considers the variability in growth across three to five domains, it is not unusual to find only two or three students in a class of 30 who function on grade or age norms in every area (Ellsworth, 1996). While we continue to rely heavily on age and grade-level norms for understanding students' strengths and needs as learners, current research on neurodevelopmental constructs reveals interrelated systems that function more like an ever-expanding web (Levine, 2002) than a series of independent rungs. Before examining the value of integrating what is known about age-related stages with emerging knowledge about the complex development of the brain, a personal experience is offered as an illustration of the need to broaden our concepts of typical and atypical development, IQ, disability, gifts and talents, the role of the educator, and the process of learning.

During my late 30s, I began advanced graduate-level work in the fields of emotional and behavior disorders, typical and atypical development, and education. I was well past the age of onset for abstract reasoning, which Piaget (1970) identified as beginning in early adolescence. I welcomed my courses, in general, with enthusiasm. Nothing required of me was unusually difficult or beyond comprehension until I encountered a relatively minor concept that stopped me in my tracks during the third graduate-level course in statistical analysis required for program completion. I have to admit that statistics had not been the easiest content for me to understand, but I had been able to keep pace with course requirements until the concept of *sphericity* was introduced.

Being a mature learner, I was well aware of my preferred style of learning and was fortunate enough to have a professor who had taught high school while working toward the doctorate that allowed him to teach at a university. He was already familiar with the need many students have to be given verbal translations for mathematical formulas prior to manipulating numbers and numerical concepts. We had worked well together during the previous two courses and had joked about coauthoring a book in the future that we planned to title, *Statistics as a Second Language.* Long before attending graduate school, I realized that mathematics could be understood linguistically through logical reasoning, and I had filled notebooks in high school with concept definitions, theorems, and postulates.

Unfortunately, meeting *sphericity,* words failed me for the first time in my educational career. No definition sufficed. I was thoroughly confused in spite of Dr. Ferron's very competent and patient attempts at an explanation. Finally, I asked for a three-dimensional model, knowing that when words failed, my ability to visualize a concept, which could then be translated into words, was my only hope. Dr. Ferron indulged me by forming a spherical shape with his fingers and describing a clear ornamental globe with data point dots scattered within the confines of the globe. He compared this model with a snow globe that had been shaken and suspended in time. In an instant, I understood and responded with, "I've got it! It's a 3-D scatter plot!" Dr. Ferron thought for a moment, laughed, and agreed with my rather inelegant definition.

The professor who cotaught the course was visibly annoyed at our exchange. He believed that graduate-level students should not need such elementary explanations. Like other educators who are well versed in their fields and rely on a linear model of cognitive development, he narrowly defined intelligence and competence within a specific content area. The ability to think abstractly without the aid of 3-D models and lengthy verbal explanations should have been established prior to entry into a doctoral-level course in statistical analysis, according to his reasoning, and yet, I was able to master the concept, earn a respectable grade in the course (the first time I took it), and apply the concept in other settings beyond the classroom.

Perhaps the ability to think abstractly is a function of cognitive growth that typically emerges during early adolescence *and* is also dependent on the interrelatedness of neurodevelopmental constructs or systems. When my linguistic system failed to be adequate, I relied on my visual system.

The problem was not a lack of intelligence, a disability in mathematics, or an inability to think abstractly. The problem was a mismatch between the professor's preferred methods for presenting the information and my neurodevelopmental web of strengths and needs. Fortunately, I knew how to ask for what I needed.

Many children do not understand their strengths and needs well enough to ask for the kind of assistance that they need. Their parents and teachers are often equally unaware. This can often lead to inaccurate labeling of learning and behavior problems and the implementation of ineffective interventions. Over time, the child is less successful, less motivated, and more at risk for continued failure. Understanding the difference between age or stage norms as discrete, unrelated indicators of growth and the interrelated nature of neurodevelopmental systems is essential to the development of effective interventions for children with mild or moderate social-emotional problems and academic achievement deficits.

Dr. Levine has developed assessment tools that can be administered and interpreted only by trained medical professionals. These tools include sections on prenatal history, infancy, family history, developmental milestones during early childhood, affect, attention, academic skills, social skills, and subcategories within the eight neurodevelopmental constructs or systems. Resources available to school personnel include social, medical, and family histories; speech and language assessments; hearing and vision screenings; the results of individually administered intelligence tests; surveys completed by parents, teachers, and when appropriate, students; behavior rating scales; and achievement tests results. These tools can provide important insight into the impact one neurodevelopmental system is having on other systems.

A child may appear to have a motivation problem when the problem is, in fact, one of maintaining adequate levels of working memory. Another child may appear to have ADHD. Further examination by the child study team reveals that her parents have recently separated and divorced and that she feels extremely anxious about the home situation. Her attention to classroom tasks is partially diverted to thoughts and feelings about her parents' divorce and the situation is further exacerbated by a mild hearing problem. She is experiencing an allergic reaction to seasonal pollen. Her Eustachian tubes are filled with fluid. As a result, she cannot hear the teacher when any background noise is present in the environment. Instead of implementing a behavior plan to address the ADHD, the child's teacher moved her desk closer to the front of the room, the guidance counselor included her in a support group for children whose parents were divorced or separated, and the child's pediatrician put her on a nondrowsy allergy medicine to help clear the fluid from the ears. Her academic achievement and behavior returned to their previously acceptable levels of performance.

Some students, however, do not respond readily to the child study team's initial recommendations. More in-depth information and program development are required for these children. A developmental profile is constructed through the implementation of a series of formal tests; structured interviews with parents, teachers, and the student; student work samples; and carefully documented observations. Brian's profile is illustrated in Figure 2.4.

Brian had been referred to the child study team because of concerns over his disruptive behavior. He frequently interrupted the class with

Figure 2.4   Developmental Profile

Name _____ Brian B. _____   School Year _____ 2005-06 _____

Assigned Grade _____ 3 _____   Teacher _____ Doc Roc _____

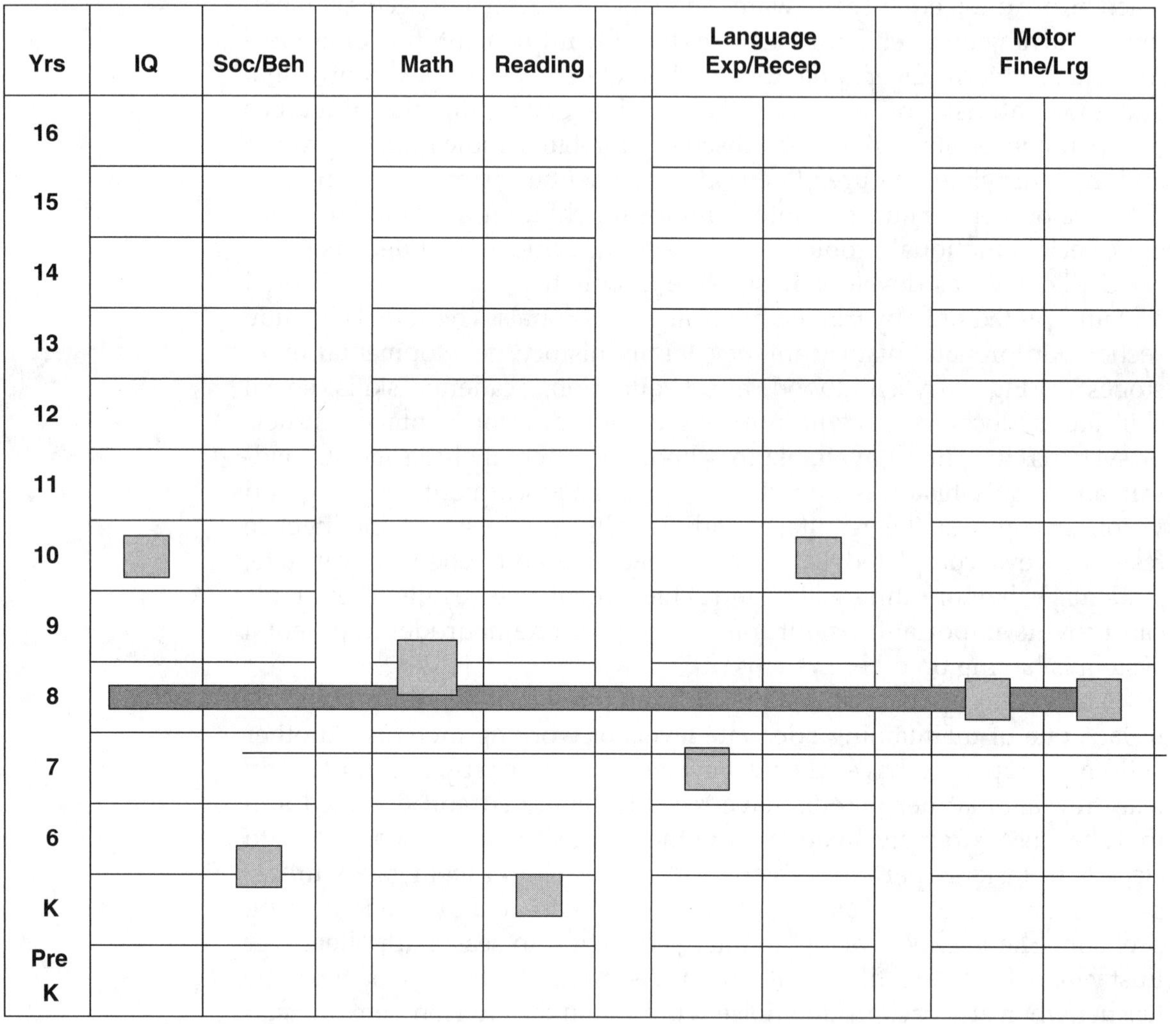

Yrs	IQ	Soc/Beh		Math	Reading		Language Exp/Recep			Motor Fine/Lrg	
16											
15											
14											
13											
12											
11											
10	▢							▢			
9				▢							
8	▬	▬	▬	▬	▬	▬	▬	▬	▬	▢	▢
7							▢				
6		▢									
K					▢						
Pre K											

inappropriate comments and drew pictures or constructed imaginative toys out of materials in his desk when he was expected to complete independent work. An individually administered IQ test revealed that Brian functioned cognitively in the superior range. In spite of a high overall IQ score, however, Brian's math ability was within the expected range for his age, and his reading achievement scores were significantly below age and grade-level expectations.

A speech and language screening revealed that Brian comprehended words, directions, and concepts that were well beyond age and grade-level expectations; but he had difficulty expressing his thoughts, feelings, wants, needs, and understandings verbally. He also exhibited difficulty with the pragmatics of speech—knowing when and how to enter a conversation; understanding the subtle nuances between types of words, tone of voice, volume, and rates of speech expected in different settings; and recognizing the need to follow the topic of conversation or request a change in topic during class discussions. Expressive language difficulties negatively impacted his behavior in the classroom as well as his ability to complete independent assignments. In addition, he had not mastered the associations between spoken sounds and the written code. This was negatively impacting his ability to read and spell. A test of his listening comprehension—in which Brian listened to a passage read aloud to him and answered oral questions by pointing to a picture located in an array of pictures that represented the answer to the question—revealed above grade-level performance. His listening comprehension score was more typical of a 12-year-old than an 8-year-old. He needed intensive work in the areas of expressive language and sound-symbol associations for reading and spelling.

Previous attempts to establish a behavior plan had failed. The emphasis had been on reinforcing desired behaviors and punishing noncompliant behaviors without the additional consideration of language-processing deficits. Additional reading instruction provided during first and second grade had also failed to sufficiently strengthen Brian's deficits in sound-symbol association. Brian's new plan was expanded to include (a) language therapy to address expressive language skills and the pragmatics of speech; (b) intensive computerized instruction designed to target recognition and recall of phonemes, their associated written symbols, and the blending of those symbols into words; (c) visual cues in the environment to prompt Brian's memory of classroom rules, academic content, and the daily schedule; (d) accommodations such as a phoneme strip attached to his desk that included picture cues to assist him in decoding and spelling unfamiliar words, an illustrated word bank, and a handheld electronic spell checker with read-aloud capacity and a headset; (e) a self-monitoring system to strengthen his attention to assigned tasks during independent work periods; (f) social skills instruction; (g) a study buddy to assist with reading and spelling tasks and social skill prompting; and (h) a reward system that included academic performance as well as compliance with classroom rules.

The entire class was trained in peer tutoring skills prior to the assignment of study buddies. Brian was paired with a student who was skilled in reading and spelling and who needed assistance with math. Brian's classmates admired his artistic abilities, so he was given the title of class illustrator. He helped design posters, murals, and three-dimensional displays aligned with science, social studies, and math content. Over the course of the year, Brian's reading achievement score increased by 24 months, his math achievement score increased by 18 months, and his classroom behavior no longer caused concerns for his parents and teachers.

If the child study team had simply assessed Brian's levels of academic and behavioral functioning without investigating processing strengths and deficits, the interventions selected to address his behavioral and academic needs might have been insufficiently intense or entirely inappropriate. Brian's behavior and academic problems were not due to a lack of motivation or understanding of expectations. His inappropriate comments were related to expressive language-processing deficits and incomplete knowledge of the implicit rules of conversation. Punishing him for noncompliance would not teach him how to interact. Rewarding him for appropriate behavior without directly teaching desired skills might have created undue levels of stress as Brian struggled to understand why he was rewarded one day and punished the next. Brian's case illustrates the necessity of looking at the whole child when assessing strengths and needs, targeting skills for remediation, and developing an intervention plan. Given the limits of time, personnel, and other resources available in school environments, how can a child study team most efficiently assess a child's needs and intervene on his or her behalf?

■ ASSESSMENT

A professional's perspective on student behavior and learning is influenced by his or her training. As discussed in Chapter 1, those who view students through a behavioral perspective believe that behavior is learned. Assessment is focused primarily on the collection of data about the frequency, intensity, and duration of a behavior within clearly identified contexts that include attention to antecedents, behaviors, and consequences. Those with a biophysical perspective investigate neurological, biochemical, and physiological components of learning. Assessments include medical tests; questions about health-related issues (i.e., diet, activity levels, sleep patterns, family history of disease); and clinical examinations. Those with an ecological perspective investigate the interaction among the environment, the required tasks, and the individual. This perspective integrates developmental, behavioral, biophysical, and cognitive components and is most holistic in its conceptualization and treatment of the student. A discussion of three essential research topics (temperament versus learned behavior, externalizing versus internalizing disorders, and neurodevelopmental constructs) is required prior to an examination of assessment tools.

Understanding the Whole Child: Essential Research Topics

The elementary school years are extremely important. If all has gone well during infancy and early childhood, the child arrives at school ready to meet the expected challenges. A sense of competence develops through (a) multiple experiences of success, (b) skills acquired while overcoming mistakes, (c) interaction with an increasing circle of friendship and adult support, and (d) opportunities to engage in a wider range of activities. Why do some students adapt while others meet with increasing levels of frustration and failure? Researchers continue to ponder that question from a variety of angles. The research on risk and resilience, described briefly in Chapter 8, provides an overview of individual, familial, and community factors at work in the self-righting process of those who labor under extraordinary challenges. For the purposes of understanding development in a more holistic manner, however, research on temperament, externalizing and internalizing disorders, and neurodevelopmental constructs is offered here as a point of reference.

Temperament Versus Learned Behavior

Researchers observed newborns and discovered what mothers had long told their doctors; children are different from their very beginnings.

Chess and Thomas (1986) describe years of research they have conducted on infants, toddlers, and young children regarding typical and atypical manifestations of the traits of temperament. They discovered through longitudinal studies of 133 individuals that temperamental traits are evident during infancy and early childhood and become established and stable by middle childhood. These traits, like the neurodevelopmental constructs identified by Levine (2002), have biological foundations determined in part by a child's genes and influenced by general health, nutrition, environmental factors, experiences with others, and the larger culture within which the child develops.

We would not think of demanding that children reach a specific height by a targeted age, wear the same shoe size based on chronological age, or have the same eye and hair color. Variations in physical traits are well understood as being beyond the control of the individual, barring surgery or other dramatic cosmetic procedures. Variations in coping skills, learning, motivation, affect, and activity levels, however, are not as easily accepted and understood as biologically determined traits. To the extent that we fail to use the research in this area, we fail to effectively nurture, educate, protect, and serve our youth.

My daughter Kala (who is in her late twenties) is a beautiful, creative, talented young woman. No one who meets her now even suspects that her pediatrician referred to her as a "mother killer" when she was two. She had a very difficult and demanding temperament. She lived life at the extremes. When she was happy, she laughed, ran, jumped, and entertained all who would give her audience. When she was angry, she screamed at the top of her lungs for incredibly long periods of time. These tantrums were often accompanied by environmental destruction. In response to being asked to pick up her toys and come to dinner, she once pulled the curtain rods out of the wall, stripped the sheets from her bed, emptied her toy box on the floor, and threw all of her clothes from her closet. This took less than 5 minutes. I could hear the destruction occurring but had to secure her brother in his high chair before going to her room to stop her. She exhibited higher-than-average activity levels and intensity for girls her age and was at the top of the chart for boys. Her self-control was low—especially when frustrated or angry. She also exhibited high levels of sensitivity to sensory input of any type and was terribly unpredictable in her patterns of sleep during her infancy. Aggravating an already volatile situation was the fact that she also had allergies to pollen, wheat, citrus, milk, and tomatoes. Fortunately, I had a wonderful pediatrician who met on a consultative basis with me during her preschool and early elementary school years. Together we developed and updated regularly a plan for her that included (a) environmental supports for biologically determined traits that she could not control, (b) educative strategies for teaching her necessary coping skills, and (c) behavioral interventions for managing behaviors that were under her control. Some teachers were willing to work with the doctor and me to extend the plan into the classroom, and other teachers were not. The years that she had teachers who were unwilling to understand her needs were difficult. By the time she was 11, she had learned to control her impulses, ask for what she needed, and function without a formal support plan at home and at school. An overview of Kala's plan is described in Figure 2.5.

Figure 2.5   Components of Kala's Plan

Traits of Temperament	Environmental Accommodations	Coping Strategy Instruction	Behavioral Interventions
High rates of physical activity, in constant motion	Keep clutter to a minimum Provide comfortable, low-maintenance furnishings Build movement into the routine: chores or classroom jobs that require lifting; climbing stairs; and brisk, large-muscle movement such as taking out the garbage, vacuuming, and stacking toys or books Do not expect her to sit through a full-length movie, a formal religious ceremony or service, a concert, or any other lengthy event; plan for breaks when avoiding those types of situations is not possible	Teach her to ask for stretch breaks and permission to move from one place to another in the classroom, to use relaxation techniques that involve tensing and relaxing muscles during times of prolonged sitting, and to substitute active games and sports for disruptive behavior Invent games for potentially difficult situations. Example: When in a confined space (such as a doctor's office) encourage her to jump as many times as she can while holding an adult's hands in a specified period of time	Kala was a bright, creative, enthusiastic, and entertaining child in spite of her high rates of physical activity; difficulty with mood, biological function, and attention regulation; and low sensory threshold. Coping strategy instruction was focused on three broad areas: Communication Self-monitoring Making good choices Kala was prompted through a variety of visual and verbal cues to apply one or more of the coping strategies she was being taught. When she communicated her needs appropriately, actively engaged in self-monitoring (as evidenced by the use of her schedule, calendar, or discussions with adults), or made good choices, she was immediately reinforced with a hug, words of approval, a smile, a pat on the back, or a small tangible reward. When she was unable to maintain an acceptable level of self-control, she was removed to a quiet area until she regained her composure. If she had made a mess, she was required to clean. If she had disrupted a social event, she was required spend an additional period of time away from the activities before returning. Whenever possible, consequences were either natural (i.e., the thrown toy broke and would not be replaced) or logical (i.e., no straws in her juice for a week after she used the straw to spit juice on classmates).
Intense reactions to changes and difficulty with mood regulation, a tendency to live life at the extremes	Keep the daily schedule as predictable as possible Prepare her in advance for changes whenever possible Provide her with age-appropriate choices (i.e., blue sweater or red sweater, apple or raisins) to encourage a sense of control over some components of the day, but limit the choices to no more than three	Teach her to use appropriate words, volume, and tone when asking for what she wants or needs Teach her to use a picture schedule and picture calendar Talk with her regularly about the schedule and calendar Model the use of the schedule, calendar, expression of wants and needs, modulation of voice	
Low threshold for sensory stimulation	Talk quietly and calmly Do not encourage active play before bedtime Remove toys and other items that overstimulate her Cut labels out of clothing Purchase clothing made of cotton and other soft, nonirritating fabrics Play soft music in the background	Teach her to go to a quiet area when she is overstimulated Teach her relaxation techniques Engage her in discussions about the activities, types of music, television shows, games, foods, and other sources of stimulation that help her calm down Make a picture chart of high energy and low energy activities and items for her to use in selecting what she needs to help herself regulate an appropriate level of stimulation	
Difficulty with regulation of biological functions (sleeping, eating, elimination)	Establish and routinely follow a schedule. An exact adherence to time is not as important as a predictable routine. For example: The going-to-bed routine included a drink of water, a bath, toileting, brushing teeth, reading one story,	Encourage the use of the daily schedule for self-monitoring	

Traits of Temperament	Environmental Accommodations	Coping Strategy Instruction	Behavioral Interventions
	prayers, a kiss goodnight, and lights out. Deviation from the sequence (to get a second drink, have a snack, read a second story, etc.) inevitably ended in attempts to negotiate a change in the lights out time and led to screaming fits and tears.		**Note:** In response to destroying her room in the anecdote of this chapter, I took all toys and clothing as well as her dresser and toy box from her room. She had to earn each item back through appropriate behavior. It took her a few months to regain all items and the privilege of making choices with regard to outfits and playtime activities. She never engaged in that level of inappropriate behavior again.
Difficulty sustaining attention	**Do one thing at a time.** If cleaning the room, for example, select one type of item at a time to put away. If playing, select one toy or game at a time. Put other items away before starting a new activity. **Take planned breaks.** When taking breaks, however, be brief and do not encourage activities that are too engaging—just stretch or do 15 jumping jacks	Teach her organizational skills and self-monitoring skills	

Chess and Thomas (1986) identified 10 traits of temperament. These traits are (1) activity level, (2) approach/withdrawal, (3) concentration or attention span and persistence, (4) intensity, (5) regularity, (6) responsiveness, (7) distractibility, (8) sensory threshold, (9) adaptability, and (10) predominant mood. The extent to which an individual trait or combination of traits presents a challenge to a child depends to some degree on the expectation of those with whom the child interacts. The physical education teacher may find a child who is active, quick to participate in novel activities, and intense a real asset to the soccer team. That same child might be the librarian's worst nightmare. Developing a plan for a child with a difficult temperament requires a period of investigation to determine which behaviors reflect biologically determined traits and which behaviors have been learned. Environmental accommodations and direct instruction in coping strategies are most effective when addressing traits of temperament. Learned behaviors may require explicit instruction in rules and replacement behaviors.

For example, a child who reacts to new situations by withdrawing and refusing to participate would benefit from advanced notifications of changes in activities and time to observe others before being asked to engage in novel tasks. Providing notification and time to observe might provide children with enough support to allow them to proceed satisfactorily. If they have learned, however, that crying will gain them access to preferred staff members and activities, the environmental supports might not be sufficiently reinforcing. They may need to be taught through a behavior support plan that (a) access to preferred people and activities will be available only if they comply with the required task, (b) they can ask for advanced notification of changes and time to observe novel activities, (c) they will feel calmer and more able to participate if they ask for and gain access to the support they need, and (d) they are capable of handling these challenges.

Stanley Turecki (2000) has written a tremendous book for parents, with application to classrooms, entitled *The Difficult Child.* In this book, he recommends that parents and teachers remain neutral when responding to a behavioral challenge. Take time to analyze the situation and determine whether the child needs an accommodation due to a biological trait that is beyond his or her control, instruction in age-appropriate rules and expectations, or some combination of the first two options. In addition, Turecki cautions adults who are engaged with a difficult child to avoid punishing traits of temperament. Children establish a sense of learned helplessness or learned optimism by the age of seven (Seligman, 1995). Punishing a child for a biologically determined trait he or she cannot control encourages the development of learned helplessness. If a punishment or consequence for a learned behavior is warranted, be brief, be firm, be calm, be consistent, and do not engage in negotiations.

Additional information on developing individualized positive behavior support plans is available in Chapter 7. Examples of behaviors that represent traits of temperament, environmental accommodations, and coping strategies are provided in Figure 2.6.

Greenspan (1995) identified five distinct groups of children with difficult temperament profiles. Each group experiences different challenges in the school environment and will need different types of responses from school personnel. The five groups are labeled (1) highly sensitive, (2) self-absorbed, (3) defiant, (4) inattentive, and (5) active-aggressive. Of those five groups, only the active-aggressive group has been associated with an identifiable pattern of parenting. Parents of these children inconsistently respond to their children's needs. The children exhibit little or no empathy, have difficulty expressing their wants and needs, and act impulsively without constructing an internal dialogue that might help mediate their tendency to act out. The highly sensitive group exhibits more instability of mood and is easily embarrassed. The self-absorbed group prefers to daydream and does not engage easily with others. The defiant group exhibits high rates of negative responses, particularly when they cannot be in control. They prefer highly concrete, well-organized activities. The inattentive group has difficulty maintaining attention to any given task for the required amount of time. This behavior has negative implications for learning as well as social interaction.

Essential understandings from the research on temperament include:

1. Tough-to-manage children do not necessarily have a disorder—they might just have a difficult temperament that will respond to environmental supports, instruction in coping strategies, and a consistently applied set of rules and consequences.

2. The assumption that a child is choosing to act inappropriately can have long-term detrimental consequences if the response to that assumption is focused primarily on punishment.

3. Even biologically determined traits can be modified (for the betterment or to the detriment of an individual) through a variety of planned and unplanned factors and experiences.

Figure 2.6   Traits of Temperament and Intervention Strategies

Traits	Environmental Accommodations	Coping Strategies
Activity level	Remove unnecessary items from the room Secure shelving units, entertainment centers, and other furniture that may present a safety hazard Place potentially harmful substances and tools out of reach unless the child is being actively supervised Adjust the daily schedule to provide frequent breaks for large-muscle activities Provide acceptable and attractive equipment for large-muscle play Include daily chores that require large-muscle activities	Teach relaxation techniques that include stretching, tensing, and relaxing muscles Teach the students to use self-monitoring and self-control skills Teach communication skills and provide acceptable alternatives to inappropriate activities when the student communicates a need for movement Teach proper nutrition and self-care (including adequate amounts of sleep) Teach sports and fitness skills
Intensity and sensory threshold	Maintain a consistent and predictable schedule Provide advanced notification of changes Model calm responses Provide a safe place for de-escalating Provide nonthreatening prompts and environmental cues to implement coping strategies Use pictures, music, and/or color cues to communicate a need for de-escalation	Teach the child to recognize his or her own level of intensity and/or areas of sensory sensitivity Teach the child to make his or her own adjustments to the environment when possible (i.e., put on a jacket if cold, wear a headset if distracted by noise, lower voice if talking too loud) Teach the child to ask for what he or she needs
Regularity	Maintain a consistent and predictable schedule Allow time in the schedule for waking up, falling asleep, eating, or other potentially difficult transitions Provide picture cues	Teach the child to use a daily schedule and weekly calendar or planner Teach the child to self-monitor and self-reinforce for following his or her schedule
Approach/withdrawal and adaptability	Provide advanced information when changes in routine, personnel, or activities are required Practice (role-play) potentially disturbing situations prior to the event Provide additional time in the schedule for "warming up" to new people, activities, or places	Teach the child to use a daily schedule and weekly calendar or planner Teach the child to communicate wants and needs—particularly for information and/or reassurance in new situations
Distractibility	Reduce the levels of activity, noise, light, odor, motion, and/or texture that are difficult to integrate Increase the attraction to the task by utilizing the child's preferences (Example: The child experiences frustration when writing stories and is distracted by other students who sit at his group table, by having to remain seated, and by the scratching noise his pencil makes on the notebook paper. The teacher tapes a large piece of chart paper to a wall on the other side of the classroom, allows him to stand while he writes, and provides him with a variety of colored markers instead of a pencil.)	Teach the child to utilize appropriate alternatives in the environment for decreasing stimulation and increasing attention to task Teach the child to self-monitor and self-reinforce for completing tasks Teach the child to communicate wants and needs Teach the child to break large tasks into smaller, more easily accomplished subsets and take brief breaks intermittently
Predominant mood	Do *not* respond to negative moods with anger, anxiety, irritation, or frustration! Be matter of fact in labeling the child's mood, remain calm, offer potentially helpful suggestions, distract the child with a commonly preferred activity, task, song, or story, and give the child time to shift gears Concentrate on acceptable behavior, not on the emotional tone or quality of the interaction Example: Joe has not smiled all morning. He uses a crabby tone of voice when responding to a question but answers the question correctly and completes his work. The teacher should compliment him on his correct answer and completed work rather than getting into an argument with him over his attitude Provide a safe place for students who are upset to de-escalate and a method for communicating wants and needs	Teach the child to recognize and label his or her own moods Teach the child to identify what he or she needs to feel more comfortable Teach the child to communicate his wants or needs Teach the child to self-monitor and self-reinforce for regulating his or her own moods A simple chart with faces illustrating different moods and the words for the corresponding emotions can be used to help a child identify how he or she feels. Children who are old enough often benefit from keeping an interactive feeling journal. The student writes about how he or she feels, what precipitated the mood, and his or her plan for dealing more effectively with the mood. The teacher responds in writing at a more convenient time and returns the journal to the student

Externalizing and Internalizing Disorders: The Question of Blame

Mental health professionals sometimes categorize different emotional and behavioral disorders (EBD) as externalizing disorders or internalizing disorders. Externalizing disorders are characterized by verbal and physical aggression, poor impulse control, lack of empathy for others, and a high need for instant gratification. ADHD, conduct disorder, and oppositional defiant disorder are examples of externalizing disorders. Internalizing disorders are characterized by thoughts and behaviors that reflect fearfulness, sadness, apprehension, guilt, helplessness, and shame. Depression, school phobia, obsessive compulsive disorder, and separation anxiety are examples of internalizing disorders. As researchers learn more about the origins and developmental trajectories of EBD, the lines become blurred between disorders once described as internalizing or externalizing. Tourette Syndrome and obsessive compulsive disorder are known to be caused primarily by dysfunctions in the brain. Both conditions are characterized by overt behaviors that others might find disturbing. In addition, children with a particular disorder do not always exhibit the same behavioral profile as adults. For example, young children with major depressive disorder may not act sad. They may exhibit chronic levels of irritability and opposition or defiance (Koplewicz, 1996).

The dangers in arbitrarily labeling a disorder as externalizing or internalizing are that (a) the reciprocal interaction of environment, emotions, thoughts, and behaviors can easily be ignored; and (b) assumptions about a child's motivations for behaving in a particular manner can easily be misinterpreted. A third danger and frequent barrier to both communication and effective behavior support plan implementation is the assumption that a child has a particular emotional or behavioral problem because of poor parenting. In some cases, parents have contributed to the EBD their children exhibit. Trauma experienced at the hands of someone other than the parent, abuse, neglect, an unfortunate mismatch between a child's and parent's temperaments, or well-intentioned but ineffective responses to a child's difficult temperament can contribute to the development of emotional and behavioral problems.

Regardless of the origin of a disorder or the constellation of factors that may have contributed to a child's behavioral and cognitive disabilities, however, blaming the parent and/or the child is an unproductive response. Parents (even the ones who are ineffective) want their children to be successful. Medical research continues to uncover the neurological and biochemical conditions that cause children to be predisposed to developing mental illness. In *It's Nobody's Fault: New Hope and Help for Difficult Children* by Harold Koplewicz (1996), blame and shame are replaced by medical facts and straightforward suggestions for home and classroom application.

Neurodevelopmental Constructs

Levine's (2002) neurodevelopmental constructs are offered as the third area of research from which an understanding of the whole child can and should be drawn in making academic and behavior plan decisions. Each of these constructs or systems works independently to contribute to a child's overall development. Other systems or constructs will be affected if one system is not working efficiently. In this way, each system is also interdependent. Levine identifies the following systems of neurodevelopmental development: (a) attention control, (b) memory, (c) language, (d) spatial ordering, (e) sequential ordering, (f) motor, (g) higher thinking, and (h) social thinking. Each system must be able to effectively (a) receive input, (b) store information, (c) use information during internal processing, and (d) provide output.

In a school environment, failure of any system to perform one or more of the four functions listed above can cause learning and behavior problems. A child who knows an answer but can't express it is different from a child who knows an answer but refuses to express it. Both children might look very much alike in a classroom, but they may need very different types of support. A list of processing deficits, characteristic classroom behaviors, and potential classroom interventions is provided in Figure 2.7. For a more complete examination of Levine's neurodevelopmental constructs, see *A Mind at a Time* (2002) and a video entitled *Developing Minds* (2002), a production of WBGH Boston, available at www.wgbh.org.

Assessment Tools: Expanding and Enhancing Their Application

Each school district has its own preferred assessment tools and procedures for determining the strengths and needs of children with challenging behavioral or academic problems. As stated earlier in this chapter, potential sources of information might include a review of the child's records that reveals information from social, medical, and/or family histories; vision and hearing screenings; speech and language assessments; and academic achievement tests. School-based teams rarely submit a request for an individualized intelligence test and other more narrowly focused assessments of cognitive and social-emotional functioning unless a particular disorder is suspected.

If a child has been given an individually administered intelligence test, examine the subtest scores. Look for patterns in the subtest scores that indicate problems with the input, memory, internal processing, or output of information. Consult charts that include information about milestones typically mastered at the child's chronological age across motor, linguistic, social-emotional, mathematics, reading, and concept development domains. Construct a developmental profile like the one completed on Brian in Figure 2.4. Compare areas on the chart in which the child is making satisfactory progress with areas in which the child is having difficulty. Identify common skill strengths and deficits across domains. The intersection of those commonalities provides valuable cues for intervention development.

Triage: A Rationale for Decision Making

Every child who presents a challenge on a given day does not need a complete child study team assessment. How can teachers and other school

Figure 2.7   Behaviors Associated With Processing Deficits and Corresponding Interventions

Processing Deficits	Common Classroom Behaviors	Potential Interventions
Short-term memory	**May appear to be highly distractible** Performance may be impaired by anxiety Performance may suffer if speed of input is increased May have difficulty following multiple step directions, completing sequential tasks such as long division or taking notes	**Keep oral directions brief** Illustrate and post sequential steps Provide frequent review Allow the student to use a tape recorder, prepared notes, and graphic organizers Establish a peer buddy system Reduce environmental distractions
Long-term retrieval	**Information is not retained over time** Recall is poor on tests Memorization of math facts, poems, states and capitals, for example, is unusually difficult	**Limit the number of new concepts presented at one time** Engage the student in brief frequent drills rather than massed infrequent reviews Teach the student to use graphic organizers Pair new concepts with concrete objects, maps, charts, photographs, or other memory aids Teach the student to use mnemonic devices such as ROY G BIV (used to remember the order of the colors in the spectrum: red, orange, yellow, green, blue, indigo, and violet) Use as many senses as possible when teaching a new skill or concept: music, dance, taste, texture, smell, sight, and so on
Auditory processing (phonemes and morphemes)	**Difficulty hearing sounds in words and in making the association between sounds and corresponding letters (decoding)** Difficulty spelling (encoding) Difficulty listening Difficulty learning a foreign language	**Provide additional training in sound-symbol recognition and blending** Use song lyrics and poetry (rhyme) during read-aloud periods to heighten awareness of sounds Sing songs and play games that emphasize awareness of sounds as well as sound-symbol associations Provide notes or a study buddy to assist with note taking
Visual processing Spatial ordering	**May have difficulty with a sense of space and orientation** May lack awareness of visual detail May have difficulty sensing visual boundaries May have difficulty with handwriting, geometry, and art	**Provide practice with enhanced cues (i.e., handwriting paper with ridges or bumps as well as visual lines to indicate where margins begin and where lower and upper case letters should extend)** Engage the student in building 3-D models and using manipulatives Engage in enrichment activities that enhance visual processing skills and hand-eye coordination such as paper folding (origami), kite construction, cartoon drawing, and simple games like pickup sticks and tiddly winks
Processing speed	**May be highly distractible** May be impaired by anxiety Often fails to complete work on time May have difficulty with timed tests May read slowly and have impaired comprehension May take longer than others to complete math problems	**Allow more time for work completion** Avoid timed tests Reduce the quantity of work and focus on the quality Limit copying tasks If copying tasks are required, structure them to make them easier to complete Allow a buddy to take notes Photocopy overhead or PowerPoint® notes Utilize fill-in-the-blank or circle-the-correct-response formats for worksheets

Processing Deficits	Common Classroom Behaviors	Potential Interventions
		Allow the student to dictate or tape-record long answers In math, allow the use of a calculator when the objective of the lesson is not related to computation mastery Teach the student to place a dot under each letter or word copied to prevent omission and/or reversals Provide the student with a highlighted textbook in content-area classes with heavy reading requirements Do not require speed or accuracy with copying tasks Teach the student self-checking strategies Provide games and other engaging activities that help the student increase fluency
Sequential ordering	**May have difficulty with concepts of time** May have difficulty remembering numbers, the alphabet, days of the week, months of the year, and other items in order May have difficulty sequencing events or topics in essays, stories, or reports May have difficulty establishing a schedule or knowing how to best organize tasks	**Provide frequent and varied review of sequentially ordered information** Construct number lines, timelines, flow charts, and other illustrated representations of content Provide the student with 3 × 5 cards on which to write tasks to be completed or subtopics within a larger topic, then have the student arrange the cards in order and number them Directly teach the student to use a planner Provide the student with a guided reading form to complete for long content-area reading assignments to enhance and highlight the sequencing of content Provide the student with an outline format to use during prewriting activities
Abstract thinking Linguistics (semantics, syntax, discourse)	**Poor comprehension of vocabulary** Difficulty answering questions about commonly known topics Difficulty with reading and listening comprehension Difficulty interpreting word problems in math Difficulty with written language Difficulty with content-area subjects Difficulty with oral language Difficulty applying information learned May have difficulty applying information and making generalizations Difficulty knowing how and when to join a conversation Difficulty expressing wants, needs, and emotions Difficulty modulating volume and tone of voice	**Encourage recreational reading and discussion of general topics** Relate new information to previously mastered concepts Preteach relevant vocabulary Teach the function and meaning of prefixes and suffixes Use manipulatives, models, charts, graphs, and photographs whenever possible Incorporate the student's interests into the explanation of a new concept (i.e., compare negative integers to a 5-yard penalty in football) Provide multiple types of graphic organizers and teach the student to apply information to the specific type of graphic representation Provide direct instruction in the pragmatics of speech and in social skills related to areas of concern Provide visual cues and verbal prompts to assist in teaching social/behavioral skills Teach self-monitoring and self-reinforcement

personnel make the best possible use of the resources available to them? Many of the details required for fully implementing an answer to that question are outlined in the remaining chapters of this book. The broad answer is best represented by the following set of questions.

1. Is the child's behavior within typical limits, given his or her gender, chronological age, and cognitive functioning level?

2. Note: Approximate cognitive functioning level is more important than chronological age level in determining how typical a child's behavior is.

3. Does the child exhibit the behavior in more than one setting?

4. Has the child consistently exhibited the behavior over a period of time (2 to 3 weeks)?

5. Is the behavior characteristic of a trait of temperament?

6. Is the classroom environment organized to meet a variety of academic and behavioral needs?

7. Does the behavior respond readily to either an environmental accommodation, direct skill instruction, consistent enforcement of the rules, or some combination of the above?

Do not submit a request to the child study team if the child's learning or behavior problems are age appropriate, are not pervasive across settings, have not persisted over time, and are responsive to classroom accommodations, direct skill instruction, consistent enforcement of the rules, or some combination of the above. Apply the combination of interventions found in this book that best fits the environment and the child's needs. Do submit a request to the child study team if the child's problems are atypical given his chronological age and cognitive functioning level and present severe, pervasive, and intense challenges. Many of the interventions described in this book will be of help. Use what is most appropriate to the setting and the needs of the child. In addition, use the expertise and support of the team. Managing severe, pervasive, and intense behavior challenges is not and never should be a solo endeavor for the teacher or the parents.

■ CONCLUSION

Parenting and educating typically developing children can be challenging at times, but it is a relatively easy and rewarding experience. One must simply stay a chapter or two ahead of the youngster in readings on child development to be sufficiently prepared for the next developmental milestones. Unfortunately, children may appear to be developing typically for a period of time and then begin to experience unexpected difficulties. If it were so easy in general, however, parents, school officials, and community agencies dedicated to children and families would not continually seek new information on best practices. New advances in medical technology are allowing researchers to study the developing brain as a child performs academic tasks. Educators, cognitive scientists, physicians, psychologists, and psychiatrists are discovering the complex neurological and metabolic processes at work across domains during the rapid developmental periods of infancy, early childhood, childhood, and adolescence.

As more information becomes available, our understanding of development has shifted from a linear stage model to an interactive, interrelated web-like model of strengths and needs. Assessment tools continue to change to reflect new understandings as well. Of particular importance to educators and parents, however, is the awareness that even the more traditional assessment tools currently in use yield tremendously important information about a child's strengths and needs. The shift in thinking for some educators and parents is in how that information is used to develop interventions. Educational and medical research has contributed the following understandings about typical and atypical development:

1. Development in one domain (i.e., linguistic, motor, social) affects development in other domains.

2. Some developmental differences are biologically determined, and some are a result of environment.

3. Interventions should include attention to the interaction of domain strengths; domain-specific interventions may fail to address quality of life issues.

4. Intervention development should include (a) environmental supports for developmental differences beyond the child's control; (b) instruction in coping strategies, self-monitoring, or self-advocacy; and (c) skill instruction in areas of skill deficit.

Understanding the strengths and needs of typically and atypically developing children is essential to the development of responsive educational environments. All children can learn. Unfortunately, many children will not live up to their potential under programs designed exclusively for the typically developing child. General educators and special educators will work most efficiently and effectively with one another in the pursuit of educational excellence for all when the inextricably intertwined web of developmental constructs is understood, anticipated, accepted, and celebrated.

An understanding of typical development in general is essential in the ongoing quest to design sound educational experiences for children of a particular age or developmental level. Group development (how groups form and what facilitates the cohesion necessary for optimal growth) is the topic of Chapter 3. Too often teachers are encouraged to implement a classroom management system with insufficient understanding of the foundations on which groups in general develop and flourish. Information on typical and atypical development (Chapter 2) and group development (Chapter 3) provide a foundation for understanding effective classroom management systems presented in Chapter 4.

3

Group Development

INTRODUCTION ■

Recently I began working with a group of primary-level students with emotional and behavioral disorders (EBD). Their previous teacher was a long-term substitute who had not completed her undergraduate training. She had not established classroom expectations, rules, routines, a predictable schedule, or a consistently enforced behavior management system. The students functioned as individual entities with no group identity, focus, or purpose. The student who screamed the loudest or became the most aggressive expected to have the adult's attention first. Group lessons were out of the question during our first weeks together. Students left their seats without permission to hit or kick others, get water or supplies, and talk with classmates. They chewed pencils, paper, crayons, and erasers and spit them at each other. When provided with water bottles after physical education classes, they would snort water into their nostrils and blow it on whoever was nearest. They would not listen to stories, sing songs while I played the guitar, play instructionally focused games, or even walk to the cafeteria for lunch without constantly and loudly interrupting each other. Any assignment, no matter how basic or within their abilities, would initiate whining, kicking, crying, and relentless screams of "I can't do this! I need help!" I felt as if I spent our early days together herding tiger cubs.

This group was unusual because the members had known each other for 1 to 3 years prior to my assignment as their teacher. They had already determined who their peer leaders were and had established patterns of behavior that predictably allowed them to get what they wanted and to avoid what they did not want. The peer leader, a forceful third grader, led the group in a vote to have me removed from the classroom at the end of our first week together. Most of the students raised their hands and loudly agreed with her proclamation that I be fired. One first grader bravely disagreed and almost suffered bodily harm for his announcement that he liked me. While I was not in the least bit worried about retaining my position as their teacher, I was fearful that I would not be able to find an activity that we could all do together and that the group enjoyed. Most teachers, after 5 days of listening to children's high-pitched screaming, are not in a panic over an inability to find a "fun" activity that all individual group members would enjoy. Our success as a group, however, rested precariously on my ability to (a) maintain physical and psychological safety for all group members, (b) assist each student in redefining his or her role in the group in positive terms, and (c) redirecting the group's energy into positive, productive goals and outcomes. The first impulse most adults (including myself) have in a situation like the one described above is to punish individuals and the group for a laundry list of noncompliant behaviors—not the least of which is staging a mutiny!

Lest you be led astray by the notion that these children had diagnosed emotional and behavioral problems and are, therefore, not in the same category as those in general education classes, I'd like to share one other anecdote from my years as a general education teacher. I was hired midyear to teach a class of inner-city third-grade students. The school was surrounded by an 8–foot-high security fence with barbed wire strung across the top like holiday garland. Teachers' cars were locked behind the fence during the school day to protect them from burglary. The entrance of the school was open and accessible to the public, but all other doors were locked and secured within the boundaries of the security fence. My classroom was on the second floor of the building, facing a city street. Each Monday, the children and I found new bullet holes in the windows. Some even pierced the doors of the stalls in the girl's restroom. It was unnerving, to say the least, to sit on a toilet and realize that a bullet would have found its way into your abdomen or head, had you been there at the wrong time.

None of the students in this group of third graders had ever been diagnosed with learning or behavior problems. Each of them did cope daily, however, with many risk factors, the least of which was living in a poverty- and crime-ridden environment. These students acted out their distrust, anxiety, and confusion by fighting and refusing to follow directions. When I turned my back long enough to write the date on the board, no fewer than five fights would break out. When I asked a young man to bring his paper to me at the front of the room, girls on his row would grab his buttocks as he walked past them. When I asked a young lady to bring her paper to me at the front of the room, boys on her row would grab her crotch as she tried to return to her seat. We could not line up for lunch because the boys were attempting to grab and pinch the girls' nipples. When I asked a teacher on my floor how she managed the extreme behavior problems these children presented, she pulled out a long 4-inch wide strip of rubber cut from an old tire. Her response to their acting out was to publicly spank them. I was horrified. She smiled and told me to just get over it—that the sooner I understood their respect for the strap, the sooner I could get on with the job of teaching. These children were capable students who did learn to treat each other and me with respect without fear and intimidation during our 4 months together. Corporal punishment is never the answer!

Before deciding how you would handle either of the two unruly groups described above, think back to Chapter 1. Foundational Principle 1 is that the only person I can control is myself. The only hope I had of influencing this group to work more productively together was to respond to their needs effectively. Rejecting or punishing them without meeting their needs would not achieve the desired outcomes, so I reviewed the remaining Foundational Principles for help in understanding and responding to the students' needs. The second most important principle is defined in Foundational Principle 2: Behavior is purposeful. Students had learned to get what they wanted and avoid what they did not want with the behaviors they were displaying. If I wanted to effectively manage their behaviors, I would need to help them learn replacement behaviors that were incompatible with the ones they were exhibiting. My goals included plans to teach them how to get what they wanted and avoid what they did not want through school-appropriate behavior. Attempting to stop unruly behavior without a plan for teaching students how to get their needs met with school-appropriate behaviors would fail miserably. Foundational Principle 4 is that punishment may stop a behavior, but it does not teach a new, more desirable behavior. Punishment may also increase the students' anger toward me and avoidance of the learning tasks I present to them. Foundational Principle 3 holds the key for working through the problems this group is experiencing: Reinforcement increases the likelihood that a behavior will be repeated and is instrumental in teaching new behaviors. I had to find items and activities that *all* group members found reinforcing. Failure on my part to meet their needs for protective limits on acting out behavior within the context of a reinforcing alternative would only encourage them to increase previously learned unacceptable behaviors.

Fortunately, my husband came to my rescue with the suggestion that I try playing Simon Says with the group of students with EBD. I rejected the idea initially. The thought of getting all of them quiet and still long enough even to begin was beyond me. I also feared that when someone did not "win" a round, screaming fits would escalate into a total loss of control. In desperation after lunch the next day, however, I thought, "What do I have to lose?" and gave it a try.

[Those of you who teach understand what I mean by not having anything to lose after lunch. I have always suspected that some chemical agent was introduced into the cafeteria via the ventilation ducts. Even students who are otherwise calm, cool, and compliant often act like alien beings for the first 30 minutes after lunch.]

Like magic, the class quieted and began to respond. We had our first few moments of genuine laughter together. They had finally experienced a safe, fun, and collaborative activity as a group. We were not out of danger by any stretch of the imagination, but we had begun an important and essential group process.

The group of third graders who attended an impoverished, inner-city school responded to a strategy described in Chapter 4. Both groups of students, however, went through predictable stages of development that required different levels of structure, different goals, and different materials and methods. The following section on group characteristics and processes describes how groups change over time and why a one-size-fits-all approach will not produce adequate results.

■ GROUP FORMATION: CHARACTERISTICS AND PROCESSES

The quality of a group's development and productivity depends on characteristics common to all groups. Think about a group that you might decide to join for the first time. This group might be a Book of the Month Club, a civic organization, or a religious congregation. What needs would you have as an individual when first entering this group? Now think about the group itself. What qualities would you find desirable in a group?

Adults have more choices about the groups they join than children do, but the individual needs that group members have and the processes a group must negotiate are common across all formal and informal settings. Researchers such as Johnson (1988) and Goldstein (1988) have identified group qualities and processes that are essential to well-functioning, productive groups. The qualities include (a) physical and psychological safety, (b) a shared sense of purpose or cohesiveness, (c) compatibility, (d) clearly identified leadership, (e) well-defined roles for group members, and (f) group norms or rules (this includes the formally stated rules and procedures as well as unstated expectations). Individuals within the group need to have positive opportunities for making personal contributions. In addition, the group's activities and tasks must have personal relevance for each member.

A teacher establishes a sense of physical and psychological safety with clearly defined behavior management procedures and developmentally appropriate learning tasks. Chapter 4 addresses classroom behavior management planning, and Chapter 5 explores the connections between behavior problems and academic achievement in depth. Methods are explored in this chapter for understanding and effectively facilitating the group's movement through stages of group development as individuals within the group and the group as a whole acquire new skills. The components of classroom management as defined in Chapter 4 remain constant, but the strategies likely to be most effective at each stage of a group's development change dramatically over the course of a school year. For this reason, an exploration of (a) the stages of group development, (b) the roles teachers and students play at different stages, (c) the very real effects of the pecking order, and (d) general methods for facilitating a sense of community precede information on establishing a classroom management plan. General educators may not encounter as many children with challenging behaviors in their classrooms. Nevertheless, the research on group development is valuable information to have and apply. Many problems can be avoided by being aware of the group's stage of development and aligning teacher behaviors, instructional strategies, and behavior management techniques accordingly.

STAGES OF GROUP DEVELOPMENT ■

Researchers have long known that groups follow predictable stages of group development: (a) forming, (b) storming, (c) norming, (d) performing, and (e) adjourning (Tuckman, 1965; Tuckman & Jensen, 1977). Unfortunately, teachers are rarely taught to understand the needs and processes that support and inhibit group growth. I have collapsed the five stages of group development identified above into three stages (see Figure 3.1) for classroom application purposes (general education settings as well as special education settings).

Stage 1

During Stage 1, the students and teacher are getting to know each other (forming). Because the teacher is the officially identified leader, it is the teacher's responsibility to establish protective boundaries for the group (otherwise known as expectations, rules, and consequences). Some students in the group inevitably object to the authority of the teacher. Other students inevitably experience conflicts with their peers. A subgroup of students often experience conflict with staff and peers. Immediately after the initial honeymoon period (during which time everyone—students and staff—are checking each other out), storming begins in earnest. I have grouped forming and storming within the same stage of classroom group development because (a) the forming or honeymoon stage can be as brief as a few minutes or as long as 3 months, (b) the group's needs during forming and storming are the same, (c) the teacher's role during forming and storming is the same, and (d) both behavioral interventions and instructional strategies are aligned for the same purposes during forming and storming.

Essentially, Stage 1 represents a critical period during which the teacher's role is one of a benevolent dictator who protects individual group members' physical and psychological safety by (a) enforcing clearly defined limits on aggressive or threatening behavior, (b) taking care of students' basic needs, (c) implementing success-oriented academic strategies, (d) finding enjoyable activities that can be experienced simultaneously, and (e) facilitating individual students' movement from a "Me" to a "We" orientation. This is a tremendous undertaking for the teacher. Being consistent, persistent, ever vigilant, positive, firm, and responsive to individuals as well as to the group as a whole will never be more important that it is during Stage 1.

(Text continues on page 64)

Figure 3.1   Stages of Group Development

	Stage One	Stage Two	Stage Three
Teacher's role	*Benevolent dictator* The teacher must maintain the dual roles of caregiver and rule enforcer with equal commitment and skill. Proactive measures should be taken to assist the group in avoiding as many problems as possible. In addition, the teacher assists the group in selecting a peer leader during this critical stage.	*Director* The teacher must continue to enforce the rules in major violations but shifts from being the primary authority in the group to assisting the group in learning the skills necessary to assume responsibility for its own management and learning.	*Facilitator* The teacher's role shifts again during Stage Three to one of facilitating age-appropriate learning activities. Students should be able during this stage to engage in all activities their peers of average cognitive ability enjoy with a minimum of concern for behavioral problems.
Group behavior patterns during the stage	During Stage One, students' behaviors are often verbally aggressive and/or disruptive. Some students will be easily provoked into acts of physical aggression. Students often have difficulty understanding and respecting personal space. They express emotions through actions rather than through words and exhibit limited abilities to problem-solve. Other common characteristics of Stage One group functioning include (a) problems quickly escalate, (b) problems usually spread from one student to another instead of remaining localized, and (c) students attempt to manipulate adults through arguing, begging, bargaining, or blackmail. This is a volatile period. Students are testing the limits of the program and the adults in charge of the program.	Groups typically have fewer problems during Stage Two than during Stage One. The problems may be as intense when they do occur, but other group members will not join the person having a problem in the disruption of the group. In addition, group members begin to talk about the group and being part of the group in positive terms. One of the problems that can occur during Stages Two and Three is a return to Stage One behavior for a period of time. Keep in mind that the stages outlined here are not rigid in their development and maintenance. A change in schedule, an impending holiday, the loss of a group member, or the addition of a new group member may create new levels of tension for the group. A nonpunitive increase in structure and additional opportunities for positive recognition will usually facilitate a return to Stage Two functioning within a week or two.	During Stage Three, the group is able to engage in age-appropriate activities with no more supervision than the average group of that age. The teacher should be aware, however, that while the group as a whole functions well during Stage Three, individual group members may not be able to maintain appropriate behavior outside of the structured environment of the classroom. As individual students who are functioning at a higher level move into other classes, the dynamic of the group will shift. A new peer leader may have to be selected. During the reorganization of the group, behavior problems that were characteristic of the group during Stages One and Two may return for a short period of time. A nonpunitive increase in structure and additional opportunities for positive recognition will usually facilitate a return to Stage Three functioning within a week or two.
Typical length of the stage	Groups range in the length of time it takes them to understand and accept the	Stage Two is a period of decision making for individuals as well as the	Once a group has established well-functioning processes

	Stage One	Stage Two	Stage Three
	limits placed on their behavior. Some groups accept the program without a lengthy period of testing. Other groups take up to 3 or 4 months to accept the program. The length of time a group engages in typical Stage One behaviors depends on (a) the skill of the teacher in providing a safe, productive program; (b) the prior experiences the group may have had with other adults; and (c) the cohesiveness of the group members themselves. Most groups experience Stage One functioning for 3 to 12 weeks.	group. Students with long histories of inappropriate behavior may not entirely trust their newfound skills. Stage Two is typically longer in duration than Stage One. The acquisition of new social skills takes time for individuals. Learning new processes for group participation is also a lengthy process for students who have had little opportunity outside of school to observe well-functioning groups. Stage Two can take from 12 to 18 weeks.	for making decisions, settling conflicts, and meeting goals, this level of group development can be maintained for the remainder of the school year. Disruptions due to holidays, schedule changes, and the loss or addition of a group member will cause some problems until the group is able to reestablish the level of communication it needs to function well.
Interaction patterns	Student-to-student interaction should be limited and monitored in the beginning. Some groups exhibit high rates of cohesiveness and congeniality even during Stage One. Until all group members know each other and are able to follow the rules, however, students should work in groups no larger than two and maintain an interaction pattern during whole-group instruction that is moderated by the teacher.	Students should be taught the skills necessary for working together as peer tutors: giving and receiving feedback, asking for clarification, and resolving differences of opinion. Cooperative learning assignments can be carefully selected to provide the students with authentic opportunities for applying concepts and skills mastered academically and for using social skills in increasingly complex situations. Behavioral expectations during peer tutoring and cooperative learning assignments should be taught directly and should be monitored closely by the teacher. Illustrated rubrics for assessing social skills after completing the assignment and teacher feedback are essential to skill mastery in this area. Limit cooperative learning groups to no more than two students.	Students can engage in any age-appropriate activity. Cooperative learning, peer tutoring, and class meetings are increasingly led by students. Expect to increase adult monitoring and assistance in new situations. Engage students in tasks outside the structure of the classroom, with students from other classes, and with unfamiliar staff members to facilitate an increase in the generalization of skills.
Social-emotional needs	During Stage One, individual group members are becoming acquainted with each other and with the	During Stage Two, students are beginning to enjoy participating in whole-group activities. A sense	During Stage Three, students have sufficient mastery over the environment, feel safe,

(Continued)

Figure 3.1 (Continued)

	Stage One	*Stage Two*	*Stage Three*
	adults. The group needs reliable, predictable, and consistent attention to issues of safety—physical and emotional. Students tend to be most interested in what is available to them personally within the setting and are not particularly motivated to engage in group-earned activities or rewards. Physical and psychological safety is of utmost importance (see Maslow in Action, Figure 3.2)	of belonging emerges. Opportunities to learn and practice age-appropriate self-monitoring, self-evaluation, and self-reinforcement as well as peer–to-peer social skills increase in importance (see Maslow in Action, Figure 3.2)	and have established a secure sense of belonging within the classroom group. Their social-emotional needs expand to include an emerging sense of self-esteem built on multiple experiences of academic and social success as well as the coping skills acquired during periods of frustration and failure. Children ages 9 and older can begin to learn to self-monitor ineffective thinking and rephrase ineffective thoughts to increase positive feelings and actions (see Maslow in Action, Figure 3.2)
Behavior management	Behavior management during Stage One is characterized primarily by the application of behavior modification principles. The teacher should begin with a careful analysis of the environment and the schedule. Prevention of over- and understimulation is very important. Expectations, rules, and consequences should be clearly defined, posted, and illustrated. Visual cues in the environment should be present to assist students in making good choices. In one class, the center activities were separated from the rest of the room with a strip of red electrical tape on the floor. Students were reminded not to step over the tape until given permission. In another room, the teacher placed strips of yellow electrical tape on the group instruction table to identify each student's personal space. This helped students remember not to touch another's instructional materials.	Behavior management during Stage Two is focused on teaching students the skills necessary for moving from external control of their behavior to internal self-control. During this transfer from external to internal control, the teacher engages the students in increasing opportunities for shared control. Students increasingly engage in the decision-making process. The teacher models the use of problem-solving and decision-making routines, asking for student input. Discussions center on more complex issues. The teacher gradually imposes less adult control as the students are able and willing to self-manage.	During Stage Three, cooperative discipline is most effective. Students have mastered concepts and skills necessary for self-management at their particular levels of development. Class meetings take less time and are not needed as often. Roles and relationships within the classroom have been established. Changes such as long holiday breaks, a substitute, or a new classmate can temporarily create stress but will not cause long-term disruption if the basic structure is maintained.

	Stage One	*Stage Two*	*Stage Three*
Affective education	Students need to know that their individual needs will be met within the context of the group. They also need to move from a "Me" orientation to a "We" orientation. Affective education should begin with each student having opportunities to identify his or her own strengths and preferences. Students can learn about different types of intelligence and different learning styles. Each student can be encouraged to make pictures, stories, or three-dimensional products that represent his/her strengths. These personal products can then be used to make a group anthology, bulletin board, or display. In addition, group members need to be taught to identify and verbalize emotions, wants, and needs in school-appropriate ways.	Affective instruction should focus on concepts and skills necessary for increased peer-to-peer interaction: taking turns, entering a conversation or activity, resolving a conflict, giving and receiving feedback, ending a conversation or activity, and communicating wants and needs effectively with peers. Problem-solving and decision-making routines should be explicitly taught and actively modeled by the teacher initially. As the students become more skilled at using the routines independently, the teacher should gradually transfer control of these processes to the students. Class officers, student courts, think sheets, and flow charts can be constructed to guide students through processes and assist them in focusing on relevant information.	Affective education should be focused on effective thinking, feeling, and behaving as identified in cognitive-behavioral curricula, self-management, organizational skills, and age-appropriate problem-solving skills. Self-efficacy is built on a realistic assessment of an individual's behavior and whether his or her performance is in alignment with his or her values, potential, goals, and needs.
Academic instruction	Academic instruction should encourage participation. Materials should (a) allow for high rates of success, (b) allow individuals to participate in a group setting without overstimulating, and (c) remain primarily at the recall and comprehension levels of Bloom's Taxonomy. Examples of effective instructional strategies for Stage One include: 1. Direct instruction 2. Response cards 3. Self-correcting materials 4. Flashcard drills 5. Games 6. Hands-on materials	Academic instruction should focus on application of mastered concepts and skills. Assignments should be grounded in age-appropriate real world scenarios. Increased complexity and problem solving should characterize learning tasks within a carefully scaffolded approach that protects students from overwhelming feelings of anxiety. The application of the scientific method to investigate age-appropriate questions and concepts, real world math problems with	Academic instruction should increasingly build on students' recall, comprehension, and application skills at higher levels of independence and complexity. All age-appropriate instructional strategies can be implemented at this time. Accommodations may continue to be necessary for students with specific learning needs.

(Continued)

Figure 3.1 (Continued)

	Stage One	Stage Two	Stage Three
	7. Developing instructionally focused projects that allow each student to make an individual contribution such as (a) an anthology of poems, essays, and drawings; (b) a town made from milk cartons and other found objects that can be used to teach social studies; or (c) a display for the school media center of a model representing a literature selection, science concept, or period in history.	manipulatives and hands-on experiences, puppets, role plays, graphic organizers for aiding in the construction and retention of deeper understandings, and interviews are excellent strategies during Stage Two. To facilitate success, however, students should be provided with step-by-step instructions, scripts, and frequent performance feedback. Students should not be expected to work in groups larger than two without an adult to help monitor. They should not be expected to organize tasks independently and will need clearly defined methods and criteria for engaging in self-evaluation.	
Enrichment and recreation	Activities in which the whole group engages for enrichment or recreation should be highly structured to maximize individuals' safety and minimize conflict. Bingo is a more appropriate Stage One game than freeze tag, for example, because (a) participants do not interact verbally or physically during the game and (b) the teacher can award prizes during the game for appropriate behavior as well as at the end of each round for covering a predetermined number of items on the Bingo board. Other Stage One activities that facilitate group development by (a) protecting the needs of individuals, (b) engaging the group in a mutually enjoyable activity, and (c) moving individuals from a "Me" to a "We" orientation include:	Activities at this stage should emphasize student-to-student interactions within a protective structure. Simple cooking activities, art projects, puzzles, and games can be made available. Stage Two favorites from previous groups include: 1. A connect-the-dot matrix game that requires each person to draw a line vertically or horizontally that connects two dots during each turn. If the line completes a square, the person puts his or her initial in the box. The person with the most initials in boxes at the end wins. 2. Completing age-appropriate jigsaw puzzles that illustrate	Activities at this stage can include all age-appropriate options. Students generally enjoy more complex projects and can work in groups as large as four without constant adult intervention. Because social skills and problem-solving skills are more sophisticated and the ability to apply and integrate skills is more highly developed, the students can engage in a wider variety of activities successfully. Stage Three favorites from the past include: 1. Developing a PowerPoint® presentation on a given topic. 2. Designing an advertisement for a newly created candy

	Stage One	*Stage Two*	*Stage Three*
	1. Making a fruit salad. Each student uses a plastic knife to cut a soft piece of fruit. The teacher assembles the ingredients and serves the salad. 2. Making holiday crafts. 3. Making cards for an elderly person in the community. 4. Constructing a bulletin board. 5. Constructing a class photograph album for sharing with guests.	an academic theme or concept (two people per puzzle). 3. Student-to-student interviews and article writing with each student serving as the interviewer and the interviewee as well as the writer and editor. 4. Marketing agents: Students select a topic to research such as whether more people like grape or orange soda. They make a prediction, interview peers and staff during recess or lunch, take data, chart data, analyze data, and report to the class. 5. Completing stories with missing words as partners. 6. Making kites, soda bottle terrariums, mobiles, and other items that require two sets of hands during construction.	bar complete with packaging options and a videotaped commercial. 3. Writing and producing their own versions of familiar fairy tales, folk tales, or stories complete with written scripts, puppets or costumes, simple sets, props, music, and sound effects. 4. Designing a "Dinner Theatre" complete with an original menu, food preparation (completed within a budget), room and table decorations, role assignments (hostess, waiters, etc.), and entertainment. 5. Constructing a nature trail on the school campus that includes research on xeriscaping prior to construction, student booklets, and teacher's manuals.
Primary theoretical/research foundation group development research from other disciplines: Tuckman (1965); Tuckman & Jensen (1977).	The primary theoretical and research foundations for this stage in a group's development include: 1. The first two levels of Maslow's hierarchy of human motivation 2. Driekurs' and Glasser's motivations for behavior 3. The first two levels of Bloom's Taxonomy of Cognition 4. Erikson's first three level of psycho-social stages of development 5. Ecological theory and research 6. Behavioral theory and research	The primary theoretical and research foundations for this stage in a group's development include: 1. The third level of Maslow's Hierarchy of Human Motivation 2. The third level of Bloom's Taxonomy of Cognition 3. Driekurs' and Glasser's motivations for behavior 4. Erikson's first three levels of psycho-social stages of development 5. Ecological theory and research 6. Cognitive-behavioral theory and research	The primary theoretical and research foundations for this stage in a group's development include: 1. The fourth level of Maslow's Hierarchy of Human Motivation 2. The fourth level of Bloom's Taxonomy of Cognition 3. Erikson's first three levels of psycho-social stages of development 4. Ecological Theory and research 5. Cognitive-behavioral theory and research

The students most at risk behaviorally and academically will most frequently test the limits of the behavior management system, the goodwill of the teacher, and the tolerance of their classmates during this stage. Children, having fewer social skills and a smaller vocabulary than the average adult, will act out when behaviors that have previously met their needs fail to work for them. Stage 1 is often referred to during off-the-record meetings among staff as the hell-raising stage because during this time, students are most frequently defiant, aggressive, noncompliant, and manipulative. As exhausting as this stage is for the teacher, it is an important period in the group's development. The teachers who are most able to fulfill the dual roles required of the benevolent dictator to meet students' needs for safety, success, and fun as well as for limits, structure, and predictable consequences facilitate the transformation of the storming so characteristic of Stage 1 into the norming of Stage 2.

Proactive Planning for Stage 1

Beyond a need for physical and psychological safety, group members need a sense of personal relevance, positive opportunities for making personal contributions, and a sense that someone cares. The fulfillment of these needs facilitates cohesiveness within the group, which allows the group as a whole to manage the inevitable conflicts, shifts in power among group members, and task-related tensions that occur when people work together. Cohesiveness is an illusive quality that includes a shared sense of purpose and set of norms for decision making, conflict management, and task completion. Cohesiveness is relatively easy to establish in groups that are formed voluntarily by highly compatible individuals. Cohesiveness is more difficult to establish in a classroom. Students may know what the function of school is but may not find school to be personally relevant. School is an artificial and forced environment. Students do not chose to come to school, do not select their teacher, and have no say over who their classmates will be. To add insult to injury, they also have no control over the curriculum, strategies, and materials with which they are expected to work. Students most at risk for behavior problems and academic failure are often the most skilled at disrupting group processes and sabotaging the teacher's efforts to maintain a quality program.

So what can a teacher do to facilitate group safety, cohesiveness, and productivity in the face of such overwhelming odds? The first step is to identify the strengths and needs of the individual members of the group. Educators typically group students for instructional purposes. Attention should also be given to other relevant grouping variables (e.g., gender, social-emotional maturity, linguistic fluency, artistic skill) when deciding which students should be seated near each other. The next step is to assist each student in identifying a positive role within the group. Some teachers establish a panel of experts that includes a variety of academic and nonacademic skills. Students' names are posted under the title that represents their area of expertise. Other teachers establish classroom jobs. Each student applies and interviews for a classroom job. Job titles and students' names are posted prominently. The third step in facilitating cohesiveness is to assist the group in developing a group focus. This can be accomplished through the development of a class anthology, a whole-group project of some type, or a mission statement that is intricately woven throughout the school day. One class decided through a series of class meetings and voting sessions to build a class theme around rockets and flight. The class motto was "Shoot for the moon!" The class officers were referred to as the flight crew. The class rules, procedures, and consequences were developed under the title of the Pilots' Code of Conduct. Each student posted a flight plan each grading period that included academic and behavioral goals, data collection charts, and an end of the grading period Flight Report. The class newsletter was titled *Rockwell's Rockets*. Each member of the class participated in the development and publication of the newsletter.

The fourth step in facilitating group cohesiveness is assisting the group in selecting a peer leader. Encouraging the growth of each individual group member is important, but the selection and maintenance of a peer leader is critical during Stage 1. If a group decides to follow a strong classmate who has few prosocial skills and no interest in helping others in the group achieve their goals, behavior problems escalate. If a group becomes committed to "hell raising" and takes on that pattern as a way of defining themselves, it is incredibly difficult to turn the group around. The class described at the beginning of this chapter is a prime example. The chaos that the group had experienced the year before had solidified the peer leader's role. She was invested in keeping her power within that group. I came along and challenged her power by establishing expectations, rules, routines, procedures, and consequences. As she experienced a loss of power, she increased her previously learned behaviors—behaviors that kept the group in turmoil. She staged an attempt at a mutiny. It failed. She wasn't ready to give up, however, and continued to antagonize peers, complain, encourage others to defy me, and model her own favorite refusal skills in an attempt to get others to follow her. She had not counted on my ability to (a) find reinforcing activities her classmates found more interesting than the chaos and (b) remain firmly and positively committed to my own role as a benevolent dictator. The goal in working through this period of conflict with the previous peer leader was not to "break" her but to enter into a shared leadership with her. She was the only girl in the group, so I appealed to her interest in fashion. I bought a brush and an assortment of ribbons and barrettes. During earned activity time, I braided her hair. She was a tremendous help with some of the less capable students in the class. I praised her for her efforts with them and gave her the official title of peer tutor. During class meetings, I called on her frequently. She eventually learned to respect the rules in the classroom and spontaneously apologized for her rude behavior during the beginning of our relationship one afternoon. I gave her a hug, thanked her, and told her how proud I was of her for her strength and loyalty to friends.

Teachers sometimes make the mistake of attempting to embarrass, punish, or dethrone a peer leader. Peers will select a leader among their ranks whether the teacher assists with that process or works to block the process. Making an enemy of the peer leader actually decreases the potential a teacher may have for positively impacting the group. The older the students are, the more important and stable the peer leader will be. If the group has not already identified a peer leader, look for a group member who is average to large in size, cognitively capable (even if academic skills are low), and perceived by other youth as being strong. Groups are not going to follow the class bookworm, no matter how positive the child's behavior might be.

As the group begins to experience success, the number of problems will decrease. Individual's problems will no longer be contagious to the group. Group members trust the teacher to manage situations calmly, firmly, and fairly. Opportunities for attention, desired activities, and other rewards are available for those who comply; so individuals invest less time and energy in behaviors that had once gained them access to adults' attention or disruptive behaviors that allowed them to avoid undesired tasks. Students begin to talk less about themselves and more about the group. Staff begins to hear them say things like, "We're the best class in the school." This signals a shift from Stage 1 to Stage 2.

Behavior Management

Students need clearly defined limits during Stage 1. Expectations, rules, rewards, and aversive consequences should be posted and illustrated. Students can assist in the development of the class plan, but the teacher needs to be the leader of the discussion, with veto power over any suggestion that would be inappropriate given the group's level of functioning and needs for safety. The group introduced at the beginning of this chapter, for example, wanted to go to the school playground for recess and asked that recess be added to the menu of options for rewards when work was done. Unfortunately, recess the year before had consisted of students wildly running into each other, standing on picnic tables, jumping off of lawn furniture in the school yard, and tearing small limbs off trees to use as weapons. When early attempts to establish safety rules with the group during an earned recess were unsuccessful, I told them that they would need to learn more self-control before we could have recess outside. I invented active games with beach balls and (clean) 30-gallon garbage cans to play in the classroom during Stage 1. Students learned to stand in line, wait for their turn, and follow the rules of the game. They loved it! After 2 months, they demonstrated enough self-control individually and as a group to attempt outside recess. Once again, it was important for me as the benevolent dictator to honor their desire and need for active play within a structure that protected their physical and psychological safety. I said no to requests that were beyond their present abilities, devised methods for teaching them the necessary skills for participation in their preferred activities, and praised them for attaining a goal relevant to them as they demonstrated mastery of the prerequisite skills.

This is a process that should be repeated throughout the school year. It is a process that is never more critical to the growth of the group, however, than during Stage 1. Behavior management during this stage is grounded in the ecological and behavioral approaches to understanding and responding to behavior. Proponents of the ecological approach examine the interaction of the individual and the environment to determine the problem. Behaviorists also consider the context of a behavior and focus on the function. Behavior is learned and is maintained because it allows the individual to get or avoid something. Points to remember when dealing with the inevitable conflicts that arise during Stage 1 include:

1. Behavior does not exist in a vacuum. The interaction of the environment and the individual or group is an essential element to consider when planning for the prevention of problems as well as when analyzing past

problems for clues to the potential for solutions. Students might act inappropriately more often at a certain time of day because they are hungry, tired, understimulated, or overstimulated. A healthy snack during the mid-morning might be more effective than an elaborate token system if the students are simply hungry due to a late lunch schedule.

2. It is easier to change the environment than to change behavior. During Stage 1, it is more important than at any other time in the group's development to make the environment work for you and the group instead of against you and the group. Students may get into conflicts because they do not keep their desks in their assigned areas. Place tape on the floor to mark their spaces. If too many toys or learning center materials are available at one time, students might leave a mess. If too few materials are available, they might argue. Scan the room for potential problem areas and make adjustments. The group described in this chapter could not have items in their desks during Stage 1. They would eat paper, chew pencils and crayons, spit the pieces on each other, and play loudly with any available item during lessons. Removal of all objects from the desks and teacher-controlled group supplies such as pencils, paper, and books dramatically reduced distractions, disruptions, and arguments over real or perceived violations of personal space.

3. Rules must be few in number, positively stated, descriptive of observable behaviors, illustrated, and posted. Chapter 4 provides examples and additional information on developing effective rules. The selection of rules, however, is another critical component of Stage 1 management. Failure to establish well-defined limits on undesirable behavior early in the Stage 1 process impedes group growth.

4. Contingent reinforcement of desired behaviors that are incompatible with undesired behavior should be the *first priority* after taking proactive measures to prevent problem behaviors.

5. Aversive consequences for undesired behaviors should be enforced calmly, firmly, consistently, predictably, and sparingly.

6. Do not use dependent or interdependent group contingencies *during this period*. Students who earn rewards should receive them. Students who do not earn rewards should not get them. This may appear at first to violate the Stage 1 goal of moving students from a preoccupation with meeting their own needs to a sense of belonging as a member of the group; but it is not. Think about the developmental progression of childhood. According to Erikson (1950), infants must first have their own needs met reliably before they are able to engage in the give and take of more mature relationships. Likewise, Maslow's (1962) theory of human motivation is built on the assumption that individual need fulfillment precedes group affiliation. Students with a history of behavior problems often have great difficulty trusting adults. If students comply, they need to know that their reward will be reliably made available. If students fail to comply, they need to know that the reward will not be made available and that, in some cases, an additional aversive consequence will follow.

7. Include a severe clause in the classroom management plan for behaviors that present real danger to the group. The severe clause describes immediate consequences for severe behavior problems such as serious physical aggression.

8. Be true to your word in all matters of classroom management.

9. Remember that a lack of positive recognition creates an aversive atmosphere. Students require constant attention during this stage in the group's development and will move forward only if the reinforcement ratio is sufficient to meet their needs.

Affective Education

During Stage 1, students are learning to comply with the rules and are getting to know the teacher and each other. Affective education should focus on teaching students the classroom rules and procedures initially and then move into teaching them vocabulary for expressing emotions, wants, and needs. Learning classroom rules and procedures should be fun. Use games such as Behavior Bingo, pantomime, and Twenty Questions to review the rules. Engage the students in role-playing and in making posters to illustrate the rules. As students are taught the hierarchy of responses to noncompliant behaviors, reward them for exhibiting desired behaviors during the role-play activities.

Many students become so used to being punished that they refuse to go to a cool-off carrel to calm down, even though they have been told that they are not in trouble. Spend a few days practicing with role-plays, invite the office staff to observe at the end of the week, and have refreshments after the students demonstrate their new skills. It might seem silly from an adult's point of view to take so much time teaching students to go to a cool-off area, but the students need the reassurance and practice if they are reluctant initially. Many problems can be avoided after the time spent training students because they understand that it is better to go to cool-off than to stay in an upsetting situation and have their behaviors escalate.

Sometimes teachers assume that students have the vocabulary necessary for expressing emotions, wants, and needs. Often, this is not the case. Consider the following statistics on the quantity and quality of words that youth from different socioeconomic areas hear per hour (Hart & Risley, 1995). Children who live in poverty hear an average of 616 words per hour. Those in working class families hear an average of 1,251 words per hour. Children in middle class homes hear an average of 2,153 words per hour. Clearly, children who hear 2,153 words per hour have been provided with a significantly different environment for vocabulary acquisition than those who hear only 616 words per hour. Of even greater concern, however, is the quality of words heard. Hart and Risley (1995) report that children living in poverty hear 5 affirmations and 11 prohibitions per hour. Those who live in working class homes hear 12 affirmations and 7 prohibitions. Children from middle class homes hear 32 affirmations and 5 prohibitions. Exposure to words that express emotions, wants, and needs may, in fact, be quite limited for many children. Curriculum is available commercially for teaching children to recognize and appropriately express their feelings. Reading comprehension and language arts lessons present additional opportunities to assist students in building a rich repertoire of skills. Lesson plan ideas and strategies as well as commercially available affective education curricula are described in more detail in Chapter 5.

Academic Instruction

The primary goals with regard to instruction during Stage 1 are to (a) teach students that they are capable of learning, (b) teach students that learning can be fun, (c) teach students to habitually complete assigned tasks, and (d) teach students recall and comprehension level skills necessary for more complex tasks later in the school year. The reason that recall and comprehension level skills (as defined by Bloom, 1976) are the primary focus during this stage is that students are experiencing sustained levels of anxiety during Stage 1 that will not be present on an ongoing basis during Stages 2 and 3. Until students feel safe and are under control behaviorally, they do not have the ability to focus on the higher order thinking skills required for application, synthesis, and evaluation.

Academic instruction should be carefully scaffolded for success. Students are often unable to manage frustration effectively during Stage 1 and may scream, cry, attempt to run from the classroom, or create a disturbance with another student to avoid academic tasks that appear to be too difficult. This a wonderful time to build fluency and mastery with recall and comprehension level skills that the students will need for higher level thinking tasks later. Use success-oriented strategies such as direct instruction and precision teaching. Use self-correcting materials and materials that the students prefer such as markers and chart paper or play clay. Students who would be reluctant to write sentences or paragraphs on notebook paper, for example, might be happy to complete the same task if given a variety of markers. Refrain from having students compete with each other. Each child should take pride in his or her own accomplishments regardless of what another child has done. *Do not attempt cooperative learning tasks at this point in the group's development.* Limits on acting out behavior are still being established and prosocial skills for managing peer-to-peer interactions have not been mastered.

Build a foundation for enhancing students' self-efficacy during Stage 1 by having them concentrate on the skills and talents that they have already developed. Students with a history of behavior problems are well aware of what they are unable to do and have already begun to think of themselves as incapable by the age of 7 (Seligman, 1995). Teaching a student with learned helplessness the skills of learned optimism takes time and requires multiple experiences at school, at home, and in the community.

As stated earlier in this section, the primary goals with regard to instruction during Stage 1 are to (a) teach students that they are capable of learning, (b) teach students that learning can be fun, (c) teach students to habitually complete tasks, and (d) teach students recall and comprehension level skills necessary for more complex tasks later in the school year. The reason that recall and comprehension level skills (as defined by Bloom, 1976) are the primary focus during this stage is that students are experiencing sustained levels of anxiety during Stage 1 that will not be present on an ongoing basis during Stages 2 and 3.

Enrichment and Recreation

The communication pattern most likely to result in positive outcomes during Stage 1 is from student to teacher. Student-to-student interactions should be kept to a minimum and monitored frequently. This makes whole-group activities more difficult to arrange and manage. In spite of the challenges, whole-group activities are an important part of the program at this stage of the group's development. I recently found a new game called Twister Moves. This game requires each person to stand on a separate mat and listen to directions called by two DJs on a music CD. The students love this game. They are able to be quite active within a well-defined space. While they enjoy entertaining themselves and each other, the colorful mats and DJ patter keep them focused.

Other games and activities useful during Stage 1 include simple cooking projects, Bingo, and academically focused tasks that allow them to contribute individually to a group product such as an anthology of drawings and writings, a bulletin board, or a three-dimensional display. Do not attempt to engage in collaborative projects such as puppet shows or plays. Students may begin to experience the fun of whole-group performances by engaging in Reader's Theater, but they should not be expected to move about the room or interact as if talking to other people in the play. (Reader's Theater involves having students read aloud from scripts they have had time to rehearse individually.) Readers should sit at their desks or on designated chairs in the room. Once again, the goals of these activities and tasks should include (a) teaching students to have fun within the limits of school-appropriate behavior, (b) facilitating interaction patterns that are primarily from students to teacher rather than from students to students, (c) experiencing fun as a group, and (d) assisting individuals within the group to move from a preoccupation with self to a sense of enjoyment in being part of the group.

Stage 2

During Stage 2, individual students will continue to exhibit problem behaviors. The group may also have problems from time to time. A change in schedule, holiday, or new addition to the group may disrupt their usual routine. Stage 2 is different from Stage 1 in the following ways:

1. Fewer problems occur on a regular basis.

2. Fewer students are involved when problems do occur.

3. Problems are resolved more quickly.

4. Students begin to take responsibility for proactive planning to avoid future problems and for generating solutions during the discussion of a problem.

5. Students begin to work cooperatively with a partner without constant adult monitoring.

6. The teacher's role shifts from benevolent dictator to director.

Behavior Management

Behavior management continues to be one of the teacher's primary responsibilities, but movement toward shared management begins in earnest. Group planning sessions for weekly reinforcement or enrichment activities are a great way to begin to teach students to manage group processes more independently. When relatively minor but persistent problems, such as talking out during lessons, repeatedly occur and involve all or most of the group, the teacher can effectively manage a class meeting. Students can be expected to assist in identifying the problem behavior, brainstorming solutions, selecting a hierarchy of responses to the problem, and implementing the plan. Group contingencies can also be established during Stage 2. Students can work together to meet a group-determined goal and celebrate their success. One group, for example, decided to celebrate by having a class popcorn party when all classmates earned an A on their spelling tests in the same week. Spelling tests had been a particularly stressful event for the class during Stage 1. In spite of having a well-structured program that almost ensured success for anyone who participated, several of the students lacked confidence in themselves and would tear up their papers, cry, and curse. After the group as a whole had exhibited enough self-control for teams of two to work together, students decided to spend part of their earned activity periods helping each other master the spelling words so all students could earn an A. This not only was a tremendous achievement academically but also signaled a new level of maturity in the group as well as increased levels of confidence within targeted individuals.

Affective Education

Affective education focuses on the mastery of social skills necessary for building relationships with peers and those in positions of authority. Some individuals and groups need more help with social skills instruction than others. Younger students will use threats such as "I won't be your friend," "You can't come to my birthday party," and "I'm going to tell my Daddy" to attempt to get others to do what they want them to do. One of my young students expressed his anger toward me by threatening to have his Dad call the police so the police could shoot me. Other students in the past have been more direct. They have called me a "f__ing b___" or an "a___hole." Older students are more apt to make fun of their peers or respond with "You can't make me!" when confronted with an authority figure. Social skills training curricula are available for all developmental levels. Before teaching a series of social skills, assess individuals and the group. Sometimes students know how and when to apply a skill but choose not to perform. This is called a performance deficit. Students with performance deficits may need more reinforcement for applying the skill rather than lessons how to implement the skill. Sometimes students have not been taught a particular skill. I worked with a young lady, for example, who had never used a fork or spoon. In her home, everyone ate out of the cooking pot. The family did not even have plates or bowls for each person. She used inappropriate table manners because she had not been taught any other way of behaving. It is best not to assume that a child is misbehaving. Even if deliberate noncompliance is occurring, it doesn't hurt to give the student the benefit of the doubt and teach the desired skill.

As an extension of the vocabulary development for expressing emotions, wants, and needs begun during Stage 1, students should also be introduced to coping styles and strategies for selecting the most effective coping style for the situation. Students can recognize coping styles and explanatory styles by the age of seven. They may also be able to talk about alternative thoughts and behaviors prior to the age of 9 or 10. Until the age of metacognition at the age of 9 or 10, however, students will not be able to think about their own thinking processes. Until the intermediate grades (3 to 5), teachers and parents can model appropriate coping and explanatory styles and help the children identify effective statements and behaviors in themselves and others. During the intermediate grades, children can be taught the thinking skills they need to dispute their own irrational thinking and, as a result, more effectively manage their own emotions and behaviors.

Academic Instruction

During Stage 2, students can begin to apply the information learned at the recall and comprehension levels during Stage 1. They have had enough academic success with lower level cognitive tasks to take greater academic risks. Stage 2 students with sufficient skill mastery levels are able to tolerate more open-ended assignments. They can begin to make effective use of graphic organizers such as Venn diagrams, story maps, and categorization charts. Because of their increased self-control, they are able to learn the social skills necessary for peer tutoring. With attention to structuring the task, students can begin to work with partners to study spelling words, review math facts, edit each other's essays, and complete two- or three-step projects. Fully developed cooperative learning assignments that require more than two team members and cognitive skills beyond the application level are not recommended during Stage 2. It is easy for the teacher to forget that the group in still somewhat unstable. Individuals appear to be more capable academically and behaviorally than they are. Students' newfound academic and behavioral successes need to be carefully nurtured during Stage 2. Attempting to move individuals and the group too quickly into activities and assignments that they are not ready to successfully manage will cause a regression in their performance. Concentrate on higher level thinking skills through the use of graphic organizers and two- or three-step projects that build on previously mastered recall and comprehension skills. A book report project, for example, might be managed through the use of a project sheet that included (a) steps for completing the project, (b) intermediate due dates, and (c) a structured format for working with a study buddy.

Enrichment and Recreation

Groups that are exhibiting Stage 2 functioning are able to work in two-person teams to accomplish predetermined goals. Two-person games such as checkers and Complete the Square-type games are possible with a minimum of conflict. Puzzles, mazes, and exploratory art activities are wonderful ways to reinforce some of the lessons taught in affective education sessions about learning from mistakes and reframing a problem as an opportunity or challenge. Academically focused group development activities that require two people to complete are also important components of the overall plan to consider during Stage 2. For example, one class decided to make a replica of the Mayflower and the Plymouth Colony for the Thanksgiving unit we were developing. Two-person teams selected a topic and a display for which they were responsible. By the end of the third week in November, the class had a complete card table-size model that was put on display in the school's media center. Two-person teams had researched and constructed a ship, garden, private homes (complete with rock and mortar chimneys), a Common house, an authentic looking Mayflower Compact, and an assortment of tools, household utensils, and foods. The model colony even contained pipe cleaner people in period outfits made of string, yarn, and construction paper. The class wrote a book about their model and bound enough copies for everyone in the class, the teacher, the administrators, and the media center.

If the behavior management strategies gradually include the students as decision makers in the building of their classroom community and the affective education, academic instruction, and enrichment or recreation activities support the group's growth, Stage 2 can be an extremely productive period in the group's development. The strategies, assignments, and activities selected must reinforce gains made during Stage 1 and motivate further movement toward independent functioning, which characterizes Stage 3. The balance of protective structure and increased responsibility is the hallmark of Stage 2 and mirrors the developmentally sensitive responses to discipline suggested in the works of Erikson (1950), Piaget (1970), and Bijou (1995).

Stage 3

Stage 3 is characterized by age-appropriate behavior. Even groups that exhibited severe problems during Stage 1 and Stage 2 settle into a comfortable level of cooperation and productivity during Stage 3, as long as the teacher continues to provide positive supervision. The teacher's role during Stage 3 shifts from that of a director of training and instruction to a facilitator of learning. During Stages 1 and 2, the teacher's emphasis is on doing things *to* and *for* students. Stage 3 marks a shift in emphasis from doing things *to* and *for* students to doing things *with* students. Educators committed to a student-centered, constructivist approach have a hard time accepting the extreme level of teacher-directed instruction and behavior management required during Stage 1 with groups of students that have limited social skills and impulse control. Most groups of children in general education settings experience such an abbreviated and mild Stage 1 that the teacher can begin with Stage 2 behavior management and instructional strategies. The goal of understanding and applying group development processes with more challenging groups, however, is to teach students the prerequisite skills they need to effectively cooperate and collaborate. Proponents of cooperative learning rarely explain how to teach students the self-efficacy, self-control, and prosocial skills necessary for participation in collaborative group efforts.

Figure 3.1 provides a summary of Stage 3-specific instructional, affective, behavioral, and enrichment strategies. Students can be expected to engage in any age-appropriate activity, once the group has reached this level of functioning. Teachers should be sensitive to changes in the curriculum, environment, schedule, or group membership that might disrupt the learning process. Disruptions can be minimized by teaching students prior to a change what is expected of them. They can help prepare for the addition of a classmate, an impending holiday, a schedule change, or a day when the teacher will not be present. Engaging students in the planning process for these types of changes increases their ownership in the success of the group, reduces their anxiety over changes, and gives them a sense of positive control.

Students and teachers assume multiple roles within a group. Stage-specific teacher roles have been addressed above. Students also play different roles within a group. Helping students identify positive roles to play within the classroom is essential to developing productive group functioning. The roles that students may play place additional demands on teachers as groups proceed through developmental stages. The following two sections address student and teacher roles.

■ ROLES THAT STUDENTS PLAY

Students play various roles in the forming and functioning of a group (Goldstein, 1988; Smith, 1988). One or more students will begin to emerge as a peer leader very early in the group's development. Other common roles include the class clown or entertainer, the bully, the victim or incompetent one, the follower, and the evaluator or critic. The teacher must take proactive measures to assist each group member in defining his or her role as positively as possible. General guidelines for facilitating this inevitable group process include:

1. Provide as many opportunities as possible for each group member to contribute to the group in meaningful ways. Class jobs are one method for including each person as a vital member of the group. Other strategies integrate students' strengths with academic content and recreational activities. In one class, students identified their top two to three intelligences as defined by Gardner's (1983, 1993) multiple intelligences. Pie charts illustrating individual strengths were posted on a bulletin board. This information was used in selecting peer tutors for specific content areas and in planning group activities.

2. Tailor academic and nonacademic task assignments with individual students' strengths and needs in mind.

3. Pay attention to nonverbal behaviors that signal tension.

4. Assist the group in learning to recognize and avoid the following barriers to communication: (a) threats, (b) commands or demands, (c) interruptions, (d) put-downs, (e) teasing, (f) insults, and (g) speaking for another person (Goldstein, 1988).

5. Directly teach effective communication skills such as "I" statements, the third person stance, paraphrasing, probes or questions, attacking the problem instead of the person, and generating win-win solutions. Definitions and examples for lessons on these skills are available in the appendices.

As stated earlier in the chapter, it is important for the teacher to shape the group's selection of a group leader, especially if the group is having difficulty deciding among potential options. One of the most potentially destructive challenges a group may face in the beginning is the tension and subgroup formation that occurs when multiple students vie for leadership. In one former group, two equally strong fifth-grade students attempted to control the climate of the classroom. One of the young men, Demond, was often grumpy and negative. The other young man, Jerome, had a violent temper when provoked but was committed to academic achievement, was a skilled athlete, and had a delightful sense of humor when not upset. I desperately wanted the group to select Jerome as their leader in spite of his occasional explosive outbursts. When he was in a pleasant mood, the group tended to follow his lead, which aggravated Demond, who would then begin to make fun of some classmates and argue with others in an effort to disrupt the group. Jerome would get angry. Demond would demand that members of the group listen to him. The tension in the group would escalate, and a fight or some other major disruption would occur. Over time, I confronted the group with the choices they were making. I pointed out that Demond often created tension in the group with negative comments. I also rewarded Jerome's attempts to support the school-based academic and therapeutic recreation programs in which the group was engaged. In addition, I talked with Jerome privately about his leadership skills and thanked him for the positive example he set for others. He liked being the "alpha male" and increased his supportive interactions with group members.

Assisting students in overcoming their negative masks and adopting more realistic and effective ways of contributing to the group requires attention to individual strengths and needs. As each student is able to contribute meaningfully to the functioning of the group, the need to act out a role (a super-competent nerd; a clown; a helpless failure; a victim; a whirling dervish of unproductive activity; a bored, uncaring bystander; an incorrigible loser; the con; or the unrealistic dream weaver) decreases. It is important for the teacher to realize that students who persist in behaving in a predetermined way instead of authentically interacting with other members of the group are often hiding behind a feeling of inadequacy. Students will only be comfortable enough to stop the coping behaviors if skills within their repertoire are sufficiently powerful to gain them a respectable alternative role in the group. Keep Foundational Principles 2 and 6 in mind here. Foundational Principle 2 is that behavior is purposeful. Students who adopt disruptive or failure-oriented roles are attempting to get or avoid something. Foundational Principle 6 is that each person has his or her own mental picture of how to best meet needs. Often the most successful plans include combining an activity the student already finds rewarding with a group goal. The application of the Premack principle (Premack, 1959) is of particular value with these students. A child who prefers to entertain classmates instead of completing academic tasks might be enticed into completing class work in exchange for time to perform weekly during a class talent show. For others, a careful reframing of their underlying strengths can be used to redirect their energy. The incorrigible loser or helpless victim can be encouraged to help a younger child. Youth who define themselves as bad are often quite gentle with younger children. They can be enticed into seeing their strengths in terms of protecting and nurturing a less able person. Students who act like a victim often need to see themselves as strong and capable. Helping someone else gives them an opportunity to feel powerful.

Attending to the development of positive roles for each group member helps individuals develop their own expanding repertoires for coping with social situations and facilitates greater cohesion within the group.

■ ROLES THAT TEACHERS PLAY

Teachers must play different roles over the course of a group's development in order to facilitate group growth. Students come into the school environment with a variety of background experiences that affect their abilities to respond appropriately to the teacher. Some expect the teacher to be a nurturing parent figure; others expect the teacher to be rejecting, demanding, and harsh. Research on the characteristics of teachers who are most effective as behavior managers describes those educators as having high levels of self-efficacy (Allinder, 1993). These teachers believe in their abilities to teach in general and to teach their assigned group of students in particular and in the ability of the students to learn. Their interactions with the students are characterized by warmth, high rates of positive reinforcement, a preference for working with the whole group, and a willingness to persist with individual students who present challenging behaviors or learning problems. Morgan and Reinhart (1991) found empathy to be associated with less teacher stress and higher rates of student achievement. Qualities of empathetic teachers include but are not limited to being spontaneous, warm, soft-spoken, relaxed, calm, humorous, analytic of behavior, able to predict another's behavior, encouraging, motivating, independent, creative, inspiring, able to give positive verbal and nonverbal feedback, accepting of differences, and low in the need to control all people and events.

During Stage 1, the teacher focuses on proactive planning and protective structuring of the environment, the schedule, academic tasks, communication patterns, and recreational activities. The benevolent dictator of Stage 1 must be conscientious in responding to students' individual needs, adaptable, and highly intuitive.

During Stage 2, the teacher's emphasis shifts to that of a director who teaches the skills necessary for group members to participate more fully in the selection and development of projects, learning tasks, and enrichment activities. At this point in the group's development, the teacher must be willing to make group members centrally involved in the functioning of the group.

During Stage 3, the teacher shifts once again to assume a new role in the functioning of the group. Children are able to engage in age-appropriate activities during Stage 3. The teacher becomes more of a facilitator of learning.

Groups of children who are characterized initially by high rates of disruption and emotional or behavioral problems require constant monitoring even during Stage 3. While the teacher's role shifts in response to the students' needs, the teacher must maintain a positive, adult leadership role during all three stages. If a new student arrives, an older student leaves, or any other significant change occurs, the group is likely to regress to a previous stage of functioning. The regression is inevitable but does not have to be unduly upsetting to the group. When regression occurs, the teacher must calmly and positively shift into the role of the appropriate stage.

Increased structure for a few days or weeks will provide the group the time it needs to self-right. Until the group stabilizes, resume stage-appropriate academic and recreational activities, engage in more teacher-directed interactions, and increase positive reinforcement. The period of reorganization within the group is similar to the process that older children in a family experience when a new baby arrives. The next section on the pecking order phenomenon further illustrates the need for differences in teacher's roles across stage development and the changes that are likely to occur in group functioning during transitions in group membership.

THE PECKING ORDER ■

Just after the First World War, Schjelderup-Ebbe discovered that chickens live within a social hierarchy he called the "pecking order" (as cited in Bloom, 1995). Chickens who are vying for the lead position will literally peck each other. The rooster who is most aggressive establishes himself as the leader of the flock. In wolf packs, male wolves fight for the alpha male position. Once the leader has been determined, the pack settles into the routines that sustain life. If the alpha male is killed or dies, the pack once again experiences a period of internal reorganization while leadership is being established.

Human groups also follow patterns of organization and disorder much like the wolves and roosters (see Bloom, 1995). This organizational phenomenon occurs even if individuals who held leadership roles in previously formed groups are assigned to the same group (Freedman, as cited in Bloom, 1995). Groups that have a clearly defined and capable leader achieve their goals more efficiently. Groups that are loosely formed and lack leadership tend to be less predictable and productive. Law enforcement officials, for example, would much rather work with a well-organized gang than one that is poorly defined. Well-organized gangs follow the directions of their leader and rarely commit unplanned antisocial acts. Poorly defined gangs are more dangerous because antisocial acts are apt to occur to meet individual member's needs or goals rather than to maintain the integrity of the gang's purposes and standards.

STRATEGIES FOR BUILDING COMMUNITY ■

Students who are most in need of a sense of belonging and community are often the most difficult to engage in productive classroom activities. The first step in building community in the classroom is establishing limits on antisocial behavior. If individuals within a classroom group are able to assist in the development of rules, routines, and procedures, a group meeting can be held to discuss everyone's ideas. For the more difficult groups, however, such invitations could be disastrous. One year, I had a group of fourth- and fifth-grade boys with severe emotional disorders and histories of violent acting out. The school district sent a clinical psychologist to the room to conduct group counseling sessions. I was instructed to sit in the back of the room and watch. The psychologist did not believe that a teacher was trained to hold group meetings and insisted that I not participate. On the appointed day, she arrived with a bucket of markers, poster board, and a smile. I retreated to the back of the classroom to watch. She opened with an explanation of the purpose of group counseling. In this case, she told the boys that they would be talking about alternative ways to handle their anger. She asked the boys to introduce themselves. They began to make silly comments but made it around the room before losing control. Then, the psychologist pulled out a large poster board and told the boys that they would need to help her develop some rules for the times when she was with them. The looks on the boys' faces ranged from open defiance to amused smirks. Before she could say anything else, they began their assault. One suggested that they should be allowed to say anything they wanted to say, including profanity and name calling. Another stood on his desk and began screaming. Every attempt on the psychologist's part to engage them in a discussion about the merits of their suggestions was followed by an increase in disruptive behavior. When all students had either fallen out of their seats laughing or were toe-to-toe with a classmate screaming such epitaphs as "butt head," "butt wipe," and "—sucker," the class leader waved his arms, signaled the others to sit down, and told them in a firm voice to be quiet. He then pointed his finger in the psychologist's face and said, "Look you know what you want us to say. We know what you want us to say. So tell us the rules and get on with it!" She gathered her belongings and left. The next time she came, she allowed me to review the classroom rules with her and the group before she began the session. She found it difficult to achieve the level of mutual respect that she had intended to establish during the first session and resigned from her position before completing her contract. So where do you start with a group that won't listen and isn't interested in collaborative group meetings?

1. *Examine the group's behavior as a whole.* If the group members function as individuals with no commitment to group rules, expectations, or relationships, then the group is in Stage 1. Be a benevolent dictator by taking care of their needs for physical comfort, success, and safety. (See Figure 3.2, Stages of Group Development and Maslow in Action.) Do not expect them to collaborate in the development of class rules, academic projects, or group contingencies. Select activities that will allow all group members to participate without requiring interpersonal skills that are beyond their mastery levels.

2. *Ask for students' input often.* Post their names on the board and place their predictions next to their names during reading and science lessons. When solving word problems together, place the operation sign that represents the action that should be taken to solve the problem next to their name during the discussion of the problem. When completing an activity or assignment, ask students to indicate their level of enjoyment or agreement using one of two methods:

A. Have students signal agreement or approval with a thumbs-up sign and disagreement or disapproval with a thumbs-down sign. Students can be asked individually to support their vote with a verbal explanation.

Figure 3.2   Stages of Group Development and Maslow in Action

Stage One		Stage Two	Stage Three
Physiological Needs	*Psychological and Physical Safety*	*Belonging*	*Esteem*
Provide food and fluids. Be aware of the possible side effects of medications. Provide adequate personal space around students' desks. Adjust furniture to the size of the students. Provide time for active movement. Provide quiet time for rest. Carefully balance active and quiet times. Provide sweatshirts and sweaters for students who are cold. Have a fan available for students who are too warm. Provide pillows or cushions for their seats. Provide adequate lighting. Block glare from windows. Make referrals to other professionals or agencies if a student is ill, has an ongoing health problem, needs glasses or some other physical aid, or has unmet needs.	Disallow aggression. Provide enough personal space for each individual. Provide safe storage for each individual's belongings. Establish and enforce safety rules. Celebrate mistakes—actively teach the value of making mistakes as part of the learning process. Provide task-specific corrective feedback (local, time limited, and internal). Provide task-specific praise. Disallow insulting remarks and unkind nonverbal gestures. Put away unnecessarily distracting items. Secure items such as paper cutters and tools when not in use. Maintain a minimum of a 3 to 1 ratio of positives to correctives. Provide structure and routine in the daily schedule. Prepare students with advanced notice when routines must be changed. Prepare students for new classmates, the loss of a classmate, and substitutes. *Never* promise a reward or a consequence that is not possible. Be predictable, honest, trustworthy, and fair! Teach social skills that will be naturally reinforced in a variety of settings. Use success-oriented instructional strategies. Use instructional strategies that reinforce personal success while contributing to the well-being of others. Structure group activities to maximize participation while minimizing opportunities for interpersonal overstimulation and conflict. Keep a record of students' successes in academic as well as behavioral areas. Actively teach the group procedures to follow when a problem arises.	Continue to use instructional strategies that move students from a "Me" orientation to a "We" orientation. Actively teach problem-solving skills, conflict resolution, and peer mediation. Involve the group in age-appropriate decisions. Actively reinforce students who use the strategies and skills taught. Use instructional strategies that involve student input and participation with peers such as peer tutoring, cooperative learning, shared reading, shared writing, service projects, mini-businesses, and plays. Keep a class collection of writings, photographs, art work, and other items that can be shared with visitors or enjoyed by students when their work is complete. Plan and execute class celebrations with the students' input and assistance. Set group goals. Have students decide how to document achievement, collect the necessary data, and report the progress. Use instructional strategies and lessons that maximize group involvement while maintaining an academic focus. Preparing foods representative of a country or culture of interest, making crafts and musical instruments, singing, and a variety of academically oriented games can increase the sense of belonging. Include all modalities in the planning of lessons. Each student's strengths should be represented during the development of a lesson. Use integrated, thematic units of study whenever possible. Involve the group in mini-business and/or service	Continue to refine the skills students have in communicating, problem solving, and planning. Fade external prompts if this has not already been accomplished. Maintain high expectations for academic and behavioral performance. Allow students to fail. Celebrate working on difficult tasks until reaching mastery. Actively reward positive acts of persistence as well as goal attainment. Develop an acceptance of personal strengths and weaknesses.

Figure 3.2 (Continued)

Stage One		Stage Two	Stage Three
Physiological Needs	*Psychological and Physical Safety*	*Belonging*	*Esteem*
	Begin to teach effective communication and decision-making skills.	projects that include schoolwide and community interaction and involvement. Rely to the greatest extent possible on the group to initiate, plan, and complete class projects, celebrations, and other activities. Allow the naturally occurring reinforcers within the environment to be recognized by actively celebrating success through group participation.	

B. Have students signal their level of agreement or approval by rais-ing one, two, three, four, or five fingers. Students should be told to raise their pointer to signal a vote of one rather than their middle finger. A vote of one would indicate extreme disagreement or disap-proval. A vote of five would indicate extreme agreement or approval. A three would indicate a neutral vote. A teacher-led dis-cussion of different points of view should follow the voting.

These methods of group participation (a) model respect for each indi-vidual, (b) model respect for differences of opinion within a controlled and nonthreatening process, (c) encourage reflection and expressions of emo-tions and thoughts, and (d) provide a foundation for increased cooperation and collaboration as individuals as well as the group acquire the necessary prerequisite skills. Asking for students' input in this way takes only a few moments and results in tremendous personal and interpersonal growth.

3. Establish high expectations and recognize all who achieve them. Building community requires cohesiveness of goals, clearly defined roles, opportuni-ties for individuals to contribute, and opportunities for success. High expec-tations are sometimes established within an atmosphere of winners and losers. If all students are expected to achieve, but only the one with the high-est grade point average is recognized, the students most at risk for failure will not be motivated to participate in the competition. If, on the other hand, all students are expected to achieve and all who achieve at a predetermined level are recognized, students who had previously thought they did not have a chance for success will be given an opportunity. Expectations should be established for behavior as well as academics. Strategies include:

A. Assigning criteria for a Student of the Week award. In my class, students must complete all class work and homework assignments, earn a predetermined level of behavioral points, and have appropri-ate behavior on the bus. Some weeks, no one earns the award. Some weeks, four or five students earn the award. Even though this is an individual award, all group members have access to it if they meet the criteria. As students who have difficult school histories discover that they can achieve in ways they had not previously thought possible, the individuals begin to value the group rules, procedures, and expectations. This increases group cohesiveness.

B. Reading logs, spelling, and math facts. Students can be challenged to read a targeted number of pages during recreational reading periods, earn 90% or higher on their weekly spelling tests for a quarter, and memorize math facts. For most of the academic goals I establish with my class, I do not assign a time limit. Some students master their multiplication facts in 3 weeks. Other students take 3 months. Everyone earns a math master ribbon and certificate when he or she meets criteria.

C. Group projects that are completed individually and contribute globally. Anthologies of writings and drawings, photo albums of class activities, bulletin board displays, models, seasonal decorations, a mini-business, a service learning project, and a class newspaper are excellent ways to (a) combine academic and social skill instruction, (b) enhance group cohesiveness, (c) provide opportunities for contributions by each group member, (d) increase students' experiences of success, and (e) provide authentic outlets for learning.

D. Develop affective bulletin boards that target skills for recognition that are specific to the students' needs and incorporated into affective lessons. Recognize students for exhibiting targeted skills by posting their names, art work, and/or a description of their good behavior on this bulletin board.

4. Define roles and expectations together. Students who are most challenging behaviorally have histories of discord and distrust with adults and peers. Teachers often talk about finding methods for getting reluctant students to "buy into" the class plan. While the teacher has the right and responsibility to define nonnegotiable limits on aggressive or disruptive behaviors, the discussion of expectations and roles can set the stage for a more collaborative relationship between students and the teacher. The following activities are helpful during the first days and weeks of school when roles and expectations are being established. These activities can be used at any time during the year to review, reflect, refine, and renegotiate roles and expectations based on students' needs.

A. What makes a good student? In spite of the challenges students may present in the classroom, they typically have an understanding of what it takes to be a good student. If they are able to work in pairs or cooperative groups of four, allow them to brainstorm prior to the whole-group discussion. Each individual or small group can be asked to generate three to five attributes. These characteristics can be written on large file cards and taped to the board as each individual or small group presents contributions. Duplicates can be eliminated by placing one on top of the other. Similar items can be combined and renamed under one title. The class should narrow the characteristics of a good student down to no more than 10. For younger groups of primary-age students, the list can be shorter. Students should also help design icons or illustrations for each attribute. The items, illustrations, and numbers from 1 to 5 next to each item can then be placed on a standard size sheet of typing paper. Students can individually rate themselves on each attribute. A one would indicate poor performance in that area. A five would indicate excellent performance. These self ratings could then be used as a basis for developing personal goals. Students can collect data to support their ratings and participate in the development of their individualized educational plans, parent conferences, and quarterly progress reports. A sample of a student's self-evaluation, improvement plan, and data collection folder is available in Figure 3.3.

B. What makes a good teacher? Students can be asked to go through the process of defining the characteristics of a good teacher in the same way that they developed the list of attributes of a good student. This process is sometimes referred to as the development of an affinity chart. Some of the characteristics of a good teacher will be the same as those for a good student. Common attributes such as being prepared, willing to help, and trustworthy should be discussed. These attributes can become the bases for a shared set of expectations more completely described in C. The values of defining the attributes of a good teacher include (a) providing students with a safe and appropriate process for discussing their feelings and needs, (b) communicating respect for students as members of a group, and (c) inviting feedback.

C. What values do we all agree to uphold? What are our shared expectations? After the class has had time to explore the characteristics of good students and good teachers, they will be able to identify qualities that they agree all people who work and play together in their classroom should exhibit. One class that I taught in the past came up with the following values or expectations: respectful, prepared, productive, cooperative, and trustworthy. The students defined each attribute, developed posters with examples and nonexamples, and used words as well as drawings to illustrate each characteristic. When the group as a whole was having difficulty with one or more of the expectations, I would ask them to identify the problem. Once the correct problem was identified, I would ask them to indicate using one to five fingers their own individual level of performance in that area. Those who indicated that they were not doing well by raising one or two fingers would be asked what they could do to improve. Those who indicated appropriate behavior by raising four or five fingers would be asked how they knew that they were performing at that level. After that very brief review, I would ask what the group needed to do at that point. They would review the behaviors reflective of appropriate behavior related to that expectation, and we would go on with the lesson or activity. This is more immediately effective with older students than with younger ones. The younger students benefit, however, from the frequent review and modeling of the self-reflective process.

5. *Establish and model problem-solving procedures.*

A. Group meetings. Group meetings should initially be very brief and focused on positive information whenever possible.

Figure 3.3   Student Self-Management Tools

Developmental Profile

Name _____   School Year _____

Assigned Grade _____   Teacher _____

Years	IQ	Social/ Behavioral		Math	Reading		Language Expressive/ Receptive		Motor Fine/Large	
16										
15										
14										
13										
12										
11										
10										
9										
8										
7										
6										
K										
Pre K										

Notes: _____

_____

My Success Plan

Name _____   Date _____

What will I be learning this grading period?

What do I already know how to do well?

What do I need to learn?

How will I accomplish my goal?

How will I know if I have met my goal? What data will I collect?

How am I doing?

Dates I will review my progress and rate my level of achievement:

_____ 1 2 3 4 5   _____ 1 2 3 4 5

_____ 1 2 3 4 5   _____ 1 2 3 4 5

Parent Signature _____   Teacher Signature _____

How Am I Doing as a Student?

• Arrive on time	1	2	3	4	5
• Bring materials	1	2	3	4	5
• Listen	1	2	3	4	5
• Follow directions	1	2	3	4	5
• Complete tasks	1	2	3	4	5
• Math	1	2	3	4	5
• Reading	1	2	3	4	5
• Spelling	1	2	3	4	5
• Language	1	2	3	4	5
• Science	1	2	3	4	5
• Social Studies	1	2	3	4	5

Ground rules for group meetings should include:

1. Speak only about and for yourself.
2. Use school appropriate language.
3. Focus on the immediate issue.

B. Decision making for fun events (voting). Students will need to have a procedure to follow when making decisions. Begin by discussing and voting on fun activities. Provide them with two or three choices in the beginning. As self-control increases, allow them to generate a list of choices. Establish a win-win process by explaining that the voting will determine the order in which fun activities will be accessed rather than eliminating options not rated number one. For example, if a group votes to make pudding for the Fun Friday activity for the present week and playing outside with a stomp rocket was the group's second choice, the stomp rocket can be put on the schedule for the following week. Once group members are able to tolerate a delay in gratification, the group can move to voting on options that include the elimination of some choices.

C. Think sheet (group and individual). Think sheets are described in more detail in Chapter 4. These include formats for clarifying and defining a problem, generating possible solutions, selecting a preferred option, implementing the plan, and evaluating the results. Before requiring individuals to engage in this process alone, students will need teacher-directed modeling during whole-group discussions. For example, one morning, my class failed to earn an activity period because no one completed academic tasks on time. I led a class meeting during which we discussed the reasons that work did not get completed. The class identified the problem, generated options for solving the problem, decided on a plan for the next morning, implemented the plan, and evaluated their success. Over a period of a few months, individuals and subgroups began to model the process without teacher guidance and prompting. Youth with the most challenging behaviors often have difficulty generating alternatives when problems arise. They benefit not only from a discussion of options, but also from a predictable process to use when problem solving. Foundational Principle 12 is particularly important to remember here: What we do *with* children is as powerful, if not more powerful, than what we do *to* and *for* them.

D. Group contingencies. Group contingencies are more effective than any other interventions designed to alter students' behaviors (Stage & Quiroz, 1997). Researchers categorize contingency options as independent, dependent, and interdependent (Litow & Pomroy, 1975). Independent contingencies are available to all group members based on a predetermined criterion. Groups characterized by high rates of aggression and low cohesion benefit initially from independent contingencies. As soon as the group has learned the class rules and is able to manage stressful situations without resorting to physical aggression, dependent and interdependent contingencies can be implemented with positive results. Dependent contingencies require a specific student or subset of students to meet criteria in order for the whole group to gain access to a reinforcer. Interdependent contingencies require subgroups of students within a whole group to meet criteria as a team to gain access to a reinforcer. With the interdependent contingency, the team functions as an individual with regard to earning the reinforcer. Cooperative learning tasks are often organized around a team approach like this. A multicomponent program can be implemented that combines group contingencies with precision requests (Forehand & McMahon, 1981), immediate reinforcement of students' behaviors, and a token economy with response cost. This multicomponent approach, described in more detail in Chapter 4, has been found to be effective in reducing disruptive classroom behaviors (Kehle, Bray, Theodore, Jenson, & Clark, 2000). A brief description of classroom-based applications of dependent and interdependent contingencies is followed by options for establishing goals, documenting progress toward goal attainment, and celebrating successes.

1. Mystery motivators (Rhodes, Jenson, & Reavis, 1993). Options for designing dependent and interdependent reinforcement programs include:
   a. Writing reinforcers on slips of paper and allowing a student to select a slip of paper once the whole group or a team has earned a reinforcer. Options for reinforcers include 3 to 5 extra minutes of recess, 15 minutes of inside game time, 1 to 5 points toward a class social, access to preferred art or music activities, "No Homework" coupons, and class dollars to spend on coupons for other privileges such as eating lunch with another class or visiting a preferred staff member in another part of the school.
   b. Targeting an individual student or subgroup of students without identifying those students prior to the collection of data on their behavior. Discuss the behaviors that will be monitored. At a predetermined time, tell the class that the reinforcer has been earned and identify the student or subgroup of students who performed successfully. If the student or subgroup of students did not perform successfully, do not identify the individual or subgroup.
   c. Identify two to five behaviors that might be targeted. Collect data on one of the behaviors. Reveal at a predetermined time whether or not a subgroup or individual met the criteria. Only name the individual or subgroup if the criteria for earning a reinforcer have been met.

2. Goals and celebrations. Establishing goals, documenting progress toward goal mastery, and celebrating successes are important components in building group cohesiveness. Start small. Set goals that can be met in a half day in the beginning. First steps toward goal setting might include a group agreement to have no more than 20 talk-outs during morning instruction. Bulletin boards are wonderful resources and are too often underutilized as a powerful motivational tool. After teaching my students about sensible

and fuzzy or ineffective thinking, students who demonstrate sensible thinking receive an Owl Award. These awards include a picture of an owl with preprinted spaces for students to record their names, the problem situation, the sensible thoughts that they had, and the behavior they demonstrated. The Owl Awards are posted on a bulletin board under the appropriate category of effective thinking. Honoring their acquisition of a new skill in this manner highlights the importance of the skill, reinforces the students for demonstrating mastery of the skill, and increases students' awareness of the skill in authentic situations.

Celebrations can be short and simple or more elaborate. Small successes should be recognized with brief, immediate celebrations. A game of Simon Says, a small snack, 5 minutes of singing or dancing, or a visit from an administrator to distribute high-fives to all are ways to celebrate small successes. Achievements that take longer to accomplish should be recognized and celebrated more formally. One year, our elementary team wrote a grant that included field trips aligned with instructional themes and student authored books. At the end of the year, students' books were put on display and shared during a formal ceremony. Parents, school-based administrators, and supervisors from the district level attended the event. With all that educators have to do, celebrations can sometimes be forgotten. Students understand the importance of their accomplishments, however, partly by observing the emphasis that adults place on them. Celebrations build a sense of community that is positive, inclusive, and goal directed.

6. Play stage-specific games. Stage-specific games have many advantages, including (a) protecting group members from overstimulation, (b) strengthening stage-specific communication and problem-solving skills, and (c) facilitating group cohesion. Goldstein (1988) identified multiple age-specific games designed to facilitate group growth. A few examples are offered below.

Stage 1 (Goal: fun! Whole-group participation with minimal student-to-student verbal interaction and no touching.)

Pass the mask: Students sit in a circle. The first person makes a face. The second person makes the same face and passes it to the next person. This continues until the mask has been passed around the circle. The person who began identifies the emotion that goes with the face. The accuracy of the mask passed is evaluated.

Clapping game. One person leaves the room for a moment. An object is identified by the group. The person returns and attempts to locate the mystery object. The group gives clues by clapping softly when the person is far from the object and loudly when the person is near the object.

Cooperative pin the tail on the donkey. The person who is blindfolded is given directions by group members about where to place the tail.

Stage 2 (Goal: communication. Student-to-student interaction in two-person teams with a specific goal.)

Beach blanket ball. Pairs of students are instructed to hold the corners of a beach towel. Without touching the beach ball, pairs throw the beach ball to another pair holding a beach towel. The other pair attempts to catch the beach ball in their beach towel. Pairs earn points by catching the ball in their beach towel.

Car and driver. Students are divided into two-person teams. One person in each team is blindfolded. The blindfolded person is the car. The other person stands behind the person who is blindfolded and places his or her hands on the blindfolded student's shoulders. The person who is not blindfolded is the driver. The driver verbally directs the car through an obstacle course.

Towering tower. Two-person teams are given bean bags, blocks, or other items selected by the teacher. Each team is instructed to build a tower as high as possible without having pieces fall from the top of the tower.

Stage 3 (Goal: generalization of social skills. Whole-group activities designed to incorporate multiple social and communication skills within a time-limited, goal-oriented framework.)

Building the monster. A model of a monster is provided in a secluded location. Each member of a four- to six-member team is given a role. Only the researcher can see the monster. The researcher tells the communicator what the monster looks like. The communicator tells the purchaser what to buy and the builder how to build the monster. The communicator can talk with all participants, but the researcher can only talk to the communicator. The purchaser and builder can only talk to the communicator. The purchaser is given a bag of beans with which to purchase parts of the monster. The parts merchant can accept no returns and does not give refunds. If the wrong part is purchased, the communicator and builder must decide on a way to make it work. At the end of the activity, the original monster is revealed. This is a great way to introduce cooperative learning processes and skills prior to beginning academically focused cooperative learning lessons.

Tug of peace. Students sit in a circle with a sturdy rope at their feet. The rope is knotted to form a circle. Students tug on the rope with enough force to allow all of them to stand.

Knots. Students join hands and begin to step over and under each other's joined hands to form a human knot. Without dropping hands, students untie the knot.

CONCLUSION ■

Understanding and responding appropriately to the stages of group development is essential in classrooms with students who have very challenging behaviors. In general education classrooms, the stages of group development are less intense and even more responsive to stage-specific teacher intervention. Stage 1 is characterized by an initial period of calm followed by the testing of behavioral limits. The teacher's role during Stage 1 is the benevolent dictator, providing careful attention to students' needs and protective levels of structure. Stage 2 is characterized by fewer challenges to adult authority. Students begin to positively identify with group membership. The teacher's role shifts to that of the director, orchestrating the transition from teacher control to shared control of group processes. Stage 3 is characterized by age-appropriate behaviors. The teacher's role shifts primarily to that of the facilitator as shared leadership with an emphasis on student responsibility for goal setting and self-monitoring become the norm.

Research-based instructional strategies and behavior management techniques are often presented to educators as equally valid in all settings with all students. Unfortunately, prerequisite social, emotional, and behavioral skills are not addressed. This can cause harm to individual students, the growth of a group, and the self-efficacy of a teacher. Knowing the critical components at work within groups at particular stages can increase the likelihood that a selected strategy, method, technique, or program will benefit all. Chapter 4 addresses the topic of classroom management with specific attention to expectations, rules, procedures, and consequences.

4

Classwide Behavior Management

INTRODUCTION ■

Hewett and Taylor (1980) identified the three major components of classroom management for students with emotional and behavioral disorders (EBD) as (1) conditions, (2) consequences, and (3) curriculum. The conditions of the classroom include the physical environment, the overall emotional climate, and the scheduling of activities. Consequences include the responses to behaviors—(a) pleasant and unpleasant, (b) planned and unplanned, (c) teacher directed and student led. Instructional content in

Figure 4.1   The *You Can't Make Me!* Model for Facilitating Cooperation

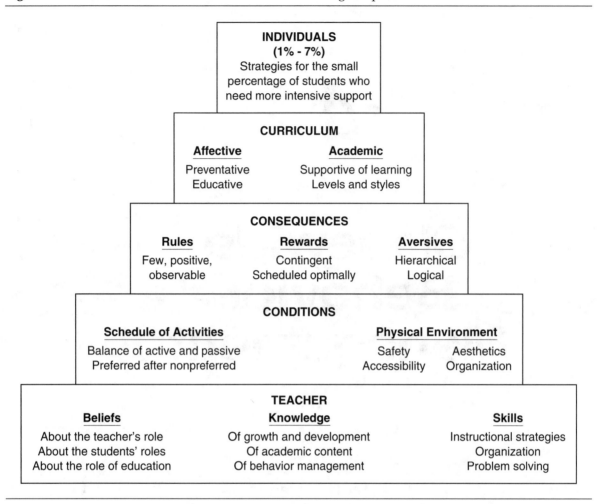

the areas of academics and behavior as well as the strategies used to deliver the content make up the category titled "curriculum." Since Hewett and Taylor's work on the orchestration and integration of critical components in the management of classroom behavior, research conducted in general education settings has expanded our knowledge of effective processes and practices in all school settings (Scott & Nelson, 1999; Sugai et al., 2000). This chapter uses conditions, consequences, and curriculum as the nuts and bolts of effective classroom management. Teachers who apply the research-based concepts and processes to their own classroom management plans are able to eliminate 80% to 95% of the problem behaviors that might occur without a plan. These are powerful tools under the direct control of the classroom teacher.

The *You Can't Make Me!* model (see Figure 4.1) for facilitating effective classroom management and instruction, which is described in the preface, places conditions and consequences on top of the foundational knowledge and skills of the teacher and under both curriculum and the individual needs of a specific student because student learning depends on the teacher's ability to manage both the conditions and consequences that occur in the learning environment.

CONDITIONS ■

Before defining and providing examples of methods for addressing conditions in the classroom, I'd like to share a story from a recent experience with students at the primary level. I walked into the classroom on the first day of preplanning to find quite a mess. The room was full of unnecessary furniture—too many desks, chairs, tables, and shelves. None of the desks were the proper size for the children assigned to the room. Whereas the students assigned to the room were in kindergarten through second grade, all of the desks were appropriate for fifth- and sixth-grade students. The children's feet would not reach the ground, and this might encourage them to put their feet on the table tops or their seats. The children's arms were too short to reach the desk tops while sitting, encouraging them to kneel or stand in their seats.

Toys and other activity center equipment were disorganized. Some of the materials were broken or had so many missing pieces that they were nonfunctional. The file cabinets were equally disorganized and full of outdated material. To make matters worse, the storage room adjacent to the classroom had so much trash in it that I could not find the instructional materials. Other teachers reported that the students had spent most of their days throwing and breaking instructional items. Very little academic work had been done. Assessment records confirmed that none of the students had gained more than 2 months of academic growth during the whole previous year. In short, the conditions and climate in that room had been characterized by disorder and dysfunction.

Children, like adults, respond at emotional and behavioral levels to the physical environment. The first thing young children do when presented with a long, wide open hall or room is run. When they walk into a room that is in total disarray, they have difficulty focusing their attention on one thing. They may jump from one topic to another during conversation or from one activity to another when told to complete a task. Priority one when designing a classroom behavior management plan is examining the physical environment of the classroom.

Physical Environment

Safety begins with the physical environment. The teacher should be able to see all areas of the classroom from every vantage point. Students' personal storage areas should be easily accessible and open to view. Students may have backpacks, cubbies with doors on them, or lockers that close, but the storage area itself should be open to visual monitoring. Desks should be placed in a way that maximizes personal space. Pathways to doors and frequently used materials should be clearly defined and free from potential hazards. All unnecessary tools and materials should be placed out of sight when not being used. Broken and forbidden items should be removed from the classroom.

Once safety measures have been taken, furniture arrangement should support activity-specific needs. A large semicircular table for small-group instruction should be separated from the area where students will do independent work at their desks. Some teachers like to put students in cooperative teams of two to four, with desks placed adjacent to and touching each other. For students with more severe emotional or behavioral problems, this arrangement is not recommended until the group has reached Stage 2 or Stage 3 functioning. If students must sit together at larger tables during Stage 1, colorful tape can be used to clearly define each student's personal space. If a special rug is used for teacher read-aloud or circle time activities, students may also need carpet squares or taped boxes to designate their assigned space on the rug. I have been known to mark each student's desk area with a large masking tape square as well. Keeping hands, feet, and other objects to oneself is easier to understand and enforce if personal space is concretely defined.

Some teachers find that using a sheet or tablecloth to cover computers and earned activity time materials such as puzzles, magnets, and other hands-on exploratory items helps students understand when to touch and when not to touch such materials. A teacher working with preschool-age students with developmental disabilities placed a wide strip of red tape across the opening to the play area and hung red curtains over the open shelves of toys. Students knew that they were to cross the red line only when the curtains were opened.

Schedule

The daily schedule is one of the most overlooked and easily manipulated variables in classroom management. Students who are young need frequent changes in activity. High-interest materials and tasks should follow less desirable activities to maximize motivation. A balance of active and passive activities should also be maintained. During reading instruction, for example, students rotate from one task to another on a predetermined schedule. They have 20 minutes of small-group instruction, 20 minutes of independent seat work, 20 minutes of computer time, and 20 minutes in a small group playing a game designed to strengthen a specific decoding skill or targeted sight words. Students must complete their independent seat work to be eligible to play the game with their assigned group. This allows each child to remain highly motivated to achieve success, allows for frequent changes in activity, encourages attention to skill mastery, and reduces behavior problems to a minimum. When using a rotation system such as the one described above, make sure to teach students to respond to an initial signal by preparing to move to the next activity. Use a second signal to direct movement from one area of the room to the next. Students will become agitated and more prone to problem behavior if they do not have time to prepare to move and clearly defined rules about when and where to move. The hour and a half spent teaching reading each day is our least problematic in terms of behavior due to the frequent changes in activity and the highly motivating tasks and materials with which students engage.

Students are often overstimulated after physical education classes or lunch. They will need a transitional activity to help them calm down and focus on academic tasks. One strategy that has worked well for me over the years is to reorient the class with a period of singing after lunch. We begin with fast-paced songs and end with quiet, slower-paced songs. Seasonal favorites as well as songs that teach academic skills such as sight word recognition, rhyming word identification, and math facts increase the academic focus while providing students with an enjoyable strategy for calming down. Some teachers use finger plays, simple stretching exercises, or reading aloud a chapter in a captivating book to help students make the transition from active, overstimulating activities to quieter, more academically focused tasks. Finding a strategy or activity that students like is essential to success. They adopt a habit of compliance when the routine is (a) sufficiently stimulating, (b) clearly and regularly followed, (c) managed through positive, reinforcing strategies, and (d) success oriented.

Climate

Classroom climate is a tremendously powerful factor in the development of a classwide behavior management system. Kounin (1970) identified teacher behaviors that contributed to an effective classroom climate. With-it-ness, a firm, calm desist message in response to misbehavior, and a high ratio of positive responses to appropriate behavior versus redirections were the essential teacher behaviors associated with a positive classroom climate. Children tend to do more of whatever adults call to their attention. If the teacher repeatedly says, "Sit down, sit down," the students will tend to get out of their seats. If the teacher repeatedly says, "Shhh. Be quiet," the students will tend to talk more frequently. It might seem a little strange to look for the few who are sitting and quiet and talk to them, but it works like magic—especially with young children. Children want the adults' attention. Thanking, praising, and regularly recognizing students by name when they comply with a request are effective strategies. When the whole class is having difficulty following a routine direction like raising their hands and waiting to be recognized before talking out or getting out of their seats without permission, try playing the "Follow First Directions" game. Place the rule or picture of the rule over a large T on the chalkboard. Write the word *teacher* over the left side of the T and the word *students* over the right side of the T. When the students forget to follow the rule, put a line under the teacher's side of the T. When the students remember to follow the rule, put a line under the students' side of the T. Students are usually content with earning more points than the teacher—no other reward is required. To make the game more motivating, however, you can offer the class an extra 5 minutes of recess or some other preferred activity if they earn more points than the teacher during a predetermined period of time. This strategy is helpful because it does not interrupt academic instruction and does not require the teacher to direct attention to the students who forget to follow the rule. If the students who remember to follow the rule are complemented by name as the line is written under the students' side of the T and the students who violate the rule are given no personal attention, the game further reinforces a positive classroom climate by responding to misbehavior without overemphasizing it.

This game should be reserved for very difficult times of the day or days that are more trying for students, such as the day before a big holiday. Its power is diminished with overuse.

CONSEQUENCES ∎

When Hewett and Taylor (1980) first referred to consequences as one of the three critical components of classroom management, they defined consequences as the reinforcements and punishments associated with students' behaviors. For the purposes of this chapter on classroom management, expectations, rules, procedures, and educative strategies are included. Research on positive behavior support at the schoolwide, setting-specific, classwide, and individual levels has broadened the scope of behavior management to include strategies for teaching desired behaviors. Specific strategies and curriculum materials designed for teaching expectations, rules, procedures, social skills, and learned optimism follow in the section on curriculum. This section on consequences explores the purposes for identifying expectations; criteria for developing rules; the differences between rules, expectations, and procedures; and a rationale for redefining behavior problems as educational opportunities.

Expectations

Expectations are broadly stated qualities or characteristics that define the way people agree to treat each other. Expectations are inclusive. Everyone, regardless of age, social status, role, or skill level, agrees to behave in ways that reflect the values identified by the expectations. Expectations do not change from setting to setting, but the behaviors that reflect those expectations may change. In classrooms or schools that use a character education curriculum, expectations would be understood easily as values. Commonly selected expectations include honesty, cooperation, kindness, and punctuality. In a class that has selected punctuality as an expectation, students would be held to a standard of timeliness with regard to arriving, beginning assigned tasks, completing instructional activities, and turning in assignments. The teacher would be expected to begin and end class on time, have materials necessary for instruction ready and organized, return graded papers in a timely manner, and assist students in learning to manage their time wisely. Expectations establish a culture within the classroom, assist students in understanding their shared responsibility for maintaining a positive classroom climate, and can be quite helpful in developing the group dynamics as defined in Chapter 3.

Rules

Rules should identify specific, clearly defined, positively stated behaviors. Classroom rules should be kept to a minimum and enforced consistently. Taking time to think through the needs of a particular group can be helpful when deciding on the wording of the classroom rules. One of the rules that work well for me is "Remain in your assigned area." If the rule states that students are to remain at their desks and the instructional activity requires movement to a group table or the floor, some students will attempt to argue over rule violations. The rule "Remain in your assigned area" allows the teacher to determine the assigned area as instructional activities change without violating a classroom rule. Another common rule is "Keep hands, feet, and other objects to self." Notice that the rule is stated positively and includes the prohibition of aggressive or disruptive behaviors such as throwing objects. Some teachers like to include rules such as "Be kind" or "Do your best." Those items do not technically qualify as rules. Both are more reflective of expectations. Unless the teacher takes time to assist the class in identifying specific examples and nonexamples of kindness, students from different cultures or socioeconomic backgrounds may act in ways that the teacher finds unacceptable. This can lead to unproductive confusion and anger. Making a rule about always doing one's best also presents unnecessary challenges with regard to establishing consequences. Behaviors such as raising a hand and waiting to be recognized before speaking are easily defined, illustrated, observed, and measured. Determining a student's best on each task is not easily defined, illustrated, observed, and measured. Take care to establish rules that reflect measurable and enforceable overt behaviors.

Procedures

Procedures should be separated from expectations and rules to avoid confusion and facilitate rule acquisition and mastery. Procedures for entering the classroom, gaining access to hall passes, sharpening pencils, and returning or gathering instructional materials should be clearly defined, placed on charts, illustrated, and displayed in the appropriate areas of the classroom. Procedures usually include several steps and are designed to make routine events, processes, or tasks more efficient. Students should know when and how to obtain permission to use the restroom, sharpen a pencil, or turn in completed assignments. Having clearly stated procedures for these routine housekeeping duties allows the students to be more responsible for their own behaviors and frees the teacher to attend to other tasks. At the beginning of the year, the teacher should identify procedures. Students can be asked to assist with problem solving later in the year if a procedure is not working smoothly or if a new procedure needs to be added.

For example, I had set aside the first 10 minutes of class each morning for students to sharpen their pencils. Problems arose when buses were late or morning announcements broadcast from the school's closed-circuit television station started earlier than usual. The students suggested that one of the class jobs be "pencil sharpener." They decided that the pencil sharpener would be selected from among the students who did not ride a bus. This person would sharpen all pencils placed in a can on the bookshelf and return those pencils to the desk of the person whose name was on the pencil before the second bell each morning. Samples of common classroom procedures are provided in Appendix A.

Reinforcement and Punishment

Reinforcement and punishment are inextricable entwined and easily confused. We all believe that we know the difference between the two concepts, but the application process is more complicated than one would expect. The types of attention, tangible items, and sensory stimulation that reinforce one person can act as a punisher for another. Failure to understand an individual's preferences can result in an increase of inappropriate behavior.

Reinforcement is defined as any attention, tangible item, event, or activity that increases the likelihood that a behavior will be repeated. Reinforcement is one of the least understood and most often abused techniques available to educators. Examples from multiple school-based observations include:

- A student who does not want to clean up a mess he has made engages the teacher in an argument and is removed from the classroom for using profanity. While he is gone, the teacher cleans up the mess.
- A student who has severe ADHD is reprimanded repeatedly for kicking the desk in front of her.
- A student is told to raise her hand and wait to be recognized before talking out and is then allowed to call out answers to academic questions during a lesson.
- A student who usually talks out 10 times in a 30-minute lesson is denied access to a reinforcer until she has a perfect day with no talk-outs in 6 hours.

Children, like adults, will repeat behaviors that allow them to avoid people, objects, tasks, and sensory stimulation that they don't like and gain access to people, objects, tasks, and sensory stimulation that they do like. Reinforcement can include the attainment of something desired. This is called positive reinforcement (Alberto & Troutman, 1990, 2002). Reinforcement can include the avoidance of something the person wishes to avoid. This is called negative reinforcement (Alberto & Troutman, 2002). Teachers and students can get into a cycle of interaction that negatively reinforces both of them. The results of this common pattern of interaction are unproductive at best.

For example, teachers usually do not want to interact with a student who is disrupting the class, destroying materials, or refusing to complete assigned tasks. Sending the student to the office can reinforce the teacher's desire to have a momentary respite from a difficult situation. The student, on the other hand, may dislike following a particular class rule or completing certain types of work. The student learns through experience with the teacher that removal from an undesirable situation will follow his open defiance of the teacher's authority. Nothing corrective occurs before or after this sequence. Over time, the student reacts more quickly and with greater force to tasks he wants to avoid and the teacher's tolerance for his behavior wears thin. The teacher is negatively reinforced by having the student removed from the room. The student is negatively reinforced by avoiding the teacher's directions and the undesired task. This pattern of mutual negative reinforcement can spread through a classroom rapidly. When this occurs, the teacher's role shifts from instructor to enforcer, the classroom climate becomes coercive, learning is impeded, and relationships between students and teachers become strained.

A few years ago, I watched a group of fourth- and fifth-grade students actively plot to remove a teacher from the classroom through various overt and covert acts of defiance. The mood in the room was so tense that I feared for the students' and the teacher's safety. They threw objects at each other and at her when her back was turned; put nonlethal but inedible substances in her coffee cup; hid her purse; and engaged in multiple minor disruptions such as dropping books on the desks and floor. The teacher screamed, cried, pleaded, threatened, sent students to the office, demanded that administrators come to her room, called parents, and eventually resigned.

I asked to take over the class after watching five substitutes in 6 weeks try to establish some order in the room and fail. One substitute left on her lunch break and never returned. Opportunities for recognition were not clearly defined and reliably made available to students. They did not know how to gain positive attention. The focus of teacher and student interactions had become so negative that students who were behaving and completing their assignments were ignored. In addition, a hierarchy of consequences was established for the whole group that included (a) gradually increasing levels of response to milder forms of misbehavior; (b) opportunities for the student to self-correct and take an active role in his or her behavior management; (c) educative strategies designed to assist the student in identifying and solving reoccurring problems; (d) corrective measures that did not allow students to avoid undesired tasks through misbehavior; and (e) methods for reconnecting the student with the teacher, his or her classmates, and the culture of the classroom upon reentry from the office. Instead of treating each individual problem behavior as a new issue, I developed a hierarchy of responses to noncompliance. The first day of the second semester, I began our time together with a discussion of the rules, procedures, opportunities for recognition, and hierarchy of consequences. Each student's name had been posted on the board. As students entered the room and sat down in their seats, they earned two stars next to their names. When they raised their hands and waited to be recognized, they earned another star. Failure to comply resulted in a warning line. Three warning lines resulted in removal to a cool-off area for 5 minutes. Cool-off was a desk placed against a wall in the instructional area that was far enough away from other student's desks to allow for some privacy. While in the cool-ff area for the first time in a day, students were allowed to complete written work, but they were not permitted to draw, color, listen to music, or play with toys. They were also ineligible for stars and other reinforcers during the time they were in cool-off. Cool-off time only started when students were seated and quiet. If they talked out or failed to follow directions while in cool off, the timer was reset and the 5 minutes started over. Once the cool-off time was completed, the three warning lines were erased, and the students returned to their seats. If they were sent to cool-off more than once in a day for the same behavior, they had to complete a think sheet. Think sheets are problem-solving sheets that help students identify the problem behavior, think about alternatives, and design a plan for their success.

Sometimes students were unable to follow directions in cool-off or exhibited more severe behaviors. They were then asked to move to a carrel in a secluded part of the classroom. This carrel was designated as an in-class suspension carrel. Students were assigned different amounts of time in the in-class suspension carrel commensurate with their behavior. Times ranged from 15 minutes to an hour. While in the in-class suspension carrel, students were required to complete academic assignments and were not eligible to earn stars or participate in class activities. If they had already completed a think sheet, they were asked to review and revise it. If they had not completed a think sheet that day, one was provided.

Failure to regain self-control in the in-class suspension area resulted in removal to another classroom for 30 minutes to an hour. I partnered with a colleague who allowed me to send students to her room. She, in turn, sent students to my room when necessary. Students worked in the in-class suspension carrel in another class for the predetermined amount of time. When they returned to class, they had to work for a minimum of 15 minutes in the in-class suspension carrel in their assigned classroom before being eligible for stars and other class activities.

I always met the students at the door with "I'm so glad you are back. Are you ready to be part of the class?" It is essential to welcome the student back to the room after he or she has had a problem. Students often think that adults don't like them or are angry with them when they have misbehaved. They also confuse their own emotions with others' emotions and think that if they are angry, others are also angry. Welcoming them to the room and asking if they are ready helps them understand that the teacher is not angry and that the responsibility for their behavior is theirs.

The purposes for a re-entry time in the in-class suspension carrel are (a) to establish the importance of taking care of problems within the room, (b) to give the teacher time to assess the student's emotional state and respond with support if necessary, and (c) to disallow avoidance as a strategy for dealing with undesired tasks or requests. Some students believe that following a teacher's directions allows the teacher to win. They understand interactions between themselves and adults as battles of will. If they escalate their behavior to the point of being sent out of the room and do not have to comply with the teacher's request, they believe that they have won, even if they receive a more severe consequence when they get to the office. Requiring a reentry period in in-class suspension does not allow students to escape or avoid the teacher's original directions.

If the student escalated to aggressive behavior or left without permission at any point in the process, an administrator was called and an office referral was written. I never needed to call an administrator or complete an office referral. The hierarchy alone did not cure the group or individuals within the group. The success of the overall plan was a result of a combination of factors: (a) a highly motivating instructional program, (b) multiple opportunities for positive recognition, and (c) a clearly defined hierarchy of responses to noncompliance that allowed the student to remain in control of his or her choices, supported the teacher's role as the positive authority, disallowed avoidance or escape as a way of dealing with undesired tasks, included educative steps, and reinforced the student's role as a member of a group.

Figure 4.2 includes a menu of reinforcers and a hierarchy of consequences to noncompliance. Both are essential in the process of building an effective classroom management plan. The menu of reinforcers needs to include choices. Some students will want primary reinforcers such as small snacks and drinks. Other students will prefer toys, art supplies, or recreational reading materials. Some will want to earn activities, passes to see preferred adults, or coupons for available privileges. Many teachers do not believe that it is appropriate to reward good behavior. They believe that students should work for the intrinsic value alone. They also worry that rewarding children for behaviors that are age-appropriate and generally expected will encourage the children to become reliant on external motivators. These are valid concerns—especially with groups of students who do not need unusual levels of external support. Offering rewards has, in fact, been shown to decrease motivation (Kohn, 1993) when reinforcement is offered for completing tasks that (a) are well within the student's repertoire,

(b) are preferred by the student, or (c) involve creative output. Motivation is also negatively impacted if the reinforcer is in full view during the completion of the required task, if the reinforcer is offered too often, if the task is perceived as being too difficult in relation to the reward, or if the intervals between reinforcements are too long. When designing a reinforcement system for a whole group of students, consider the following factors: (a) the ages and developmental levels of the students in the group, (b) behavior patterns that are common for members of the group, (c) the average attention span of group members, (d) known likes and dislikes, and (e) methods for fading the reinforcement when it is no longer needed.

Figure 4.2   Menu of Reinforcement and Hierarchy of Consequences

Menu of Reinforcement

Nonverbal signal: Smile, thumbs up
Oral and verbal praise
Written compliment

Tangible
Food
Drink
Small school-related item: pencil, eraser
Small toy: miniature car, balloon
Token to be used later to purchase
    items or activities
Student of the Week certificate
Turnaround Student of the Week certificate

Social
Being seated near a friend
Eating lunch with another class

In-class activities:
    Preferred classroom jobs: line leader, teacher's helper
    Peer tutor
    Access to preferred magazines and books
    Access to games, puzzles, or toys
    Access to science artifacts or equipment
    Computer time
    Access to art supplies
    Access to music through headsets
    Access to taped stories or video

Out of class activities:
    Access to the library
    Extra P.E., music, or art periods
    Time with a preferred staff member
    Peer tutor in another class
    Office helper
    Media center helper
    Cafeteria helper
    Messenger

Positive call to parent
Positive referral to a support staff member
Positive office referral

Hierarchy of Consequences

Nonverbal signal: Frown, thumbs down
Oral or verbal reminder
Written warning
Change of seat, same activity
Change of seat, different activity
Observation time-out in the classroom
Time-out in another classroom
Call to a support staff member
Classroom discipline referral, call to parent
Office discipline referral, call to parent
In-school suspension
Out-of-school suspension

Severe Clause: Physical aggression or leaving class without permission will result in an immediate call to the office.

Note: The list of potential reinforcers is noticeably longer than the hierarchy of consequences. This sends a clear message that the teacher is more interested in recognizing "good" behavior than in tending to "bad" behavior.

Educative Strategies

While reinforcement does increase the likelihood that a behavior will be repeated, the desired behavior must be within a student's repertoire. Some problem behaviors occur because the student is capable of performing the desired behavior but finds it easier or more rewarding to act inappropriately. This is called a performance deficit. Other problem behaviors occur because the student does not know what to do. This is called a skill deficit. Classroom groups may exhibit performance deficits because of insufficient reinforcement for appropriate behaviors or because the inappropriate behaviors are more efficient. A teacher may offer to reward students who raise their hands with praise, positive notes to the parents, and special privileges. If, however, the quickest and easiest way to get the teacher's attention is to talk out, many students will talk out. Classroom groups may exhibit skill deficits due to insufficient instruction in how and when to follow class rules and procedures. School is often a foreign environment for children. They do not have to wait in a long line at home to use the restroom, get their meals, or take their turn at a water fountain. They are not expected to raise their hand or respond to a change in activity on a single cue. Even if the students have been in school for a few years, differences in previous school experience may not have prepared them for the expectations, rules, and procedures in a new class.

For these reasons, time and attention must be spent on teaching desired behaviors and ensuring that those behaviors work for the students. If it is more efficient from the students' points of view to act inappropriately to get want they want or avoid what they don't want, the reinforcements and punishments defined in the teacher's plan will be ineffective. Strategies for teaching rules, procedures, and expectations are similar to those used to teach academic skills. The two basic types of knowledge required are concept knowledge and skill knowledge.

Concepts represent about 80% and skills represent about 15% of the knowledge taught in schools. Concepts are words that represent a category of attributes such as competition, triangular, and cooperation. Skills represent sets or subsets of sequential behaviors such as washing hands, entering a room, and requesting assistance. Teachers already know how to teach concepts and skills but rarely think of behavior management strategies in those terms.

Teaching concepts: To learn any concept thoroughly, students need to understand the definition of the word, examples of when the concept applies to a particular circumstance, and examples of when a concept does not apply. Young children will learn the concept of *doggie.* They understand that *doggie* applies to animals that walk on four legs, have pointed or floppy ears, and hair. When out on a walk with Mom and Dad, they point to all four-legged creatures with pointed or floppy ears and hair and say, "Doggie." This works well for them until a cat runs up a tree. "Doggie." "No, Sweetie. That is a kitty." The child persists. "Doggie." Mom and Dad smile and continue the walk. A few moments later, the child sees a horse. "B-I-G D-O-G-G-I-E!" the child cries. "No, dear. That is a horsie." And so the walk continues. The child has the beginnings of an understanding of the concept of dog and has been introduced to a few examples. The problem at this point for the child is that he hasn't been provided with enough nonexamples to fully understand the concept of dog. Sheep, goats, horses, cats, and zebras have some of the attributes he associates with dogs. Lack of sufficient experience and an incomplete definition leave him vulnerable to misunderstandings.

Students experience the same confusion with concepts related to social interactions that we expect them to understand. Concepts such as respect, honesty, kindness, cooperation, and compromise require complex and abstract understandings of emotions, behavioral responses, self-management, and context. Showing respect at a football game is not exactly the same as showing respect during a class discussion. Being honest when the teacher asks if you took a toy off the shelf is not the same as being honest about an opinion regarding another's appearance, work, or skill at kickball. Many children have not had enough experience in multiple social settings to fully understand how their present situation affects how they should behave. Other students have been taught ways of behaving with regard to respect, honesty, and kindness at home and in their neighborhoods that do not align with classroom expectations. For these reasons, time taken to actively teach social-behavioral concepts is time well spent in the development and implementation of an effective classroom management system.

Begin by identifying concepts to be taught. Most, if not all of the classroom expectations will fall into the category of a concept. Decide on a definition for the concept. Identify critical attributes of the concept. Select

Figure 4.3   Concept Development

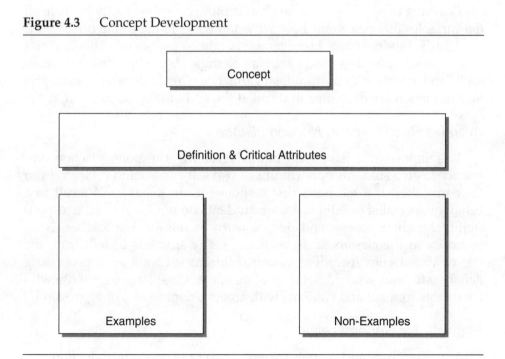

examples that illustrate the correct application of the concept. Select nonexamples that include part of the definition or some of the attributes but differ from the targeted concept in one or more areas. The graphic organizer shown in Figure 4.3 illustrates one method for involving students in the concept development process. Defining concepts such as *respect* in words that young children can understand can be quite difficult. Dictionary definitions are sometimes helpful. Older students can get into groups and brainstorm critical attributes, examples, and nonexamples. Students should then be encouraged to present their work and adopt a classwide definition, list of attributes, examples, and nonexamples that everyone agrees represent the concept. Students can then illustrate and display these mini-posters for use throughout the year.

Teaching skills: Skills are sets or subsets of sequential behaviors such as regrouping for addition, following a set of written directions, and accessing assistance during instruction. To teach any skill effectively, the following components must be present in the lesson: (a) the identification of the skill, (b) the purpose for using the skill, (c) application cues, (d) the sequential behaviors to be applied, and (e) a method for self-checking. Think about the process of teaching a student when to use a particular type of end punctuation for a sentence. Students must first understand the concepts *sentence* and *punctuation.* The purpose of end punctuation is to signal the reader that a complete thought is finished. The sequential behaviors for teaching the application of the skill include (a) reading the group of words to determine that they represent a complete thought, (b) deciding whether the thought is a statement, question, or exclamation, and (c) placing a period, question mark, or exclamation point at the end of the sentence. Self-checking for this type of skill might include rereading the group of words or checking the context of the sentence.

Learning to apply behavioral skills is more complex, partly because all the variables that determine how, why, and when to use a skill can be hard to identify. Students can, however, be taught to use social skills in classroom and schoolwide settings with appropriate instruction, frequent feedback, and multiple opportunities to practice. Curriculum and strategies for instruction are described in detail at the end of this chapter.

Aversive Responses to Noncompliance

It is important to have steps in the hierarchy of responses to noncompliance to give students opportunities to (a) self-correct and (b) learn from their mistakes. If a teacher's first response to misbehavior is a call to a behavior specialist or administrator, students do not learn to take responsibility for their actions and do not learn to rely on the teacher as an authority in the classroom. In addition, many students benefit from the use of visual cues including young children; students with processing deficits; students who do not speak English as a first language; those who are unable to read; and students with anxiety, depression, or aggression.

Planning for Generalization

Many teachers and parents express concern over the introduction of a classroom management plan that includes external reinforcers. They fear

Figure 4.4   Components of Skill Mastery

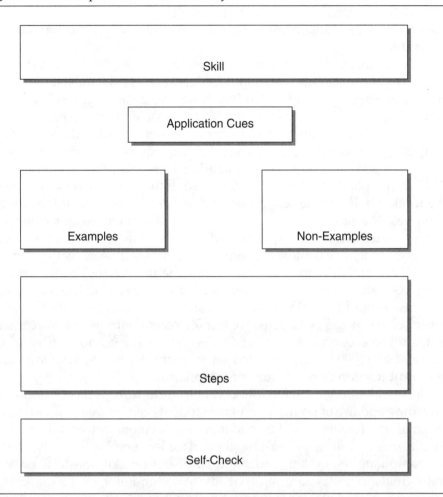

that the students will become dependent on the rewards and will refuse to work or behave unless the adults promise them a treat or privilege in exchange for their behavior. This is not likely to become a problem if the adults make plans from the beginning to fade the tangible reinforcers by (a) pairing the distribution of tokens or points with social reinforcement such as praise and a smile delivered promptly and in close proximity to the child, (b) telling the children in the beginning that the program is a game that will change as their skill levels and needs change, (c) training children in multiple settings, (d) involving different adults in the training process, and (e) building logical and natural reinforcement into the process.

Kehle et al. (2000) describe a multicomponent intervention program designed to reduce disruptive classroom behavior that includes strategies outlined previously. The teacher implemented a dependent group contingency that included a mystery motivator. A subgroup of students not identified to the whole group was monitored throughout the day on the frequency of off-task and talking-out behaviors. Rewards such as stickers, pencils, extra recess time, and time in the classroom to engage in preferred activities were listed on individual slips of paper and placed in a box. The teacher told the students that they would be playing a game to help them learn to remain on task and talk when it was their turn. The mystery motivator would be selected from the box if the subgroup of students earned the reward for the whole group. The teacher only revealed the identities of the targeted students if they did, in fact, perform to the desired level.

In addition to the mystery motivator, the teacher implemented a precision request program (Forehand & McMahon, 1981), moved about the room frequently to monitor student behavior, posted class rules, implemented a token economy system with response cost, and paired the distribution of tokens with immediate social reinforcement in the form of eye contact and descriptive praise. The precision request program requires the teacher to wait 5 seconds after delivering a request to the student. If the student complies, the student is reinforced. If the student does not comply, the teacher delivers the request again and waits 5 seconds. If the student complies, the student is reinforced. If the student does not comply, a reductive technique is implemented such as the removal of a token. Initially, students earn tokens immediately and with each act of compliance. Over time, the intervals of time or the number of times a student complies before a token is earned should be increased. The social reinforcement should remain constant. As students master the targeted skills, other behaviors can be targeted for reinforcement with the token economy or the token economy itself can be faded. The token economy used in the Kehle et al. (2000) study included an awarding of points for compliance and a subtraction of points for noncompliance.

In my classroom, I have found it helpful to turn decisions about the awarding and use of points over to the students as a strategy for fading the external reinforcers. As the students take a more active role in self-monitoring and decision making, they place less emphasis on attempting to manipulate the system and more emphasis on skill mastery. Because individuals in a class are rarely ready to self-monitor simultaneously, a combination of whole-group monitoring and individualized self-monitoring may emerge during Stage 2. Providing the class with a menu of options that includes social as well as tangible rewards allows for the differentiation of the reinforcement system and the transition from external to internal evaluation processes. Specific information on teaching students to self-monitor is offered in Chapter 7.

■ CURRICULUM

Teaching Rules

Teaching rules is not unlike teaching other concepts and skills. The first step is to determine if any unfamiliar concepts are embedded in the rules. A rule such as "Complete tasks on time" might not need any additional explanation. The same rule worded differently, "Be punctual," might require attention to the concept of punctuality. Either rewrite rules that have difficult concepts embedded in them to make them more easily understood by the students, or conduct lessons on the more challenging concepts using the steps outlined earlier in the chapter. Once students understand all concepts embedded in the rules, the students will need to practice the rules. A variety of activities should be used to reinforce rule acquisition. A few of the tried and true include:

Behavior Bingo: Make a Bingo board template using pictures to represent rules on some squares, single words on other squares that represent class expectations, and category names or pictures for class procedures (i.e., sharpening pencils, attaining a pass to the restroom, etc.) on other squares. Give each student a blank template and one with the pictures and words. Have the students cut the illustrated template apart and past the illustrated squares in any pattern they desire on their own blank templates. When they are finished, discuss the meaning of each picture and word or set of words. Retain an illustrated template that has been cut apart for use during the game. Draw one of the squares from a bowl and give the students a hint about the rule, expectation, or procedure. Students raise their hands and wait to be recognized before identifying the square representing the clue. All students mark that square on their cards with a button or lima bean. The game continues until someone has a diagonal, horizontal, or vertical row of squares covered. Students sometimes like to play until a class member has each corner square covered. They call this "four corners." Playing until all squares are covered does not work in this game because all students have the same items on their boards. The only differences are in the order of the items.

Play this game often in the beginning as students are learning the rules. I like to laminate each student's board and make a few extras for new students who might arrive later in the year. The game boards and other items needed for playing are stored in a large manila envelope and become part of the substitute packet. Behavior Bingo is a positive method for students to use in reviewing rules with a substitute or a new classmate and on days that are more challenging such as before or after a major holiday.

Pantomime: Students usually enjoy getting up in front of the class and acting out a mystery word or phrase. Use the illustrated squares from the Behavior Bingo game for prompts. Allow students to select one square and silently act out the meaning. The person who guesses correctly can be allowed to have the next turn, or the student who has best followed the rules while waiting for his or her turn can be chosen next.

Role-play: Role-play requires students to interact. Students work in pairs or teams of four to act out a common classroom event to illustrate a rule. When using role-play, however, it is important to require students to act out appropriate behaviors. This is not the time for students to practice or illustrate nonexamples.

Children's literature: Children's stories are often rich with examples and nonexamples of rule compliance. Aesop's fables are wonderful resources for discussing the importance of moral action. The Amelia Bedelia series by Polly Parrish illustrates Amelia's good-natured attempts to follow directions, even if she is misguided at times. Another useful collection is The Berenstain Bears series by Stan and Jan Berenstain. The characters in the Berenstain Bears books get into trouble and resolve their problems with the help of teachers, parents, and other positive authority figures. The stories included in the students' required reading materials are also often overlooked as resources for facilitating an understanding of the importance of following rules. The section on teaching learned optimism at the end of this chapter provides sample worksheets and activities that can be used to extend the typical language arts and reading curriculum used in elementary grades.

Puppetry: Puppets are great fun for young children. Many who are reluctant to speak during a role-play will come alive when given a puppet. As with role-plays, students can write their own skits or be given a teacher pre-pared script. One very challenging group of fourth- and fifth-grade boys with severe EBD actually cooperated long enough to write and produce a brief videotaped puppet show complete with handmade puppets, hand-made stage sets, and musical accompaniment. We read the traditional version of the Three Little Pigs and then the revised version by Jon Scieszka, called "The True Story of the Three Little Pigs." In the revised version, the story is told from the point of view of the wolf instead of the pigs. The young men loved the twist on the old tale and wrote their own script. Their video won an honorable mention in the county media contest later that year. Of greater significance, however, was their heightened awareness that differing points of view can affect how people view their actions as well as the consequences of an event. Teaching rules to older students, particularly ones who have had multiple experiences of school failure socially and behaviorally, sometimes requires attention to more than rule comprehension and behavioral mastery. That is one of the advantages of using literature, puppetry, and role-play to extend the lessons.

Think sheets: Think sheets or problem-solving sheets are question-and-answer style prompts that assist students in thinking about their behavior, identifying their emotions and thoughts, clarifying the outcomes, and generating alternatives with more potential for success. Students who are most prone to violating rules are typically least able to identify the contributing factors in a problem and generate solutions. They need practice with this skill when they are calm enough to process information. Think sheets are educative and can easily be included in the hierarchy of consequences to noncompliance. A reproducible example of a think sheet is provided in Appendix A.

Teaching Social Skills

Direct instruction of social skills is a highly effective method for dealing with problem behaviors. Social skills instruction should be used in combination with a predictable, well-structured environment, multiple opportunities for practice in a natural setting, and frequent corrective feedback and praise. Some teachers select a social skill for a week to teach the whole class as a preventative strategy. The first skill in most curricula is listening. That has always amused me. When I have had classes that did not already have that skill in their repertoires, teaching listening in the pre-scribed manner was impossible. In the most recent group with which I worked, the children were not able to participate in a formal social skills lesson for the first 6 weeks of school. Whenever they were asked to sit at their desks and listen to a speaker, they would yell out irrelevant statements, call each other names, fall out of their desks, climb on top of their desks, and cry. The behaviors they exhibited were more typical of 2-year-olds than of 7-, 8-, and 9-year-olds. As mentioned earlier, our first success-ful activity as a whole group was playing Simon Says. Before going any further I would like to make a few points about teaching appropriate behavior.

1. You cannot teach a child to do nothing. Attempting to stop one behavior will only result in the child selecting another (usually more disturbing) behavior to exhibit. Instead of concentrating exclusively on what you want the child to stop doing, look for a replacement behavior that would make the targeted behavior impossible to perform. For example, the class built a town out of milk cartons and other items decorated to look like houses and stores. The boys began to use the toy trucks and cars provided for pretend play in the model town as torpedoes. They bombed buildings, rolled the vehicles off desks into walls, and began racing the cars across the room in an effort to hit people. For one day, the cars and trucks were locked in the closet. We had a class meeting to discuss options. Together we decided that the cars must remain on the roads that decorated the area rug. All traffic rules must be followed. Any driver failing to follow the safety rules would have his or her car impounded. A race track was constructed out of a large piece of cardboard. Racing cars were no longer permitted in the town or on the rug. The replacement behaviors for throwing toy cars were (a) keep vehicles on the roads printed on the area rug, and (b) keep racing cars on the track.

2. When identifying replacement behaviors, engage the group.

3. Make every attempt to select a replacement behavior that (a) is acceptable to the group, (b) addresses the function of the behavior, and (c) is as easy, if not easier than the behavior being replaced. Individuals will abandon the replacement behavior if it is embarrassing, boring, frustrating, ineffective, or too difficult.

4. Social skills, like academic skills, are categorized hierarchically with prerequisite skills such as listening and asking for assistance being taught before more complex skills like apologizing. Before teaching a social skill, refer to the scope and sequence provided in the curriculum guide and determine the skill level of the group, subgroup, or individual. Teachers would not even consider asking first graders to write a five-page composition with references. Expecting an individual or group to master social skills without providing training and practice in prerequisite skills violates the same instructional protocol as expecting first graders to write term papers.

Teaching a social skill is no different from teaching any other skill. The first steps include defining the skill and establishing a rationale for applying the skill. Once students understand what they are to learn and why it is important, they are ready to learn the steps for mastering the skill. Generally these steps are explained and demonstrated by the teacher. Students are not permitted to role-play the inappropriate behaviors—only the steps associated with the skill. Application cues are then discussed. Role-play with feedback should be done in natural settings to increase the likelihood that the actions will be repeated. Focusing a group's attention on a specific skill for a week, 2 weeks, or a month can be quite effective as a preventative strategy. These lessons are far less time consuming than dealing with repeated misbehavior. Once students have learned the steps for skill mastery, a discussion of application cues and methods for self-monitoring should be conducted. During the initial period of learning, students need high rates of praise for exhibiting the targeted skill. While it is impossible in a large group of students to reward each and every occurrence of the targeted skill, consistent and contingent recognition of students' positive behavior is essential to the learning process.

A variety of social skills curricula are available commercially. *Skillstreaming the Elementary School Child* by McGinnis and Goldstein (1999) includes lesson plans, homework formats, observational checklists for informal assessment of students' needs and progress through the curriculum, and additional information on enriching and extending the instructional process. *Social Skills for Tough Kids* by Rhodes, Jenson, and Reavis (1990) is less extensive in terms of the scope and sequence but includes reproducible mini-posters illustrating the context and application of each skill. Fourth and fifth grade students appreciate illustrations that depict older children and respond positively to the visual aids. An expanded list of affective curricula is provided in the Appendices.

Reinforcement, punishment, educative behavioral strategies, and attention to the environment as well as the academic instruction are tools that must be well integrated and managed. Of growing concern to many educators and researchers, however, is the lack of attention to the cognitive and emotional components of behavior management. Glasser (1998) identifies the four components of behavior change as (1) observable behavior, (2) physiological reactions, (3) thoughts, attributions, or beliefs, and (4) emotions. As children grow, they learn to judge people and events that affect them. They begin to develop an understanding of themselves, expectations for people in particular roles, and ideas about what they believe to be their ideal. Externally imposed behavior management systems and social skills instruction address only overt behaviors. The children who need more include those with EBD, the ones who have experienced trauma, and those who have had learned helplessness modeled by the adults in their lives.

Martin Seligman (1995) has conducted longitudinal studies on youth in general education classrooms from the fourth through the tenth grades. He took one group of fourth grade students who scored highest on an assessment of learned helplessness, taught them the components of learned optimism, and followed them into high school with annual assessments. Another group of fourth grade students who scored highest on an assessment of learned helplessness received assistance with academic and behavioral needs, but students were not taught how to change thoughts of helplessness to thoughts of optimism. At the end of the longitudinal study, Seligman (1995) found that the group that had been taught to self-monitor for learned helplessness and self-correct those thoughts maintained higher rates of academic achievement and appropriate school behavior than those who had not been taught learned optimism. In addition, the students who had been taught learned optimism did not decline significantly during adolescence in their abilities to apply the optimistic thinking skills. Students who had not been taught the optimistic thinking skills became increasingly pessimistic in their thinking over time. Seligman likens the effect of explanatory style instruction to penicillin for the mind. A brief explanation of the components of teaching optimism follows. For those interested in fully incorporating such curriculum into their behavior management and instructional routines, I highly recommend purchasing one or more commercially available curricula.

Teaching Optimism

Children establish their explanatory styles by the age of 7 (Seligman, 1995). Explanatory styles are most easily defined as the ways that people explain the reasons for the good and bad events in their lives. A person's orientation toward optimism or pessimism is determined biologically to a degree. The good news for parents and teachers is that even with a biological predisposition to pessimism, a child or adult can learn to be more optimistic. Why is this important? Because people who are more optimistic have better relationships with others, experience fewer illnesses and accidents, are more successful, make more money over their lifetime, and live longer. Improving the likelihood that students will get along with each other, persist with difficult tasks, and be happier in general is tremendously important. How is optimism learned? Seligman (1995) has identified three ways that children learn helplessness and optimism.

1. Children model the adults around them. If adults reflect pessimism in their words and actions, children are more apt to talk, think, and act pessimistically. This is especially detrimental if adults explain unpleasant or traumatizing events as if such experiences reflect the general condition of the world. Some adults will make comments like, "You just can't trust anyone" or "There's no point in trying. Nothing is going to go our way anyway." Because children have limited experiences, they are unable to judge the accuracy of adults' observations. Over time, children are susceptible to adopting the worldview of the adults who care for them.

2. Children learn from the feedback that adults give them. If adults talk about them as if they are incapable of learning or changing, they will adopt thoughts and actions that reflect the adults' perceptions. One little guy with whom I currently work had decided that because of his ADHD, he would never be able to perform successfully at school. The first day we met, he said, "Hi, I'm Chris. I'm ADHD. I'm bad." He then proceeded to run around the room, climb on furniture, kick toys, and fall over a desk. Chris has an above average IQ, functions more than a grade level above his peers in math, and is on grade level in reading. In spite of his obvious ability to learn, he had already decided by the age of 8 that he would never be accepted or acceptable in school. I'm happy to report that Chris is being mainstreamed into a general education class at this time. He still has more difficulty than most containing his exuberance for life, but he no longer defines himself by his disability and openly tells staff, "I used to be bad. Now I am good. Now I know how to behave at school."

3. The third way that children learn to be optimistic or pessimistic is through life experiences. Children who have experienced trauma or who live daily with multiple risk factors such as poverty, parental substance abuse, and so on are at higher risk for developing a sense of learned helplessness. Teachers certainly cannot shield students from unfortunate events at home and in the community, but educators can assist students in processing disturbing situations and understanding them in ways that facilitate learned optimism. I once worked with a group of students who were all facing the death of a parent or grandparent. In each case, the students were close to the people who were dying and were old enough to be aware of the pain and suffering of the person they loved. We were able

to access assistance from Hospice. With parent or guardian permission, grief counseling groups were established. With another former group, all the students lived in homes at or just above the poverty level. Winter holidays and talk of what Santa would bring brought out the Grinch in each of them. With the help of the school's guidance counselor and behavior specialist, we organized a whole unit of study around alternative ways to celebrate and discussed the importance of showing love to our friends and family in ways that do not require great amounts of money. We taught them to make simple wooden items, to sew, cook, and crochet. They made many of the gifts that they planned to give. In addition, we asked local merchants for donations—not of toys for the children but of items they might give to their family members. Throughout the month of December, they earned Santa Bucks for completing academic tasks and following school rules. On the last school day before the winter break, they went shopping with the Santa Bucks they had earned. Sometimes the worst feeling, the most helpless feeling of all, is not being able to give. Our students received toys, clothing, and food from local charities. What they needed was the ability to earn meaningful rewards and to give of themselves.

Seligman (1995) outlines strategies for teaching learned optimism in a book he wrote for parents and educators titled, *The Optimistic Child.* Over the 30 years that he has researched learned helplessness and learned optimism, he has discovered that three categories of beliefs affect a person's explanatory style: (1) internalizing versus externalizing, (2) situation-specific versus global, and (3) time limited versus pervasive. People who are optimistic tend to take responsibility for (internalize) their successes and externalize their failures—not to the point of refusing to take responsibility for future action, just enough to ease the sting of defeat. For example, a student with a history of achievement will say, "I did well on the test because I studied and I'm smart" when the grade is high. When the grade is low on a particular paper, the same student will say, "I did poorly on the test because the test was poorly written. And anyway, I didn't have time to study because I had to practice for the homecoming game." A student with learned helplessness, on the other hand, would externalize the success and internalize the failure. On receiving a high test grade the student would say, "I did well because the test was easy, the teacher likes me, and I was just lucky that day." When receiving a poor grade, the same student would say, "I just stink at math. I'll never be any good at it."

Students with a sense of learned helplessness often react badly to praise. Some will politely discount a teacher's kind support words. Others will withdraw with a scowl on their faces, curse, throw the nearest object, or tear their work into pieces. This can be confusing. Adults then sometimes assume that the child doesn't care or is too rude to manage. If we look at the student's perception of the interaction, however, the anger and frustration make sense. The student believes that he is incapable, that he has never done well and will never do well, that he has no control over the whims of others—especially in school. The genuine praise a teacher offers can be perceived as condescending or mocking. Even if the student believes that the teacher is sincere, he has been convinced through a series of prior experiences that she is wrong. Being a failure is hard enough without someone suggesting things could be different after a student has decided nothing can be done. Now this presents a real dilemma. Praise and success are essential to learning. Like some medicines, however, praise and success feel like salt in a wound. How can teachers address students' needs for positive reinforcement and success without triggering thoughts, emotions, and behaviors representative of learned helplessness?

1. Model optimistic thinking. When unpleasant events occur, talk about the cause in realistic terms. Stress the temporary nature of the problem, and highlight unaffected components of the situation that remain intact and operational. On rainy days, students are often disappointed that they cannot go outside for recess or physical education, for example. Take the opportunity to teach about cold fronts, how clouds form, or some other related science topic of interest. Remind the students that bad weather is never permanent, and then ask them to identify games they like to play inside—games that they might never have the time to play until it rains. Providing students with a positive model for thinking, feeling, and acting during times of stress is helpful in redirecting misguided energy and establishing a positive classroom environment.

2. Provide corrective feedback that models the three components of optimistic thinking: People with learned optimism accept appropriate levels of responsibility for their successes and failures and expect that they will be able to perform adequately over time and across domains (social, cognitive, physical, etc.). Generalize success. Limit failures to a specific time and task. Attribute success and failure to factors students can control. "Good job" is not as effective as "Everyone completed at least 17 out of 20 math problems correctly. I can see that this group understands making change!" To increase the effectiveness of the praise, include references to time and other areas of functioning. "I'm not surprised that you are doing so well learning to make change, because you learned so many other difficult things this year in spelling, reading, and social studies. I believe we are going to have our best year ever!" Likewise, when students make mistakes, focus on factors under their control and limit the problem behavior to a specific time and task. Instead of saying, "This is the worst group I have ever seen—you never walk in the hall like students," try saying, "I am concerned about our behavior in the halls. The rest of the school does not get to see how well behaved and helpful each of you can be like I do when we are working together in the classroom. What can we do to improve?" Engage the students in a discussion of behaviors under their control. Remind them of times when they are able to follow rules and tasks at which they are successful. Then engage them in a problem-solving discussion.

3. Keep proof of their success available for review. Teach students to keep "good work" folders, portfolios, and data collection charts on individual goals. Select one or more academic and behavioral goals. Chart group progress and display prominently. Some methods for doing this include: (a) bar charts illustrating group attendance percentages, group averages on spelling test grades, or homework completion rates for the group; (b) paper chains that include a link for each student's contribution to a class goal; (c) bulletin board displays. Bulletin boards can be decorated with a seasonal or academic theme. In October, I like to place purple background paper on the bulletin board with large, leafless trees arranged along the bottom of the bulletin board. Students are provided with small, blank, ghost-shaped pieces of white paper on which to write their names and their contribution to a class goal intermittently throughout the days and weeks of the month. Once a day, the ghosts are collected and stapled to the bulletin board. At the end of the month, the group record of success can be transformed into individual records of success by having each student make a Halloween scene to laminate and take home for a placemat. Variations on the bulletin board themes include (a) elves with cash register tape records of academic and behavioral success, (b) a football field with a "Let's Make That Goal" banner that spans from one goal post to the other, (c) featherless turkeys that earn feathers through students' academic and behavioral success, (d) hot air balloons that gain altitude as they slide up on a long strip of paper threaded through the basket of the balloon and attached at the bottom and top of the bulletin board as students achieve goals; and (e) golden, glitter-outlined coins with students' names and achievements recorded on them added to the leprechaun's kettle and scattered about the ground under a rainbow.

4. Assist students in monitoring thoughts, emotions, and behaviors. Before the age of metacognition, children are unable to think about how they think. When students are 9 or 10 years old, they can be taught to check the validity of their thoughts against evidence available in the environment and reframe those thoughts. Reframing requires students to challenge their thoughts, dispute inaccuracies, and redefine their perceptions based on new information. Before the age of 9 or 10, students should not be expected to reframe their thoughts. Adults will need to provide disputing evidence and assist the students in generating alternative scripts. They can, however, begin to monitor thoughts, emotions, and behaviors. One method for beginning the process for younger students is to teach them about coping styles through the use of stuffed animals and puppets. The think sheet for younger children displayed in Figure 4.5 includes animals that represent thinking styles and emotions. The shark represents uncontrolled anger and aggression toward others. The donkey represents anger expressed through refusal to cooperate. The ostrich represents refusal to take responsibility for self through a lack of ownership of feelings and actions. The teddy bear represents an attempt to get attention and avoid undesired tasks by acting helpless. A fifth animal, the owl, represents a coping style characterized by taking a moment to assess the situation (stop and think) before deciding how to act. When students repeatedly exhibit a problem behavior and are asked to complete a think sheet, they first identify the problem. The second step is to circle the picture and/or words that represent their emotions at the time of the problem. The third step is to circle the animal that represents the thoughts or coping style they applied in that situation. While coping styles can become habitual responses to stress, by making students aware of their choices and offering them a strategy for selecting a style most likely to result in positive outcomes, they learn that self-monitoring and self-control can result in increased control over how they think, feel, and behave. Prior to using the think sheet as part of the classroom discipline plan, students should be introduced to the animals. Role-plays or puppet shows can be used to depict typical classroom scenarios. An animal that represents an ineffective but commonly displayed coping style would be presented with a problem situation and express emotions and thoughts representative of that coping style. The owl would then enter the scenario; ask questions about emotions, thoughts, and expected outcomes; and model more appropriate thoughts, emotions, and behaviors. In the beginning, the teacher can provide the scripts. Once the students understand the coping styles of each animal, they can be asked to write the scripts. To further extend the lessons, stories, books, and videos can be introduced. As stated earlier in this chapter, however, most required reading texts also contain many stories that illustrate the relationship among thoughts, emotions, and behavior as well as the powerful effects on emotions and behavior of changing the way one thinks of a situation. Open-ended questions and graphic organizers designed to help students understand coping styles can be used in addition to or in place of standard comprehension questions with the prescribed academic curriculum.

Tremendously useful commercial curricula are available that address the associations among thoughts, emotions, and behaviors. These curricula are easy to implement with whole groups, subgroups, or individuals and support the character education initiatives authorized in many school districts. Combining these curricula with targeted social skills instruction, academic instruction, and behavior management strategies increases students' mastery of concepts and processes. Some personal favorites include:

1. *Thinking, Feeling, Behaving: An Emotional Educational Curriculum for Children, Grades 1–6* (Vernon, 1989)

2. *Positively! Learning to Manage Negative Emotions* (Kerr, 1990)

3. *Thinking, Changing, Rearranging* (Anderson, 1988)

When combining these curricula with social skills instruction, the following schedule provides enough variety to keep students actively engaged and enough repetition to facilitate skill mastery.

Monday: Introduce the skill

Establish a rationale for learning the skill

Require each group member to identify a specific application for the skill

Complete a graphic organizer of the skill components

Role-play demonstration

Tuesday: Review the components and rationale for skill mastery

Engage students in role-plays specific to their identified applications

Make mini-posters to illustrate skill application

Wednesday: Review the components and rationale for skill mastery

Identify the coping styles associated with failure to apply the skill

Use relevant lesson activities from the rational-emotive curricula

Figure 4.5   Think Sheet for Coping Style Instruction

Think Sheet

What was the problem? _____

How did I feel?   Mad   Sad   Glad   Afraid

How did I act?

Shark   Donkey   Ostrich   Teddy Bear   Owl

What would the Owl think? _____

_____

What would the Owl do? _____

_____

What did you do that was helpful? _____

_____

What will you do the next time? _____

_____

How will you reward yourself? _____

_____

_____

Thursday: Read a story or watch a video that illustrates the rational-emotive concept and the social skill targeted

Identify the characters that demonstrate effective and ineffective coping styles and skill application

Rewrite the script to result in a successful outcome for unsuccessful characters

Friday: Play a game or engage in a cooperative activity that requires the application of the targeted skill

Provide corrective feedback and contingent praise

Engage the students in self-evaluation

CONCLUSION ■

One of the repeating themes throughout this book is that what we do *to*, *for*, and *with* children sends powerful messages. Focusing only on what is to be done *to* and *for* a child renders the child helpless—an object on which we apply our knowledge and skills. Thinking, rather, in terms of what we will do *with* the children to facilitate their developing understanding of themselves, of the world, and of their valuable place in this world should be the goal. Just yesterday a third grader who had spent 2 years prior to this school year screaming, threatening, attacking, and throwing furniture said to the school resource officer, who was visiting our classroom, "Corporal Dean, do you remember when I was mean? I'm not mean anymore!" Comments like that always touch me deeply. No one was telling this child that he was a mean person. He defined himself as mean. His inability to control aggressive impulses left him believing that he was incapable of being successful at school. In response to that child's comment, others in the class said, "Yeah, we used to be the worst class in the school. Now, we're good!" Corporal Dean had watched the group spin out of control regularly. He knew their history as a group and agreed that they had indeed learned many new skills.

The class that had attempted to vote me out of the group by the end of our first week together eventually decided that they liked behaving, earning recognition for their achievements, and mastering new academic content. When we began the year together, students avoided academic tasks and demanded one-on-one attention. They ignored class and school rules. The days were a struggle for them and for those charged with teaching them. In four months, their behaviors, emotions, and thoughts about school, each other, themselves, and their futures had changed dramatically. They sat in their desks, raised their hands when they wanted to ask a question or make a comment, waited for their turn for help, completed academic tasks without complaint, and proudly earned recognition for social skill mastery. They talked about moving up a grade level in reading and memorizing multiplication facts as if they were capable of such lofty goals! Their parents even noticed changes at home. They were calmer, more confident, and more positive. One young man in particular had given his mother a fight every morning before school. He hated to go and resisted her attempts to get him ready at every turn. He now jumps out of bed and is dressed before anyone else in the family. He likes school. Even more important, he likes who he is at school.

Children want and need positive adult authority and guidance. The way we discipline them directly and indirectly teaches them who they are and who we expect they will be. If we are negative, punitive, condescending, or unnecessarily enabling, we teach them that they are not capable or worthy. If we are positive; design educative strategies for correcting their social and behavioral mistakes; explain their behavior in terms that express our belief in their abilities to grow, learn, and take charge of their goals; and surround them with a supportive, structured environment; we teach them that they are capable and worthy.

A school psychologist who was serving as a behavior specialist in an elementary school talked with me at a county-level training about a teacher in her school who refused to adjust her classroom management system to meet the needs of her students. The teacher had taught for many years and stated emphatically that she knew what she was doing. Unfortunately, her classroom management system was extremely negative. Students' misbehavior was posted publicly. Their appropriate behavior was recorded on point sheets, but no one was allowed to see the point sheets until the end of the day. Students earned access to preferred activities only if they had a "star day." No other system of recognition or reinforcement was included in the plan. Students regularly "lost" their star days within the first hour or two of school. Once that occurred, those students became angry, defiant, and impossible to teach. The behavior specialist asked me how to get through to the teacher.

My first response to teachers who have a punitive approach to managing behavior is to ask them how motivated they would be if their principals took notes daily on their mistakes and posted them for their colleagues to see. I don't expect an answer. The question is simply food for thought. Another thought-provoking story is offered as an alternative after a few moments of reflection.

A famous baseball pitcher was interviewed after one of his most successful seasons. The interviewer asked how he managed to so consistently pitch the ball into the strike zone. The pitcher replied that he never missed once during his initial years of learning to throw. His dad painted a large target on the side of the barn. The pitcher spent hours as a young boy pitching the ball at the target. As his aim become more consistent, his father made the target smaller. Over time, he was able to aim directly at a very small zone and hit it with certainty. He never felt inadequate to the task. He always believed that he could learn the skill. He never failed. Those early lessons learned from his dad carried him through a successful career.

Our task is to shape behavior in the classroom in much the same way that the pitcher's dad shaped his pitching as a child. He began with a wild and unpredictable throwing motion. With practice, he learned self-control. He became stronger and more consistent with his performance. The target provided structure, a reachable goal, a visual prompt, and immediate feedback about his performance. Our classroom management systems should do no less.

■ NOTE

Portions of Chapter 4 have been reprinted with permission from the Council for Exceptional Children from Rockwell, S. (2006.) *Tough to Reach, Tough to Teach: Students With Behavior Problems* (2nd ed.) Arlington, VA: Council for Exceptional Children.

5

The Behavior-Achievement Connection

INTRODUCTION ■

Several years ago, I worked in a segregated center school for students with emotional behavioral disorders (EBD). Their average annual rate of achievement prior to the implementation of strategies outlined in this chapter was a dismal 2 months growth per year at the primary level and 4 months growth per year at the intermediate level. After documenting this alarming statistic through pre- and posttesting of all elementary-level students in the program, the principal gave the staff permission to design a multifaceted approach to address the academic challenges our students presented. Because all of the students enrolled in this school were identified as having severe EBD, many teachers and administrators had assumed that (a) behaviors would need to be brought under control before teaching could occur, and (b) the students were unable to learn, given the frequency and intensity of their emotional and behavioral outbursts. Our students would throw pencils and flip desks in response to requests to write sentences. Many of them climbed under tables, cried, screamed, and tore bindings off books when they were asked to read. Math computation worksheets were usually accepted without major incidents until the teacher dared to introduce a new skill. The battle to increase academic skills was a daily struggle. Students clearly defined our attempts to teach reading, writing, and math as attacks on their self-worth, violations of their zones of comfort, and threats to their images of an ideal world. What motivates such outrageous, resistant responses? The simple answer is a need to escape or avoid an aversive task. The simple answer is incomplete and can lead to a misapplication of rewards and punishers if not examined more closely. The following characteristics of students who are at risk for academic failure highlight the complexity of the challenges as well as the potential solutions for students and those interested in helping them. The opening anecdote described achievement rates for students identified as having severe EBD. There are students in general education classrooms with similar academic achievement profiles who exhibit less intense behavior problems. Their needs are also addressed in the research, and suggested applications are presented in this chapter.

■ LEARNERS WHO ARE AT RISK

Children with diverse learning needs who do not develop academic skills at the same rate as peers are often described as lazy, noncompliant, disorganized, or passive when presented with an academic task. Researchers have discovered, however, that the challenges these students must overcome are more complex than surface behaviors alone might indicate. In addition, the complexity of the learning challenges creates a cumulative effect on achievement as students move from one grade level to the next (Collins, Dickson, Simmons, & Kameenui, 1995). An expanded list of characteristics common among learners with diverse needs is provided below.

1. Low-achieving students lack sufficient knowledge of (a) self as a learner (Billingsley & Wildman, 1990; Palincsar, David, Winn, & Stevens, 1991); (b) task demands (Billingsley & Wildman, 1990; Palincsar et al., 1991); (c) how, when, and why to apply skills and strategies (Billingsley & Wildman, 1990); and (d) the resources needed to complete a task (Billingsley & Wildman, 1990).

2. Low-achieving students require explicit instruction in skills and concepts. Their abilities to learn incidental or tacit knowledge is poor (Chan, Cole, & Barfett, 1987; Rottman & Cross, 1990; Schunk & Rice, 1992).

3. Low-achieving students require explicit instruction in generalization strategies. They do not make connections between skills and concepts within one content area or between skills and concepts across content areas without direct, teacher-mediated instruction (Chan et al., 1987; Schunk & Rice, 1992; Simmonds, 1990).

4. Low-achieving students often lack background experiences with content-related prerequisite skills and concepts (Weisberg, 1988).

5. Low-achieving students require explicit instruction to link prior knowledge with current content (Weisberg, 1988).

6. Low-achieving students benefit from instruction in self-monitoring. They often make poor use of time and other resources because they don't know what they don't know (Malone & Mastropieri, 1992; Schunk & Rice, 1992).

7. Low achievers attempt to avoid feelings of failure by engaging in one or more of the following behaviors: (a) withdrawing, (b) feigning interest, (c) shifting blame to an external agent, (d) selectively forgetting assignments or completing the wrong assignment, (e) procrastinating, (f) cheating, and (g) lowering expectations of self (Paris et al., 1991).

8. Low-achieving students often generalize a sense of failure in one area to a low perception of competence across all academic tasks. They exhibit a sense of low perceived competency in spite of average or high ability (Johnston & Winograd, 1985; Paris et al., 1991).

9. Low-achieving students benefit academically from attribution training. In studies that included academic strategy instruction without direct instruction in the covert cognitive components associated with learned helplessness, students did not exhibit increased academic achievement levels to the same degree as those who had instruction in academic strategies and attribution training (Schunk & Rice, 1992).

A STRATEGY SELECTION FRAMEWORK ■

Scholars at the National Center to Improve the Tools of Educators (NCITE) synthesized 30 years of research on instruction across all academic content areas (Dixon, 1994; Dixon, Carnine, & Kameenui, 1992; Grossen & Lee, 1994; Kameenui et al., 1994; Miller, Crawford, Harness, & Hollenbeck, 1994). They set aside debates on the merits of one philosophical approach over another and concerned themselves with a single critical question: Which empirically validated characteristics are essential to the efficacy of curriculum and instruction for diverse populations of students? The answer to this question was summarized in the identification of the universal access principles for instruction and curriculum development. These principles include (a) identifying major concepts, (b) activating prior knowledge, (c) using conspicuous strategies, (d) providing mediated scaffolding, (e) strategically integrating content, and (f) engaging students in judicious review (Kameenui & Carnine, 1998).

■ A MULTIFACETED APPROACH IN ACTION

The students introduced at the beginning of this chapter were being taught by highly motivated teachers. The district provided a full array of curriculum options and ample instructional support. The missing link in the educational process for these students was a lack of understanding on the part of all involved about the nature and needs of learners who are at risk. These students require explicit instruction in the major concepts of a unit. They do not make associations among content areas and generalize concepts across settings without direct, teacher-initiated instruction. Support during periods of skill acquisition is essential. Their lack of confidence and history of past failures quickly leads to anxiety, frustration, and a need to fight or flee what appears to them to be an overwhelming obstacle. Our early work in redesigning instruction for the children who were most resistant to reading included sight word recognition games and total mastery of all words in a text prior to putting a book in the students' hands. These students were only willing to risk making mistakes during the learning process after multiple experiences of success. Errorless learning initially was a required prerequisite to higher rates of success and active participation in the exploration of concepts and skills later. Frequent and varied forms of review were integrated into the overall instructional plan as well.

The universal access principles for curriculum development and instruction as defined by Kameenui and Carnine (1998) served as a framework from which to develop a research-based approach that was effective and manageable. Our restructured, multifaceted approach included (a) norm-referenced pre- and posttests of basic skills; (b) individualized curriculum-based measurement conducted and graphed twice weekly; (c) interdisciplinary instructional units aligned with a scope and sequence of basic skills as well as state standards in reading, writing, and math; (d) explicit instruction in the use of graphic organizers, support materials, rubrics, and low- as well as high-tech accommodations; (e) attribution training for students with learned helplessness; (f) multiple and varied forms of review, often in game format; and (g) authentic opportunities for the integration and application of skills. In the first year of implementation, our students exceeded our expectations by increasing their growth in reading from an average of 2 months for the primary-level students and 4 months for the intermediate-level students to an overall gain of 8 to 10 months respectively.

We were thrilled, of course. The transformation in the school was dramatic. Behavior problems decreased significantly. Student work decorated classroom walls and the halls. Children no longer hid under tables or cried when asked to read. The principal was pleasantly amazed to find children requesting permission to stay inside instead of going to recess so they would have time to complete letters to senators about saving the whales during a unit on ocean life. Children who had at one time fought all attempts to be taught because they believed that they were too dumb to learn shared their work proudly with any adult willing to take the time to listen.

The remaining sections of this chapter are devoted to information and processes proven to be effective in addressing the instructional needs of students who are at risk of school failure and associated behavior problems. The body of research from which the interventions, strategies, and process were derived crosses the general education and special education spectrums. Students in general education achieve at higher rates when these interventions and processes are applied in the classroom. Students with special needs fail to achieve when these interventions and processes are omitted. What is nice to do for some is essential for others. The good news is that these are not general education- or special education-specific.

THE ROLE OF ASSESSMENT ■

As stated in Chapter 1, the proportion of students with EBD in a given school population ranges from 10% to 20% (Brandenburg et al., 1990; Kauffman, 2001; U.S. Department of Health and Human Services, 2001). Only a small proportion of those students will be served in special education programs. Assessment for identification and placement in special education includes prereferral data, a review of school records, identification of critical strengths and needs, and the ongoing assessment of the program developed to meet the identified needs (McLoughlin & Lewis, 2001). Schoolwide, district, and state-level testing is mandated by the No Child Left Behind Act (NCLB) (2001). Assessments designed to test school, district, and state achievement levels often provide little useful information regarding the strengths and needs of students already identified as at risk, particularly when those students are required to take the tests developed for their assigned grade level rather than their identified instructional level. Complete texts are devoted to the pros and cons of various assessment procedures.

This section serves as a quick reference to research-based, best practices for assessing individual students in a classroom setting. The purpose of this section is to provide the reader with a basic overview of assessment options in alignment with the overall focus on meeting the needs of students with diverse needs. References cited in this chapter provide the reader a good place to begin if additional in-depth information is desired.

Assessment is an integral component of instruction. We too often jump into teaching a unit without assessing students' prior knowledge. This wastes valuable instructional time and, even worse than that, can lead to student frustration. Out of a desire to "cover the curriculum," we too often move from one unit to the next without assessing students' mastery of skills and concepts within the newly completed unit. We can sometimes delude ourselves into thinking that we work so closely with our students that we know what they need without engaging in some form of assessment.

Last year's group of second and third graders proved me wrong on that score one day when we were editing a paragraph together on the board. For several days in a row, I had made the mistake of writing the sentence, "today is _____" and completing the blank with the day of the week. The following sentences in the paragraph always contained other capitalization and punctuation errors, including proper nouns that had not been capitalized. Unfortunately, three of my students had wrongly assumed that the third word in each sentence needed to be capitalized. They had extrapolated their own rule for identifying proper nouns, one that had nothing to do with nouns in general or proper nouns in particular. My lack of attention to a critical component of the instruction-assessment cycle had led to their confusion.

Both standardized and informal assessment techniques provide valuable information to the student, teacher, and parents. Purposes for each are outlined below along with commonly available resources.

Standardized Assessments

Standardized tests require uniformity in administration and interpretation of results. These norm-referenced tests allow for comparisons among students of the same grade or age level. Norm-referenced tests are administered to a large number of individuals, representing identified subgroups within a targeted population. The performance of the individuals on the test becomes the standard or norm by which individuals who are given the test are compared. Age, gender, geographic region of residence, ethnicity, and socioeconomic status are among the variables used to identify a norm group. The advantages of norm-referenced assessments include (a) the ability to compare an individual student to a larger group of students representative of a regional or national sample, (b) the standardization of administration and scoring processes, and (c) easily interpreted scores that illustrate a profile of growth when examined over multiple testing sessions (Wallace et al., 1992). Disadvantages include (a) a lack of information about specific instructional needs, (b) potential discrimination of various subgroups within a culture, (c) the overuse of or emphasis on total scores instead of item analysis in developing the educational plan for a particular student, and (d) overgeneralizations or misuse of test results (Wallace et al., 1992). In spite of potential disadvantages, individually administered achievement tests and diagnostic assessments can provide valuable information about a student's strengths and needs.

Achievement tests: Group-administered achievement tests are typically given on an annual basis to students in general and special education. The results of these tests are used to evaluate overall achievement; the tests are not designed to provide in-depth diagnostic information. Commonly administered batteries include the California Achievement Test (CAT) and the Comprehensive Test of Basic Skills (CTBS). In addition to group-administered achievement test batteries, individual achievement tests with diagnostic components are also available commercially.

Diagnostic assessments: Diagnostic batteries include multiple items for assessing specific skills. Individually administered achievement tests typically provide only a few items at each level and for each skill, making an in-depth analysis of learning problems unlikely. Many of these achievement tests do, however, provide some diagnostic information through the analysis of response patterns. The Kaufman Test of Academic Achievement

(KTEA), the Peabody Individual Achievement Test—Revised (PIAT-R), the Wide Range Achievement Test—Revised (WRAT-R), and the Brigance Diagnostic Inventories are among the individual achievement tests that provide some diagnostic information in the areas of letter identification, decoding skills, sight word recognition, computation error patterns, spelling error patterns, reading comprehension skills with regard to answering specific types of questions, and math concept development during the application of math knowledge. The KTEA, PIAT-R, and WRAT-R include norm-referenced scales that allow the teacher to compare the individual student's performance with a national sample.

Informal Assessments

Criterion-referenced tests: Criterion-referenced tests (CRTs) are not used to compare a student's performance with a class, a district, a national sample, or any other predetermined norm group. These tests measure student performance on criteria required for mastery of a sequentially developed set of subskills. Goals for each student within the list of skills identified on the CRT and mastery levels for each are determined based on the individual student's strengths and needs. Some curricula contain CRTs that are closely aligned with instruction. Some CRTs represent a scope and sequence typical of curricular goals and objectives. The Brigance Diagnostic Inventories are examples of commercially available CRTs. Grade-level equivalents for subskill sets are available, but these grade-level scores are reflective of skills taught at typical grade levels rather than the scores of a national sample of students or norm group. Some CRTs are developed at the state or district level to measure state-mandated standards.

Regardless of whether or not the CRT is a commercial assessment or a locally developed assessment, the purpose of the CRT is to measure individual achievement toward curricular skill objectives. CRTs can be helpful in aligning a student's educational goals and daily instruction with general education curriculum. CRTs are helpful to students and parents in identifying individual areas of strength and need. CRTs are also useful tools for motivating reluctant and discouraged learners. Increments of progress are usually more discretely defined. This allows the student, teacher, and parent to identify benchmarks that are attainable in a few days or weeks instead of waiting for an annual assessment score. The list of skills for each content area and grade level provided in Figure 5.1 can be used as an informal assessment of progress. Teachers and parents should consult their state and district standards for more in-depth information on local grade-level expectations.

Curriculum-based measurement: Curriculum-based measurement (CBM) is a measure of a student's performance on a critical skill in reading, writing, or math using materials and procedures directly aligned with instruction. CBM is typically completed with a one-minute probe that is repeated frequently (twice weekly) and monitored regularly as a strategy for informing further instructional practice and for assessing student achievement (Deno & Fuchs, 1988; Fuchs, 1995; Shinn & Hubbard, 1993). CBM includes the graphing of data from each one-minute probe. This allows the teacher to

Figure 5.1   Scope and Sequence of Basic Skills by Content Area and Grade Level

	Reading	*Written Language*	*Math*
Kindergarten	Identify rhyming sounds Match sounds with pictures Understand prepositions (on, under, etc.) Understand concepts of size Organize objects into categories by attribute(s)	Begin to experiment with writing	Rote counting to 10 Recognition of numerals to 10 One-to-one correspondence Simple addition through the joining of objects from two sets into one group
Grade 1 *Sight Word Mastery* Dolch Word Lists Preprimer Primer Grade 1 *Fry's First Hundred Words*	Recognize letters of the alphabet Identify initial consonant sound Identify final consonant sound Identify medial consonant sound Identify sounds made by consonant blends and diagraphs Recognize short vowel patterns Recognize long vowel patterns Understand plural endings Understand verb endings Understand synonyms, antonyms, and homonyms Understand simple compound words	Write name Begin to spell simple, common pattern words (i.e., bat, cat, rat, fat) Copy, complete, and/or compose simple sentences Begin a sentence with a capital letter End a sentence with a period or question mark Follow a left to right progression Form letters legibly Space letters and words legibly	Rote counting to 199 Read and write numbers to 99 Place value: ones and tens Identify equivalent and nonequivalent sets Addition and subtraction facts Solving for missing addends Symbol recognition: +, −, = Skip counting by 2s, 5s, 10s Odd and even number recognition Identify 1/2, 1/3, 1/4 Addition of numbers with two to three addends without regrouping Identify multiples of 10 to 100 Simple real-world problems
Grade 2 *Sight Word Mastery* Dolch Second-Grade List *Fry's Second Hundred Words*	Identify elements of a story: setting, characters, problem, actions, and problem resolution Identify r-controlled vowels Identify medial vowel sounds Identify three-letter consonant blends Identify diphthongs Understand suffix *er* Understand *y* sound variants Identify vowel diagraphs	Write words in alphabetical order by the first consonant Capitalize names of people, months, days, and words in a title Use a comma in writing dates, cities and states, and after greetings and closings in a letter Compose correct sentences Avoid running multiple sentences together with *and*	Place value to the 100s place Read and write numerals to 999 Regrouping for addition and subtraction Understand meaning of x and y in problems with missing addends Real-world problems using simple addition and subtraction of like fractions, whole numbers, and money Begin multiples of 2, 3, 4, and 5 with products of 0–25
Grade 3 *Sight Word Mastery* Dolch Third-Grade List *Fry's Third Hundred Words*	Identify elements of a story: setting, characters, problem, actions, and problem resolution Understand *er* and *est* Understand possessive Use contractions Identify syllables Recognize multiple spelling patterns for the same long vowel sound Know how and when to change *y* to *i* before adding endings Understand pronoun referents	Write words in alphabetical order by the first and second letter Identify and capitalize proper nouns Use periods at the end of sentences and abbreviations Use apostrophes in contractions Use commas in a series Understand and use some suffixes and prefixes Recognize and use singular, plural, and possessive forms of nouns Use exclamation points Use a variety of sentences and descriptive words Identify verbs Avoid choppy or run-on sentences Remain on one topic Sequence ideas	Count and write numerals to 1,000 Roman numerals to XII Three-digit addition and subtraction without and with regrouping Multiplication facts Division facts Multiplication of two- or three-digit factors by one-digit factors Perimeter Area Real-world problems using money, fractions, and whole number operations

	Reading	*Written Language*	*Math*
		Indent the beginning of each paragraph Learn to proofread	

Grade 4
*Sight Word
  Mastery
Fry's Fourth
  Hundred Words*
	Identify elements of a story: setting, characters, problem, actions, and problem resolution
	Identify main idea and supporting details
	Paraphrase
	Identify word meaning in context
	Apply a variety of word attack skills
	Identify author's purpose
	Make inferences
		Write words in alphabetical order to the third or fourth letter
		Capitalize the names of organizations, geographical names, and the words *mother* and *father* when used in place of their name
		Apostrophe to show possession
		Comma setting off an appositive and between words of explanation and a quote
		Colon after the salutation of a business letter
		Identify and use adjectives and adverbs
		Recognize singular and plural pronouns
		Make a simple outline with a main idea and supporting details
			Read and write numbers to 1,000,000
			Understand fractions as parts of a whole as well as subsets of sets
			Proper and improper fractions
			Add and subtract mixed fractions with like denominators
			Multiply three-digit factors by two-digit factors
			Real-world problem solving with fractions, money, measurement, and whole number operations

Grade 5
*Sight Word
  Mastery
Fry's Fifth
  Hundred Words*
	Identify elements of a story: setting, characters, problem, actions, and problem resolution
	Identify main idea and supporting details
	Outline after reading using two or three main headings
	Paraphrase
	Identify word meaning in context
	Apply a variety of word attack skills
	Identify author's purpose
	Make inferences and draw conclusions
		Capitalization in outlines, commercial trade names, and the titles used with names (i.e., President Lincoln)
		Colon in writing time
		Quotation marks around titles of stories and poems
		Underline titles of books and movies
		Avoid unnecessary pronouns and correctly apply gender and number to pronouns with regard to their referents
		Use correct verb tense and number
		Compose sentences with compound subjects and predicates
		Compose an outline on one topic with multiple subheadings
		Use more than one paragraph in the description of a single topic
			Relationship between proper, improper, and mixed fractions
			Add and subtract fractions without like denominators
			Decimals and place value
			Multiplication with multiples of 100
			Two-digit divisors
			Real-world problem solving using all units of measure, fractions, and whole number operations

Grade 6
*Sight Word
  Mastery
Fry's Sixth
  Hundred Words*
	Identify elements of a story: setting, characters, problem, actions, and problem resolution
	Identify main idea and supporting details
	Paraphrase
	Outline after reading using two to three main headings
	Identify word meaning in context
	Apply a variety of word attack skills
	Identify author's purpose
		Capitalize proper adjectives and the abbreviation of proper nouns
		Select words for courtesy, effectiveness, and appropriateness of the intended audience and style of composition
		Proofread compositions for punctuation, capitalization, spelling, organization of thoughts, grammar, the use of
			Express numbers using exponents
			Multiply fractions
			Divide fractions
			Add positive and negative integers
			Multiply decimals
			Divide decimals
			Real-world problem solving using all units of measure, fractions, and whole number operations

(Continued)

Figure 5.1 (Continued)

	Reading	Written Language	Math
	Make inferences and draw conclusions Evaluate	descriptive language, good introductory and concluding sentences, and accuracy of facts Research skills Correctly identify references throughout the manuscript Bibliography	

Note: Each state identifies the standards of learning and instruction in each subject area for each grade level. Most classrooms are characterized by groups of students who are working on many different grade levels. This figure represents common grade-level expectations and can be used as a guide in planning instruction as well as an informal criterion-referenced test in the evaluation of individual students. Content for each grade level was identified through a variety of sources and is not meant to be used as a formal evaluation of student progress.

respond quickly to and correct student errors; identify instructional strategies that are the most effective for a specific student; communicate clearly with the student, parents, and other professionals about the student's progress; and provide the student with concrete evidence of progress, which increases motivation. CBMs are conducted more frequently than CRTs and can be more useful in the daily diagnostic teaching process for that reason.

Rubrics: One of the more frequent criticisms of special education has been the lack of attention to the development of higher order thinking skills in the typical special education instructional format. Students learn to complete folders of worksheets that contain short-answer, recall-type questions; but they are unable to apply information and think critically about a task. The inclusion of rubrics in the instruction-assessment cycle provides a framework for students to begin to apply discrete skills to a more broadly defined product and think more critically about the processes they use as well as the value of their work (Andrade, 2000). A good rubric should (a) address content and performance objectives for the required task, (b) include levels of mastery within the content and performance objectives, (c) contain vocabulary and illustrations or symbols that students understand, and (d) be sufficiently specific with regard to performance standards that multiple users consistently score the products at the same level of proficiency (Andrade, 2000). The student-generated rubric provided in Figure 5.2 was used as a strategy for guiding their work as they completed their "My Dream Club House" projects as well as a self-assessment once their projects were completed.

A blank rubric form and a description of how to engage students in the development of rubrics for different assignments are provided in Appendix A. Students who are reluctant to complete writing assignments and those who become too anxious even to begin other types of projects are often motivated to begin after helping to construct a self-evaluation tool. In one second grade class of students with EBD, students decided to make the design of a colorful border around stories and essays part of the rubric score of a 4. Papers at each level of the rubric were posted for students to examine. Once the students had a model example, everyone became determined to submit 4s. The teacher was delighted at their academic progress and with their newfound confidence in themselves.

Figure 5.2   My Dream Club House

Your parents finally cleaned out the storage shed in the backyard. They said that you and your friends could fix it up for a club house.

The shed has a standard size door with a window in the top half of the door. The back wall has no windows, but the side walls each have a 4' × 6' window that opens. The inside of the shed is 10' × 14.' It has a cement floor. The walls are 9' high and have never been painted. Your parents have given you a $500 budget to buy paint, tile, rugs, and/or furniture. Design your dream club house. Keep a list of the materials you would purchase and the cost of each. Describe how you would complete the project. What steps would you take? How would you decide the order of the steps? Describe the finished product, why you like it, and what you would do if you had more money in your budget. Provide drawings or photographs, a floor plan, and a list of resources used to determine costs.

Project Rubric

	Content	Illustrations	Format	Mechanics
4	Additional information provided Difficult subject or topic	Photographs and samples Data graphed using different colors and symbols	3-D display Organization highlighted with colors and/or different types of font	Correct spelling, capitalization, and punctuation as well as the use of a higher level of vocabulary, formulas, or report construction
3	All required sections completed	Data graphed Hand-drawn pictures	Placed on a poster in an organized fashion	Correct spelling, capitalization, and punctuation
2	60% or more of the content included	Data included, but not graphed	Placed on notebook paper Disorganized Not labeled properly	A few mistakes with spelling, capitalization, and punctuation
1	Less than 60% of the content included	Incomplete data	Written entirely in pencil Messy Difficult to read	Many mistakes with capitalization, spelling, and punctuation

READING INSTRUCTION   ■

Essential Elements for Effective Reading Instruction

Students with reading deficits are often characterized as passive, unmotivated, and inattentive. They exhibit deficiencies in one or more of the following elements essential to effective reading:

1. Sufficient prior knowledge (Johnston & Pearson, 1982)

2. Age-appropriate vocabulary and concept development (Baker, Simmons, & Kameenui, 1998; Becker, 1977)

3. Phonemic awareness (Adams, 1990; Hurford et al., 1993; Mann, 1993; Torgesen & Mathes, 1998)

4. Skillful application of phonics in decoding and encoding words (Ehri, 1998)

5. Reading fluency (Adams, 1990; Lyon, 1998; Stanovich, 1991)

6. Adequate levels of comprehension attained by the flexible and efficient use of metacognitive strategies such as self-monitoring, selecting

the most appropriate strategy for the demands of the task, self-evaluation, and understanding the structure of the content within a given reading selection (Chan et al., 1987; Chan, Cole, & Morris, 1990; Cornaldi, 1990; Malone & Mastropieri, 1992; Pressley, Borkowski, & Schneider, 1989; Schunk & Rice, 1992; Simmonds, 1990; Wong & Wong, 1986)

7. Motivational beliefs, which include beliefs about their (a) overall competency (Borkowski, 1992), (b) the ability to master specific types of tasks (Schunk & Rice, 1992), (c) the ability to effect outcomes (Swanson, 1989), and (d) the belief that strategy application will result in beneficial results (Schunk & Rice, 1992)

Students with diverse learning needs benefit from explicit instruction in the major concepts necessary for achieving mastery in reading. The development of metacognitive knowledge and the application of metacognitive strategies are essential to achievement and motivation. Because learning to read is a developmental process, however, the amount of time and attention allotted to each component of reading instruction will vary with the skill level of the students. While formal assessments and curriculum-based, formative assessments should drive lesson development for individual students, the guidelines in Figure 5.3, gleaned from the research on reading instruction and summarized in *Put Reading First: The Research Building Blocks for Teaching Children to Read* (Adler, 2001) provide a foundation for making general decisions about instructional materials, scheduling, and overall curriculum planning.

Students with diverse learning needs begin school with experiential deficits and neurological developmental lags that impact their readiness to benefit from formal reading instruction. The application of the universal access principles for curriculum and instruction benefit these students by providing them with direct instruction in areas insufficiently experienced prior to attending school. These areas include:

1. Interactive oral language manipulation with adults

2. Exposure to a wide variety of print genres

3. Indirect exposure to useful, content-related vocabulary

4. Direct exposure to content-related experiences in the world beyond the classroom

Students with developmental delays benefit from direct instruction in clearly defined skills necessary for effective reading. These students are characterized by poor abilities to learn critical skills incidentally. In addition, these students typically require more frequent exposure to and practice with targeted skills than the average student in order to reach mastery. Beginning a well-structured, carefully monitored reading program early provides benefits to all students.

Over time, students with diverse learning needs have been found to (a) lack sufficient self-knowledge to correct skill deficits and (b) lack sufficient motivation to persist with difficult tasks. Their success in elementary, secondary, and postsecondary educational settings depends on instruction

Figure 5.3   Components of Reading Instruction

	Definition	Rationale for Teaching	Instructional Guidelines
Phonemic awareness	The ability to hear, identify, and manipulate individual sounds in spoken words	Improves word recognition, comprehension, and spelling	Use small-group instruction Use letters when manipulating phonemes Make the connection between phonemes and reading explicit Adjust the time allotted to the needs of the students in group—in general, time allotted to this type of instruction is brief compared to the other four components of instruction Teach only two types of phoneme manipulation at a time
Phonics	Letter-sound associations—the alphabetic principle: Each sound in the spoken language has a corresponding symbol in the written language	Improves word recognition, spelling, and reading comprehension	Group students for phonics instruction according to need after the second or third grade Use a systematic program of phonics instruction characterized by (a) a clearly defined sequence of letter-sound relationship skills and (b) a direct teaching model for delivering instruction
Fluency	The ability to read accurately and quickly	Improves reading comprehension	Model fluent reading by reading aloud to students Engage students in reading text aloud frequently Have students read the same text aloud at least four times
Vocabulary	The oral and printed words required for effective communication	Improves reading comprehension	Indirectly introduce new vocabulary in conversations, lesson development, and during read-aloud sessions Be aware of the levels of word knowledge during instruction (unknown, acquainted, and established)
Comprehension	Purposeful and active understanding of text	Comprehension is the purpose for reading	Directly teach words that (a) are important to concept understanding and mastery, (b) have multiple meanings, (c) are idiomatic, and (d) will be used often in different contexts Directly teach strategies through (a) direct explanation, (b) modeling, (c) guided practice, and (d) application Use graphic and semantic organizers Teach students to (a) monitor comprehension through teacher-directed and student-generated questioning, (b) recognize the purpose for reading a particular text, (c) recognize the structure of the genre, (d) summarize, (e) paraphrase, and (f) access prior knowledge Encourage students to use multiple strategies flexibly as the comprehension task and the learners' needs dictate Provide time for students to work in cooperative groups as they learn to apply strategies to content-area readings

in effective self-monitoring and early, sustained experiences of success. The universal access principles for curriculum development and instruction provide a framework from which teachers can select the most powerful tools educational research has to offer.

■ ALGEBRAIC THINKING

The acquisition of skills and concepts requiring the application of algebraic thinking depends on two major components: (1) mathematical thinking tools and (2) fundamental algebraic ideas (Kriegler, 2002). Mathematical thinking tools include problem-solving skills, reasoning skills (inductive and deductive), and representational skills. Algebraic thinking tools include the ability to understand and use algebra as abstract arithmetic, as the language of mathematics, and as a tool to study functions (Kriegler, 2002). Experts in the field of mathematics define algebraic thinking as the ability to think abstractly about representations of number patterns, about relationships among the represented numbers, and about the impact of computation on the structure of a problem, given the context and purpose of the investigation (Greenes & Findell, 1998; Kieran & Chalouh, 1993; National Council of Teachers of Mathematics, 1989). Battista and Brown (1998) are among the experts who emphasize the necessity for instruction that focuses on reflection and sense making rather than rote symbol manipulation. Butterworth (1999) reports that humans as well as animals are hard-wired for understanding number concepts. As early as the first week of life, infants demonstrate an awareness of number. Difficulty with mathematical tasks can be attributed to two main causes: (1) a genetic disorder called *dyscalculia* that affects 3% to 6% of the population and (2) inadequate instruction in basic mathematical concepts (Butterworth, 1999). The majority of students who function below expected achievement levels in mathematics failed to develop satisfactory understandings of foundational concepts.

Key Elements That Facilitate Algebraic Thinking

Conventional math instruction is characterized by two phases. In the first phase, the teacher demonstrates the process for completing a problem while students observe. Teachers typically demonstrate only one to four examples. The students are not actively engaged in asking questions or discussion. Following this passive student phase, independent work is assigned. Teacher monitoring and feedback are typically inconsistent. This model of instruction is ineffective for the majority of students. Those with diverse learning needs are unable to acquire the skills and concepts necessary for algebraic thinking without active participation in instruction, guided practice with teacher-mediated scaffolding, frequent monitoring to prevent repetitive practice of mistakes, corrective as well as positive feedback, and direct instruction in self-monitoring strategies. Dixon, Carnine, Lee, Wallin, and Chard (1998) describe a three-phase process for effective instruction that facilitates skill and concept mastery.

Phase 1: Teachers demonstrate, explain, and engage students in a discussion about the concept or skill. Definitions, critical attributes, examples, nonexamples, and sequences or patterns are fully developed through interactive questioning and discussion with students. Students are actively engaged.

Phase 2: Teachers provide additional examples of the concept or skill for students to work through with assistance. During the guided practice phase, students are provided with teacher-mediated scaffolding in the form of charts, calculators, peer buddies with advanced skills, and other learning aids. Teachers monitor students' progress and provide frequent corrective feedback. Teacher-mediated support is gradually faded as students demonstrate mastery.

Phase 3: Teachers assess students' mastery levels in basic skills and their ability to apply skills and concepts to problem solving. Students demonstrate their ability to independently recall basic facts and to generalize or transfer their knowledge to new problem-solving tasks.

In addition to using effective instructional formats, adequate time for mastering each new concept or skill and the sequencing of skills need to be carefully considered. Students with recall deficits benefit from repetition. Sequencing the order of skill instruction to ensure that each skill builds a foundation for the next skill and that no skill is ever entirely dropped from the instructional content is helpful. One middle school math department addressed students' needs for adequate time and repetition with each skill area by realigning the curriculum. Sixth-grade students concentrated on whole number operations and place value. Seventh-grade students concentrated on ratios, proportions, and measurement. Eighth-grade students concentrated on statistical representations of data, interpretation, and analysis. As seventh-grade students concentrated on ratios and proportions, whole number facts and operations were continually revisited. A deeper understanding of place value and the mental math associated with place value helped students to grasp decimal fractions and metric units. Entering eighth graders began their study of statistics and problem solving with a solid foundation in whole number facts, fractions, and place value. By the end of the eighth grade, all students had mastered the arithmetic skills and concepts necessary for fluent problem solving.

Usiskin (1997) defines algebraic thinking as a language that has five major components (1) unknowns, (2) formulas, (3) generalized patterns, (4) placeholders, and (5) relationships. By incorporating those five components of algebraic thinking into each phase of the targeted arithmetic concept and skill set for specific grade levels, students with diverse learning needs were provided with adequate time, sufficient repetition, and a facilitative sequence that allowed them to reach high levels of achievement. Resisting the pressure to teach too many topics each year is one of the challenges that educators of students with diverse learning needs must address. To facilitate a deep understanding of a broad range of skills and concepts, the required content must be realigned and sequenced to allow for mastery of content over a period of years (Grades K–2, 3–5, 6–8, 9–12).

UNIT PLANNING ■

Curriculum mapping and interdisciplinary unit planning bridge the gap between research and application by systematically integrating the universal access principles for curriculum development and instruction (Deschler, Ellis, & Lenz, 1996; Kameenui & Carnine, 1998). Once again, whole books have been written and multiple workshops have been developed over the past decade to address this effective, research-based practice. The purpose of offering a set of guidelines and a step-by-step process in such an abbreviated form is to encourage thought and action. Some school districts are on the cutting edge of this approach. Other school districts have not even begun to address this body of research.

While it is preferable to have all teachers of a grade level as the smallest group at work on this level of instructional planning, individual teachers can embrace this approach regardless of the mandates at the local level and realize unequalled successes. Whether the initiative begins with an individual teacher, with a grade-level team, or at the district level, however, care should be taken to begin slowly and work methodically over a period of time to reach full implementation across academic content areas. Our school took a full year to prepare the first year of curriculum and committed to an additional 2 years, as well as placing a teacher on special assignment to ongoing multiyear curriculum development. The district did not allocate an additional teacher to the school, but the administration and teachers were so impressed with the increase in student achievement that teachers agreed to take additional students into their classrooms to allow one teacher to devote 100% of her time to assessment, instructional strategy training for the elementary team, and multiyear curriculum development. Start small, take joy in baby steps, and dream big! (At the end of this chapter, you will find some sample materials showing how to proceed from an annual plan through a unit organizer to a weekly plan and a single lesson plan.)

Identifying Major Topics, Process Skills, and Concepts

Begin by identifying and organizing major topics, process skills, and concepts across content areas. Examine interdisciplinary similarities. Targeted reading comprehension skills include the identification of the main idea and supporting details. Math curricula include real-world problem solving. Being able to solve real-world math problems depends on the ability to identify the main idea and relevant supporting details of a word problem. It is important to teach process skills such as main idea and supporting detail identification across content areas simultaneously. Students who are at risk for school failure do not generalize a skill from one content area to another without direct, teacher-initiated instruction.

Similar concepts should also be clustered to enhance student achievement. A county-required unit on economics, for example, can be taught at the same time as a math unit on money. A study of the ocean, a rain forest, or some other ecosystem provides a rich array of opportunities for strengthening research skills; developing expository writing skills; identifying main idea and supporting details; using and analyzing different types of measurement, graph, and map reading; and applying the scientific method to a student-generated question. Some of the units, concepts, and skills commonly taught during the elementary years are listed in Figures 5.4 and 5.5.

Figure 5.4   Process Skills Across Content Areas

	Reading	*Math*	*Written Language*	*Science*	*Social Studies*
Identify main idea	Comprehension	Word problems	Expository and narrative writing	Comprehension	Comprehension
Identify supporting detail(s)	Comprehension	Word problems	Expository and narrative writing	Comprehension	Comprehension
Identify irrelevant information	Problem solving	Word problems	Expository and narrative writing	Problem solving	Comprehension
Make inferences	Comprehension	Word problems	Expository and narrative writing	Problem solving Comprehension	Comprehension
Draw conclusions	Comprehension	Word problems Concept development	Expository and narrative writing	Comprehension Problem solving	Comprehension
Compare two or more concepts or topics	Comprehension Concept development	Concept development	Expository writing	Concept development and comprehension	Comprehension
Contrast two or more concepts or topics	Comprehension Concept development	Concept development	Expository writing	Concept development and comprehension	Comprehension
Sequence information	Comprehension	Problem solving	Expository and narrative writing	Problem solving Comprehension	Comprehension
Predict	Comprehension	Problem solving		Problem solving Comprehension	Comprehension
Generalize	Problem solving	Concept development and problem solving	Expository and narrative writing	Concept development and comprehension	Concept development and comprehension
Evaluate	Comprehension	Concept development and problem solving	Expository and narrative writing	Problem solving Comprehension	Concept development and comprehension
Synthesize	Comprehension	Comprehension and problem solving	Expository and narrative writing	Problem solving Comprehension	Comprehension

Note: Selecting one or two process skills to emphasize during each week of instruction during a unit strengthens students' understanding and application of the skill(s) across content areas and increases the likelihood that students will master the skill(s).

Strategic Ordering of Content

After identifying state- and district-mandated topics, skills, and concepts, examine the content across disciplines for developmentally sensitive instructional sequences. A unit on fractions at the primary level can be inserted into the instructional sequence without regard to instructional sequencing because primary units on fractions require students only to identify a few common fractions and manipulate those with common denominators. Students at the intermediate level may require instruction in multiplication and division facts before being taught to add and subtract fractions with unlike denominators.

Figure 5.5   Topics and Concepts Across Content Areas

Reading	Written Language	Math	Science	Social Studies
Poetry	Spelling	Numeration	Scientific method	Map and globe
Elements of fiction	Grammar	Whole number operations	States of matter	Geography
Elements of nonfiction	Capitalization	Money	Properties of matter	State history
Phonemic awareness	Punctuation	Fractions	Plants	Economics
Phonics	Sentences	Measurement	Animals	Government
Sight word mastery	Paragraphs	Time and calendar	Ecology	Cultures
Fluency	Poetry	Geometry	Earth science	Local and national holidays
Comprehension skills	Narrative writing	Perimeter and area	Weather and space	American history
	Research skills	Algebraic thinking	Simple machines	
	Expository writing	Problem solving	Human body/health	

Note: These isolated topics and concepts can be organized under broad headings and units of study to enhance concept development through integrated units of study.

The semester or annual curriculum map should reflect the integration of topics, skills, and concepts across curriculum content areas. This integration should be flexible enough to allow for teacher innovation and students' strengths and needs as learners. This map is more than an organizational tool. It provides the teacher, students, and parents with (a) an overview of the major concepts and skills; (b) a timeline for instruction and learning; (c) a logical, developmentally sensitive flow of content; and (d) opportunities both to preview future concepts within the context of the entire semester or year and to link prior knowledge with new content. The ability to identify a discrete concept or skill within a larger context strengthens the learner's understanding, motivation, and retention of information.

Prime Background Knowledge

Making the ordering concepts and skills explicit allows students to make connections between and among different units of study. Information is not memorized for the test and promptly forgotten if it has relevance to past and future content. The anchoring of present content through an exploration of background knowledge should be a regular feature of the instructional process. Curriculum mapping makes this easier by engaging students in an ongoing review of critical questions related to the major concepts. Students should be expected to reflect on the critical questions for a unit and identify which question is being addressed during the day's learning activities. Plans for pre- and posttesting as well as frequent applications of CBM should also be built into the semester or annual curriculum map. Regular attention to the acquisition of discrete skills facilitates growth over time and strengthens the student's ability to make connections between prior knowledge and new concepts.

Integrated and Scaffolded Learning Supports

Learning supports fall into two broad categories: accommodations and conspicuous strategies. Accommodations include (a) items such as highlighters, handheld spell checkers, and colored transparencies for covering reading selections; (b) environmental supports such as small-group instruction, frequent breaks, and preferential seating; and (c) teacher-directed strategies such as reducing the number of items on a page, clarifying written or oral directions, and providing pictures or symbols with written or oral directions to enhance understanding and memory. Accommodations should not change the level of instruction in terms of student learning. Accommodations should simply level the playing field so that a student with a disability can participate in acquiring the same learning goal as a same-age peer.

Conspicuous strategies make the implicit processes of a task explicit. Students who are at risk for school failure often require direct instruction in the unstated rules and procedures others are able to understand and apply without assistance. Skilled writers know how to identify the audience for a particular writing assignment, select a topic, organize supporting details, write the composition, edit the draft, and produce a satisfactory final product. Students who are at risk need direct instruction in the organization, composition, and editing processes of such a complex task. They can be expected to complete a final product, but they may need step-by-step instructions, graphic organizers, a timeline, and a study buddy to help them through the various stages of the project. Building the instruction of conspicuous strategies into the overall instructional plan facilitates higher levels of performance in all students.

Frequent and Varied Review

The review of previously mastered concepts and skills is easier to manage when one unit of study is planned as a logical or developmental prerequisite of the next unit of study. Few skills and concepts are discarded as last week's content. The curriculum has meaning across subject areas and across time. Last year, I taught second and third grade students with EBD; during the first quarter of the school year, they learned the following skills and concepts: (a) the scientific method, (b) the concepts of evaporation and condensation, (c) states of matter (solid, liquid, gas), (d) properties of each of the states of matter, and (e) the difference between a solution and a mixture. We conducted a number of experiments using saturated sugar solutions, gelatin, popcorn, corn starch, and baking soda. Throughout the year, these skills and concepts were repeated and reviewed in response to science, social studies, and literature-related content. Skills and concepts learned during the first quarter were revisited when we studied weather, volcanoes, earthquakes, and rain forests. During a unit in math on geometric shapes and their properties, the students learned the concepts of symmetry and congruence. We applied these concepts to a reading selection on origami, the examination of pictures depicting fractional parts, the study of area and perimeter, and the construction of various shapes with attribute blocks.

At the end of the year, we played Inside Olympics, a three-day academic competition in which teams as well as individuals competed for prizes and recognition of mastery in specific areas. The behavior specialist watched as I asked two second grade students if a paper shape in my hand was symmetrical. They both nodded in agreement that the shape was symmetrical. When I asked how they knew, one replied, "Because if you folded it in half, each side would be congruent." The other student added without prompting, "Congruent means that the shapes are the same size and the same shape. The color or design on the paper does not matter." With this, the behavior specialist raised his hand to his head in amazement and told the young men that they were too smart for him.

Critical Components in a Unit Plan

1. Clearly define the major concepts and skills to be mastered.

2. Sequence the skills within each content area developmentally.

3. Align content-area concepts and skills across disciplines.

4. Identify targeted learning outcomes for each content area.

5. Include formal and informal assessment processes in the plan.

6. Develop a few critical questions that focus students' attention on the major concepts and skills included in the unit plan.

7. Design authentic learning experiences that integrate learning across content areas.

8. Integrate conspicuous strategy instruction, graduated levels of support, and judicious review into the overall plan.

Critical Components of a Lesson Plan

1. Clearly define the skill(s) and/or concept(s) to be addressed in the lesson. Be aware of critical lesson components for each of the four types of knowledge (see Figure 5.6): concepts (Williams & Carnine, 1981), skills and rules (Carnine, Kameenui, & Maggs, 1982), laws and law-like principles (Rosenshine, 1971), and evaluative knowledge (Blatt & Kohlberg, 1975).

2. Identify three levels of achievement with regard to student learning: (1) what all students will know, (2) what some students will know, and (3) what a few students will know by the end of the lesson.

3. Clarify the relation of the lesson objective(s) to the overall unit plan: Which critical question does it address? Which major concept(s) and/or skill(s) does the lesson cover?

4. Determine the types and levels of prior knowledge required for successful participation in the lesson: How will prior knowledge be accessed, enhanced, and used?

5. Identify different levels and types of academic support needed for students to successfully participate in the lesson.

6. Determine the conspicuous strategies students need to know how to apply in order to complete assigned tasks; common strategies

Figure 5.6 Four Types of Knowledge

Concepts (80%)	Skills and Rules (15%)
Concept knowledge lessons include an understanding of a definition, critical attributes, examples, and nonexamples. Failure to address these components of a lesson on concepts could lead to an incomplete or erroneous understanding of a concept. Most of the information (80%) learned during the grade school years falls under the category of concept knowledge. Concept development is critical in reading, language arts, math, science, social studies, art, and music (Williams & Carnine, 1981).	Skills lessons include a clearly defined rationale for applying the skill, application cues that indicate the need to use the skill, step-by-step directions for applying the skill, and a method for self-checking. Skill knowledge occurs in grade school curriculum at the rate of approximately 15%. Some skills (such as those required for completing a long division problem) must be followed in a specific order. Teaching students a memory strategy to help them remember the steps (such as Please Excuse My Dear Aunt Sally for the order of operations to use in computing algebraic equations) is essential for some students' success (Carnine, Kameenui, & Maggs, 1982).
Laws and Lawlike Principles (< 5%)	Evaluative Knowledge (< 5%)
Law and lawlike principles include statements of cause and effect. The conditions for the cause must be clearly identified. The effect must be linked directly with the cause. Laws and lawlike principles are characterized by "I\if this, then that"-type statements. Law and lawlike principle knowledge accounts for less than 5% of the grade school curriculum, but it is important in the areas of science and math (Rosenshine, 1971).	Evaluative knowledge is different from opinion alone because evaluative knowledge includes a set of predetermined criteria for making a decision. Students engaged in the regular development and application of a rubric will understand that evaluative knowledge begins with a consideration of criteria and a method for making an analysis of an object or product based on the criteria. Evaluative knowledge accounts for less than 5% of the curriculum for the grade school years, but it is an invaluable skill for self-evaluation and decision-making purposes (Blatt & Kohlberg, 1975).

Figure 5.7 Lesson Planning Format

Subject(s):		Type of Knowledge:
Objective(s):		
A.		
B.		
C.		
Whole-Group Activities:		
Lesson Introduction/Prior Knowledge Hook:		
Instruction/Concept Development:		
Guided Practice:		
Students with mild to moderate disabilities or low-functioning general education students	Students working on grade level with or without accommodations	Students working above grade level
Independent Practice:	Independent Practice:	Independent Practice:
Evaluation of Learning:	Evaluation of Learning:	Evaluation of Learning:

Figure 5.8   Accommodations

Modality Input and Output	Social Configuration
Oral	Independent
Visual (print and/or pictures, graphs, artifacts)	Peer buddy and/or tutor
Tactile-kinesthetic	Cooperative groups/teams
Level of Support	*Content Orientation*
Technology	Analytical
Adult/peer	Practical/functional
Strategy instruction	Creative/artistic

include outlining, categorizing, mnemonic strategies, and establishing intermediate time and task completion goals.

7. Select a method of assessment: How will students know if they have successfully fulfilled the requirements of the lesson?

8. Build choices into the lesson design to accommodate learning styles, student preferences, and those with disabilities; what choices do students have for accessing information and demonstrating mastery?

9. Conduct mid- and end-of-lesson reviews.

■ ELEMENTS THAT FACILITATE LEARNING FOR STUDENTS WHO ARE AT RISK

1. Provide a context or "big picture" for each skill taught. Do not assume that the students will understand how a skill or concept relates to the overall goal(s) of a lesson or unit.

2. Carefully sequence skills and concepts within a lesson and the overall unit to facilitate mastery in small, incremental steps.

3. Demystify complex concepts by directly relating new ideas or vocabulary to previously learned information.

4. Provide frequent, distributed reviews of previously mastered skills and concepts.

5. Assist students in breaking large assignments into smaller, more manageable tasks through the use of checklists, graphic organizers, and daily goal setting within a weekly or monthly goal target.

6. Informally assess students regularly to provide immediate feedback and focused reteaching experiences.

7. Build a system of self-monitoring into the overall instructional plan to assist students in recognizing what they know and what they don't know.

8. Use multiple modalities when teaching, reviewing, assessing, and sharing concepts and skills.

9. Carefully pace and scaffold lessons to maximize student success.

10. *Provide opportunities for students to make choices as often as possible.* The easiest way to avoid a power struggle is to give the students shared responsibility and a sense of control over some part of their learning. Sometimes something as simple as the choice of using a pencil or a marker to practice handwriting skills will be enough to motivate a reluctant student.

CONCLUSION ■

In the past, reform efforts targeting the improvement of instruction have often been narrowly focused and insufficiently researched. The targeted student population and subject area content of primary concern have tended to shift with demographic changes in student populations, political agendas, and economic conditions. The impetus to implement universal access principles for curriculum and instruction is different from former initiatives for two major reasons.

1. The six universal access principles for curriculum and instruction listed earlier were derived from 30 years of research across multiple target groups and academic disciplines.

2. The six universal access principles for curriculum and instruction represent a framework from which to select and organize effective strategies rather than a one-size-fits-all approach to diverse student populations and complex instructional factors.

Accommodating learners with diverse needs is sometimes as simple as allowing students to choose between writing with pencils or markers. Unfortunately, too many students fail to make adequate yearly progress because of a need for significant changes in curriculum planning and instructional practices. Students with diverse learning needs make connections between previously mastered concepts and new content by accessing prior knowledge and practicing skills such as sequencing and categorizing across interdisciplinary subjects. Through strategic repetition of process skills, students learn to organize their thinking and maximize mastery in multiple content areas simultaneously. Skills and concepts that had appeared to be disconnected, lacking in meaning, and irrelevant begin to "make sense" to children who had previously avoided classwork and homework assignments. Accommodations for a particular child might include individualized provisions for accessing content and demonstrating mastery. The more completely the accommodations are developed as part of the overall plan for instruction, however, the more effective and efficient the accommodations are likely to be for the greatest number of students.

Ramps for wheelchairs that are added to older buildings long after the initial construction are often poorly designed. The person who needs the ramp often must travel far from the flow of traffic, extending the time and effort it takes to use the ramp. The ramp itself is often visually distracting, cumbersome, and out of place aesthetically. Instructional accommodations added after instructional planning and implementation have occurred can be similarly distracting, inefficient, cumbersome, and out of place. Developing unit plans, lesson plans, instructional routines, and instructional environments that accommodate a wide range of learner needs saves time and energy for the teacher as well as the students. Behavior problems decrease. Academic achievement increases. Everybody wins!

■ NOTE

Portions of this chapter have been reprinted with permission from Rockwell, S. (2006). *Tough to Reach, Tough to Teach: Students with Learning and Behavior Problems* (2nd ed.). Arlington, VA: Council for Exceptional Children.

Reorganized Annual Plan

	Reading	*Written Language*	*Math*	*Science*	*Social Studies*
How do we get started on the right foot? (health, sportsmanship, and consumer education)	Poetry Identification of main idea and relevant, supporting details Prediction Fact versus opinion	Spelling Rhyming words Writing poetry Writing descriptive sentences	Numeration Skip counting by 2s, 5s, and 10s Money/consumer math Measurement (volume/weight) Simple fractions Problem solving Algebraic thinking	Scientific method Human body/health	Map and globe Economics
Where did that come from? (cultures and customs)	Elements of fiction Folktales Fact versus fantasy Elements of nonfiction Biography "How To" selections Sequencing Compare and contrast Draw conclusions	"How To" compositions Narrative writing	Whole number operations Geometry Measurement (linear) Perimeter and area Problem solving Algebraic thinking	Simple machines Plants Earth science	State and/or national history Cultures Local and national holidays Government
What makes things fly and fall from the sky? (matter and laws of physics)	Elements of nonfiction Predict Compare and contrast Make inferences	Research skills Expository writing	Numeration and place value Measurement (temperature/ratios/proportions) Time and calendar Problem solving Algebraic thinking	States of matter Properties of matter	Geography
How is our home like a spider's web? **(interdependence: life forms and nonliving matter)**	Elements of fiction Folktales Elements of nonfiction Compare and contrast Evaluate Synthesize	Research skills Expository writing	Measurement Ratios and proportions Problem solving Algebraic thinking	Earth science Ecology Animals	Cultures Geography

Unit Organizer: What Makes Things Fly and Fall From the Sky?

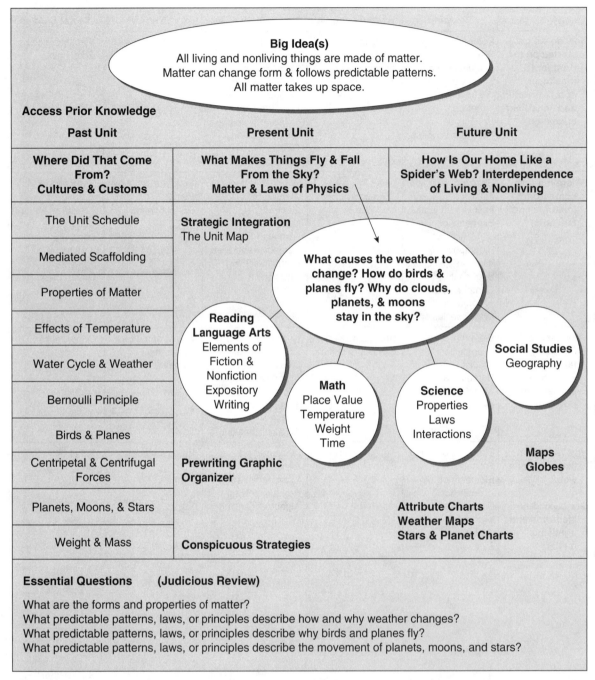

Note: Unit planning routine adapted from Lenz, Bulgren, Schumaker, Deshler, and Boudah (1994). Universal Access Principles as defined by Kameenui and Carnine (1998).

Week 1: What Makes Things Fly and Fall from the Sky?

Overall Weekly Goals	Reading	Written Language	Math	Science	Social Studies
Targeted skills: *Sequencing* major actions in the story, steps in completing the recipe for oobleck, expanded notation in the place value lessons for math, and steps in the science experiment *Categorizing* states of matter and attributes in science, geographical formations in social studies, and concepts considered during an exploration of prior knowledge and current content. Conspicuous Strategies: Concept map Attribute chart Prewriting planning sheet Proofreading Checklist	Whole-group read-aloud selection: *Bartholomew and the Oobleck* Identify: A. Elements of fiction: setting, characters, problem, major actions, and resolution B. Types and categories of precipitation in the kingdom prior to oobleck C. The sequence of major events D. The moral of the story	Creative writing *Topic:* If I were the king/queen I would command my wizards to invent _____. A. Complete a concept map of previously learned and predicted unit content B. Select one of the topics related to content from a previous unit (i.e., machines) to use in conducting a guided writing lesson that includes: 1. The completion of a prewriting planning sheet 2. A rough draft 3. Proofreading with the aid of the proofreading checklist 4. A final draft with illustrations	Place value and expanded notation A. Review place value concepts B. Engage in mental math exercises using place value concepts C. Write numbers in expanded notation D. Measure the weight and size of various objects E. Compare weight and size F. Experiment with temperature, for example: 1. Compare the temperature of items in the sun and in the shade 2. Determine the difference between the temperature of an item in the refrigerator and an item in the freezer	States and properties of matter A. Identify the three states of matter B. Identify properties of each state of matter C. Categorize matter by state D. Identify the properties of oobleck E. Review the scientific method Determine if oobleck is a solid or a liquid Targeted vocabulary: Solid Liquid Gas Properties Attribute chart Texture Viscosity Density Shape Colorless Odorless Precipitation	Review map and globe skills Identify different types of geographical formations Categorize Targeted vocabulary: Bay Island Plain Mountain Valley Isthmus Continent Ocean Lake Plateau River Desert Equator Tropics Tributary Barrier Reef

Week One: What Makes Things Fly and Fall From the Sky?

Subject: Science   **Type of Knowledge:** Concept

Objectives:

A. The students will identify the three states of matter.

B. The students will identify attributes of each state of matter.

C. The students will complete an attribute chart after examining representatives of each state of matter.

Whole-Group Activities:

Lesson introduction/prior knowledge hook: What fell from the sky in the story about Bartholomew and the Oobleck?

Instruction/concept development: Provide students with examples of solids, liquids, and gases. (Use one state of matter as a nonexample for another state of matter.) Discuss attributes.

Guided practice: Give students a blank attribute chart. Determine attributes of matter together (i.e., takes the shape of the container, holds its own shape, is hard, takes up space, etc.). Instruct students to write the attributes on the chart. Complete two or three examples on the attribute chart together as a group.

Students with mild to moderate disabilities or low-functioning general education students	Students working on grade level with or without accommodations	Students working above grade level
Independent Practice: A. Examine 10 items. B. Identify the state of matter for each. C. Identify attributes specific to the state of matter for each. D. Record answers on an illustrated attribute chart Evaluation of Learning: Completed attribute chart.	Independent Practice: A. Examine 10 items. B. Identify the state of matter for each. C. Identify attributes specific to the state of matter for each. D. Record answers on an attribute chart. E. Identify one additional example of each of the states of matter from personal experience and categorize the attributes of each. Evaluation of Learning: Completed attribute chart.	Independent Practice: A. Examine 10 items. B. Identify the state of matter for each. C. Identify attributes specific to the state of matter for each. D. Record answers on an illustrated attribute chart. E. Identify one additional example of each state of matter from personal experience and categorize the attributes. F. Select a simple machine from the last unit. Describe how the attributes of solids, liquids, and/or gases could be used to make the machine work better. Evaluation of Learning: Completed attribute chart and machine application.

6

Managing the "You Can't Make Me!" Moments

INTRODUCTION ■

From the behavioral research, we have learned that behaviors are learned and serve a function. Behaviorists take careful note of the antecedents and consequences of a behavior within a given context. Only overt behaviors are analyzed. For most classroom and school-based behavioral concerns, the analysis of observable, measurable behavior is sufficient. Students' emotional, cognitive, and physiological reactions are within normative ranges that respond satisfactorily to adjustments in the environment, task requirements, materials used, or contingencies placed on performance. Some students, however, do not respond positively to environmental changes and other supportive or corrective strategies. Many of these students have physiological, emotional, and cognitive reactions to stress that overwhelm their abilities to react in socially acceptable ways (Glasser, 1998). They may believe that they are incapable of learning to read, feel ashamed and embarrassed in front of their peers, and experience a rush of adrenaline, cortisol, and other stress hormones that prime them for a fight or flight response.

■ FOUR COMPONENTS OF BEHAVIOR

Brad, introduced in Chapter 5, represents a student for whom attention to overt behaviors, emotions, beliefs, and physiological reactions was required. Brad responded well to an individual support plan designed to extinguish the use of sexually inappropriate comments. Getting Brad to complete simple math facts and read kindergarten-level stories, however, required attention to all four components of behavior. Brad believed that he was incapable of learning. He had an average IQ and was quite knowledgeable about topics related to natural science. His memory for details, when presented with information through discussion and hands-on experiences, was remarkable. Unfortunately, Brad had a learning disability, ADHD, and a long history of school failure in addition to an emotional disorder exacerbated by his mother's alcoholism and the sexual abuse he experienced at the hands of his older sister.

Brad was repeating third grade for the second time and knew that he was still at or below first grade level academically. He not only found concentrating on printed material to be painfully tedious at a physiological level, but also experienced a tremendous sense of failure and embarrassment during instruction when he could not keep pace with peers or remember skills he had learned in earlier lessons. Brad employed a variety of escape and avoidance behaviors. He would scream and cry, crawl behind or under furniture, climb into 30-gallon garbage cans (with or without discarded food items from breakfast and lunch), or engage in sexually explicit behavior such as public masturbation, full frontal nudity, or feigned sexual intercourse with a classmate.

Given the severity and duration of Brad's acting out behavior, previous teachers had given up and given in to his demands to be left alone to play or draw. I asked him one day during our first week of working together what he hoped to accomplish with his screaming and crying. He stopped long enough to explain that his kindergarten and first-grade teachers had allowed him to sit in a bean bag chair, hold a stuffed toy, and listen to music when he screamed and cried. I explained that he would only have access to those activities when his work was complete. He calmly said, "I know," and began screaming again.

Brad eventually learned to complete his work and made dramatic advances in reading and math achievement. He stopped screaming and crying, climbing into garbage cans, and exposing his genitals in class. The road to success with him, however, was multidimensional. The following strategies were implemented to address Brad's observable behavior, beliefs about himself as a learner, emotional reactions, and physiological responses to academic tasks.

Observable Behavior

The environment was the easiest place to start. Furniture was arranged to limit Brad's access to hiding places. The garbage can was locked in a closet when not needed during breakfast and lunch. Brad's favorite activities included looking at pictures of animals, drawing, and building designs with a variety of attribute blocks. Those favored items were incorporated into his academic lessons to encourage participation. Full access to art materials and other highly desired creative toys was made contingent on his participation in lessons. When Brad refused to complete instruction with the teacher, he was placed in a room with limited adult attention and several simple paper and pencil tasks to complete. Brad disliked working in isolation and preferred the interactive instructional materials used in class to the more passive pencil and paper tasks done in isolation.

Beliefs

Like many students with learning problems, Brad was not skilled at self-observation. He was not aware of his own strengths and needs as a learner and could not accurately identify what he knew and did not know. Attribution training included (a) having Brad identify through learning games that he had a talent for recognizing word configurations, identifying initial consonant sounds, and identifying patterns in words; (b) teaching Brad to chart his own progress on specific targeted skills; and (c) requiring Brad to rephrase statements such as "I'm just stupid." Brad helped generate a list of alternative self-statements such as "I made a mistake that time. I'll do better on the next one." In addition, Brad was assigned to help a student working at the first grade level who did not know his consonant sounds. Brad made learning games for the student and was taught how to be a peer tutor. Part of the peer tutor training included work on how to give corrective feedback. This was valuable instruction that Brad used when he himself began to feel discouraged over a mistake.

Instruction in reading progressed slowly at first. Brad had experienced so much failure prior to his second year in third grade that he was not given a book to read for the whole first semester until he had demonstrated word recognition mastery of every word in the book. He could not be taught to read with books printed at his instructional level because any failure to perform with 100% mastery increased his belief that he was stupid and set off his fight or flight response at emotional and physiological levels.

Emotional Reactions

Emotional reactions to reading instruction were intensely negative in the beginning. High-interest, success-oriented materials were used initially instead of books and other commercially available support materials. Brad outlined the shapes of words, constructed an illustrated dictionary, and made lists of rhyming words that followed patterns he identified on word cards. He matched pictures and words using teacher-made puzzles, played computer games designed to reinforce targeted words and skills, and made bar charts at least three times per week to illustrate his growth in word recognition. His oral language skills were average or slightly above. Comprehension was not a concern.

To further encourage positive emotional reactions to reading instruction, he was sent to the office once a week with his bar charts. The secretary, bookkeeper, principal, and assistant principal praised him lavishly for his efforts. For the first time in his school career, he began to enjoy the learning process, take pride in his accomplishments, and look forward to the positive recognition that others gave him for making progress academically.

Physiological Reactions

Physiological reactions can continue to occur even after a student understands at a cognitive level that the threat has been reduced or eliminated. Brad tended to remain in a heightened state of excitability during instructional periods, even with the other supports put in place for him. He required direct instruction in how to recognize that he was feeling stressed and what to do to help himself calm down and focus on the task before him. We took time to talk with him about where he felt tension. He said that his arm and leg muscles became tense first and that if he kept working, his head would begin to hurt. He learned to use simple tensing and relaxing exercises at his desk whenever he began to feel upset. Allowing him to stand during some activities helped as well.

As instructional periods and independent work assignments lengthened, he learned to set incremental goals for himself and take short stretch breaks. Brad also asked to have worksheets folded or cut in half. He felt less apprehensive about a task if he could break it into smaller chunks. Over a period of 5 months, he required less teacher-assisted structure as he learned to self-monitor and make adjustments on his own.

■ THE ANATOMY OF A CONFLICT

Conflict and power struggles are common. Children often lack the social skills necessary for resolving differences among their peers and for effectively communicating with adults when conflicts arise. If a supervisor were to ask an adult employee to complete a task that the adult believed to be too difficult, unfair for some reason, or simply distasteful, the adult might (a) request a meeting with the supervisor, (b) offer mutually agreeable alternatives, (c) comply for the moment while looking for another job, or (d) resign. In a school setting, the student rarely has the cognitive and social-emotional skills necessary for negotiating a more acceptable alternative and is not allowed to resign. Given the constraints of the setting and children's immature skill sets, power struggles are inevitable.

Avoiding power struggles and defusing them once they have begun requires an understanding of how they begin, maintain momentum, and either spin out of control or end with a positive resolution. Before examining the components of a power struggle, consider alternatives strategies Ms. Marks might have used when dealing with Zane.

Zane is a third grader who is repeating the third grade for the second time. He is quite tall for his age. He has a specific learning disability in reading and has emotional and behavioral disorders (EBD). His previous teacher had allowed him to bring toys from home to keep him from screaming, falling on the floor, and disrupting the class. On Zane's first day in Ms. Marks's class, he arrived with a large stuffed duck. He cuddled the duck under his arm, kissed it, and talked to it in a high-pitched voice much like the voice adults use when talking to babies. The other students in the class began to laugh, call Zane names, and make fun of the stuffed toy. In response, Zane called the other students curse words and threatened to beat them to death. Ms. Marks demanded loudly in front of the class that Zane give her the duck. When he refused, she grabbed it from him and locked it in a closet. Zane hit and kicked her before being restrained and placed in a secured seclusion room.

Take a look at the components of a power struggle as a cyclical series of events (Morse, 1985; Wood & Long, 1991) illustrated in Figure 6.1. Zane's stressful event began before he got to school. He knew he would be going into a new classroom. He felt nervous and believed that the teacher and students would not like him. He brought the stuffed duck to help him feel more comfortable. The other students' reactions created a new stressful event. His fear that he would not be liked was confirmed and escalated. He attempted to defend himself by cursing and threatening. Ms. Marks responded by forcibly taking the duck from him. This became Zane's third stressful event. By now, he was afraid, angry, and determined to get revenge. He believed that his peers and teacher disliked him and were treating him disrespectfully. He hit and kicked the teacher. Other staff members restrained him and placed him in secured seclusion. Unless another intervention occurs before Zane is returned to class, the conflict

Figure 6.1   Anatomy of a Power Struggle

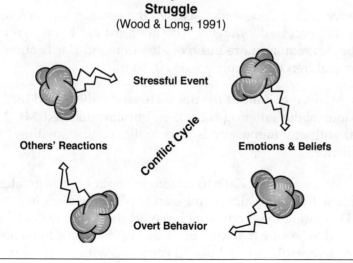

The Anatomy of a Power Struggle
(Wood & Long, 1991)

Stressful Event

Others' Reactions

Conflict Cycle

Emotions & Beliefs

Overt Behavior

cycle will repeat. Nothing has been resolved. In fact, Zane is even more angry and fearful than when he first entered the room. What could Ms. Marks have done to defuse the situation?

Consider the following series of events as an alternative to the stress-enhancing scenario described above. Ms. Marks calls Zane's mother and asks to speak with Zane. She tells Zane that the class has prepared a special snack in his honor and is looking forward to meeting him. He sounds excited to meet his classmates and says that he understands the rule about no toys at school. His mother thanks the teacher for explaining the rule to her and for welcoming Zane. On the morning of Zane's first day, Ms. Marks greets him at the door. He has a large stuffed duck under his arm. Before he can enter the room, she tells him that the duck is quite impressive and reminds him of the rule about no toys at school. Zane explains that the duck is not a toy. He tells her that the stuffed animal is his pet. Ms. Marks asks what the duck's name is. Zane replies that the duck is named Sammy.

"Well, Zane, as much as I like Sammy, this classroom is for students only."

"I know," Zane whines, "but Sammy is my pet. He has to stay with me."

"I understand that Sammy is very important to you. You want him to be safe."

Zane nods. "Come into the room. I will show you a safe place for Sammy to wait for you. You can check on him before we go to lunch and during earned activities when your work is completed."

"OK," Zane whines reluctantly. Ms. Marks allows Zane to select the best spot for Sammy to wait in the supply closet. He places the duck on a shelf, and then Ms. Marks shows Zane to his desk. The other students take turns welcoming him and serve him the snack they prepared the day before. Zane is quiet and hides his face. A classmate asks him what is wrong. He replies, "I miss my pet." The others begin to talk about their pets. He joins the conversation, eats his snack, and completes his morning assignments with everyone else.

Ms. Marks took several steps to avoid and defuse potential power struggles.

1. She welcomed Zane and discussed the issue of toys before a problem had occurred. Students who are most apt to engage in power struggles require more positive attention and clarification of rules than children who rarely engage in conflict.

2. Ms. Marks met Zane at the door. This not only helped him feel less anxious about entering the room, but also allowed Ms. Marks to deal with any unmet needs or potential conflicts without the peer audience.

3. Ms. Marks allowed Zane to remain in control to the greatest extent possible by giving him permission to place the duck in a safe place and by letting him know that he could check on the duck later if he needed to be sure that the duck was safe. She gave him choices that were acceptable to him but still complied with the class rules.

4. Ms. Marks respected Zane's feelings about the duck. She did not tell him that he was being silly or inappropriate to call a stuffed animal his pet.

5. Ms. Marks prepared the class to welcome and accept Zane by engaging them in the preparation of the snack and in getting Zane's desk in order.

6. Ms. Marks did not allow Zane to violate the rule about toys at school because he was anxious. If she had done this, the other students would have been angry with Zane for having a privilege they did not have. In addition, Zane would have escalated his attempts to bring and keep toys at school in the future.

If Zane had persisted in his attempts to keep the duck at his desk, Ms. Marks could attempt to gain his cooperation by making two or three requests in rapid succession that he is likely to execute. Examples may include selecting the color pencil that he prefers, identifying the activity he would like to earn when his work is complete, and taping his name tag to his desk. Children sometimes get into a power struggle and do not know how to get out of it gracefully. Having them follow through on two or three nonthreatening tasks allows them to comply with the original request without feeling that they are being coerced. When supportive strategies fail to produce desired results, another staff member may need to intervene. Sometimes youth get locked into a battle with one person but will comply if taken out of the situation and given a chance to discuss options with another adult. There are times when a child's behavior must be stopped to maintain the physical and/or psychological safety of that child and others in the group. The stages of aggression and strategies for effectively intervening at each stage are described in the following sections.

STAGES OF AGGRESSION ■

Anxiety: Nonverbal Cues

During the anxiety stage, students express their distress primarily through nonverbal cues. Some twist a lock of hair, some tap their pencils, and others begin to clench their fists or breath faster than usual. The teacher should intervene at this level whenever possible. Avoiding a power struggle and the escalation of aggression by meeting a student's needs at this level is the desired goal. The teacher can offer to help the student, bring the student a needed item such as a pencil or ruler, ask the student if he or she wants to talk, and engage the student in light conversation for a moment to defuse tension and assist the student in regaining perspective on the task or distressing situation.

Stress: Minor Behavior Problems

Once students begin to experience an overwhelming sense of stress, minor behavior problems begin to occur. They may express a desire to escape the situation, get out of their seats and begin pacing, crumple up their work, or break a pencil. At this point, the teacher needs to take a calm but firm approach. Offer the student choices that would be helpful to the student such as the use of different, more motivating materials; a quiet place to sit; an opportunity to work with a partner; or a brief break. Do not threaten the student with a loss of privileges or an impending punishment. Do provide the student with clear, briefly stated expectations.

Defensive: Verbal Aggression

The student who has reached the defensive stage may threaten, curse, call people names, and openly refuse to comply. The time to be supportive and offer assistance has passed. The student now needs calm, firm directions. Keep commands brief: "You need to sit down now." This is not the time to bargain with the child. For a younger child, it often helps to count to three to give the child a sense of the time frame for decision making. Older children can be given a 1- to 2-minute time limit. Explain to them that a good choice at this point will result in a favorable outcome and that a bad choice will result in a punishment. Always state the positive first. When youth are upset, they will tend to hear only the first thing said. If it is negative, they will escalate. If the student is prone to escalating to physical aggression or is highly motivated by peer attention, removal of the student's audience should occur at this point as well. Sometimes students will leave the room with an adult who was not involved in the stress-provoking situation. Call for another adult if talking does not appear to be effective in helping the child to calm down.

Physical Aggression

If a student in distress has not responded to supportive and directive interventions, physical aggression may occur. Remove the student's audience by either removing the child from the room or removing the other students from the room. Most children will calm down more quickly once the audience has been removed. Give the student sufficient personal space. Do not attempt to restrain the student unless the student is in danger or is endangering those monitoring the situation. If restraint is determined to be necessary, it should be conducted by personnel with specialized training. Restraint should always be considered the intervention of last resort.

Tension Reduction: Crying or Verbal Venting

As students calm down, they may cry and talk about what has happened. This is a critical period of intervention. The teacher, an administrator, a school psychologist, a guidance counselor, or a behavior specialist should take time to process the problem with the child and make plans for the future. Older children may feel embarrassed, especially if restraint was involved. They will need to regain composure, a sense of positive self-control, and reassurance that those involved with them care for and respect them. If the teacher is not able to be with the student during this stage, the teacher should at least take a minute or two to welcome the child back to the classroom and express positive expectations for the student's behavior upon return (Johns & Carr, 2001; Walker, Colvin, & Ramsey, 1995).

PREVENTION AND EARLY INTERVENTION ■

When students begin to feel unhappy or afraid, they have three choices. They can act out the emotion, defend against the emotion, or own and take responsibility for the emotion (Wood, 1996; Zionts, 1996). Students who act out the emotion often scream, cry, hit, kick, or throw things. Those who defend against the emotion try either (a) to escape through withdrawal or regression to thoughts, emotions, and behaviors more typical of a younger child; (b) to deny responsibility for their actions through displacement, compensation, or sublimation; or (c) to make substitutions through repressions, projections, or rationalizations. The preferred option for managing emotions and behavior would be for students to be honest about how they are feeling and accept responsibility for their choices.

Appropriate Reasons for Interfering With a Behavior

Adults have four choices when responding to a student's behavior. They can permit the behavior, tolerate the behavior, prevent the behavior, or interfere with the behavior (Zionts, 1996). Prevention requires attention to the environment, scheduling, materials used during instruction, rules, procedures, and instruction in targeted social skills. Before a teacher decides to interfere with a behavior, however, the motivation for interfering should be clearly understood. Actions taken to interfere with a behavior should be aligned with one or more of the following reasons:

1. Provide psychological and physical safety. Students should be protected from their lack of maturity by having the teacher select activities that are within safe limits for their developmental levels to protect them from injury. Attention should also be given to protecting them from bullying and the potentially harmful psychological effects of being exposed to developmentally inappropriate content—including overexposure to news accounts of disasters (Elkind, 2001; Healy, 1990; Terr, 1990), violent programs or games (Elkind, 2001; Healy, 1990), and sexually explicit information (Elkind, 2001).

2. Prevent overstimulation. Young students can have difficulty with self-regulation if they experience too many large-group, interactive activities for an extended period of time. Care should be taken when developing an instructional schedule to alternate high-energy, interactive tasks with more passive, independent activities. Many teachers dread holiday seasons because students often become more distracted and harder to manage. This can be avoided, or at least mediated, by attending to the students' needs for increased structure and opportunities to engage in calming activities.

3. Protect the integrity of an ongoing program. With recent attention to functional behavioral assessment and individualized positive behavior support planning, many educators have assumed that the individual's needs must supercede the needs of the class. Redl (1966) used the term *marginal antiseptis* to refer to the critical balance that must be maintained between the needs of individuals and the functioning of the group. An intervention that disrupts the group's functioning should not be implemented, even if an individual would benefit, unless the intervention can be integrated into the overall class plan. Likewise, an individual child's behavior should not be permitted or tolerated if it creates an overwhelming imbalance or disruption for the group. In my classroom, for example, students must complete work to gain access to preferred activities. A child who refuses to work should not be allowed to play with toys just to prevent him or her from screaming, crying, kicking, and throwing things. The integrity of the overall program would be violated and would invite the next issue, negative contagion, to surface in the group.

4. Prevent negative contagion. Kounin (1970) identified effective teacher behaviors such as with-it-ness that positively impact classroom behavior. Teachers who possess with-it-ness stop inappropriate behaviors quickly to prevent the ripple effect. The ripple effect occurs when other students begin to exhibit an inappropriate behavior first initiated by a single student. Pencil tapping, talking out, wandering around the classroom, and using inappropriate language are a few of the behaviors that are often exhibited when the ripple effect occurs.

5. Highlight a value area. Sometimes a behavior needs to be addressed because it represents a classroom expectation or value that is important to the group. Honesty, respect for personal space, and a willingness to share or cooperate are at the top of many teachers' lists of expectations. Addressing these value areas can set a positive tone for the class; assist in the avoidance of other, more disruptive problems; and strengthen students' commitment to following the classroom rules.

Ineffective Responses to Conflict

A cautionary note should be added here regarding inappropriate reasons for interfering with a behavior as well as ineffective responses to students who exhibit problem behaviors. Teachers are able to positively affect about 80% of the behaviors that occur in the classroom (Rosenshine, 1986; Sugai et al., 2000). This is an incredibly empowering statistic. Ineffective, unproductive teacher responses, however, undermine the potential for successful classroom management. The following teacher behaviors should be monitored and avoided:

1. Counteraggression. When students use profanity, offer threatening comments, or make unreasonable demands, teachers sometimes react with verbal and nonverbal threats, demands, or rude responses of their own. This tends to invite increased aggression and noncompliance from students, who are already upset. Students need adults to respond to their misbehavior with calm, firm, consistent, brief, and easily understood directions.

2. Rigid and unrealistic expectations. Some teachers establish standards for behavior and academic achievement that are beyond the abilities of certain students. Demanding that a child perform a behavior or academic task that is beyond his or her mastery level invites power struggles.

3. *Bad mood.* Occasionally, even the most skilled teacher will simply be in a bad mood from lack of sleep, an unresolved personal issue unrelated to the classroom, a minor illness, or some other stressor. Children may not be able to understand the change in attitude nor respond appropriately to differences in nonverbal cues the way adults would. On days when teachers are not feeling up to par, regardless of the reason, it is important for them to be more aware than usual of their responses to the children's behaviors.

4. *Accusation of a prejudged student.* Every classroom group has one or two children who habitually engage in specific types of misbehavior. Unfortunately, those children are often accused first and asked about their behavior second. Take care not to accuse children before conducting a fair and impartial investigation.

5. *"You" messages.* Even when children have engaged in misbehavior, they are not likely to respond well initially to statements that begin with *you* and end with a description of either a behavior or how the behavior impacts others. Instead of saying, "You make me crazy, angry, or frustrated," try saying, "I feel impatient when I am asked to repeat instructions."

6. *Confirmation of self-fulfilling prophesy.* One music teacher with whom I worked began our weekly lessons with a description of the misbehavior of targeted students over the past year. She ended her diatribe with the prediction that the student would amount to no good like siblings and cousins she had taught before the victims currently in her class. Nothing positive will come from telling children that they are doomed. Keep such thoughts to yourself.

Surface Management Techniques

Fritz Redl and his colleague David Wineman pioneered some of the early work on effective practices for working with students with EBD in classroom settings. Those strategies are as useful and relevant in today's general education and special education classrooms as Redl and Wineman found them to be in the 1950s and 1960s. Redl's (1966) Techniques for Managing Surface Behavior are listed and described below. These strategies should be among those most frequently used to avoid or defuse classroom conflict and power struggles. The order of the first 11 techniques does not suggest a hierarchy of preference or likelihood of success in any given situation. All 11 techniques should be within a teacher's repertoire and among the strategies selected as a first response, given the context and function of a particular child's behavior.

1. *Planned ignoring.* Mild behaviors that are not being repeated by other students and are not creating undue disturbance to other students are often best managed through planned ignoring. Children tend to repeat behaviors that get attention. By ignoring one behavior but giving a child attention for a more desirable behavior—especially if the more desirable

behavior is incompatible with the behavior being ignored—the teacher increases the likelihood that the behavior being ignored will stop over time. One example is students' kneeling rather than sitting in a chair. Some students kneel because the chair is not the appropriate size for them. Other students, particularly those with ADHD, kneel or squirm in their chairs because they need to release excess energy. Students can be taught how to sit during a lesson on active listening. Those with ADHD can be taught to wiggle their legs under their desks as an alternative to kneeling and squirming. Teaching students sitting skills and rewarding those behaviors instead of repeatedly reminding them to place their bottoms in their chairs and their feet on the floor is more effective. Behaviors that should not be ignored include physical aggression and loud, disruptive behaviors that interfere with learning.

2. *Signal interference.* Signal interference is an effective way to communicate with students through the use of nonverbal cues. Students who are not skilled at self-monitoring and self-management often benefit from a predetermined signal. This can be a private cue between the teacher and a particular student or a cue the whole group understands. With younger children, it is often effective to wear a laminated card that has a stop sign on one side and a go sign on the other. When the student is performing the desired behaviors, the go sign is visible. If the student begins to exhibit undesired behaviors, the teacher turns the card over to reveal the stop sign. Nothing is said to the child unless he or she self-corrects. When this happens, the card is turned to reveal the go sign. Praise or some other form of reinforcement might accompany the return to desired behavior, or the go sign might be all the feedback the child needs. With older children, I have used tapping my nose, pulling my ear, and pointing to a poster illustrating strategies for self-calming. Older students in particular appreciate not being corrected verbally in front of others. This technique does not interrupt instruction and does not require a large investment in time. It can be an essential step to take during the teaching of self-monitoring as long as the teacher is aware of the need to fade the prompt as the student gains greater self-awareness and self-control.

3. *Interest boosting.* Sometimes students simply are not interested in a particular topic or lesson format. Teachers can punish those who do not comply with the assigned tasks, but this often escalates conflict and power struggles instead of defusing them. Changing the materials, pace, or tasks can boost students' interest significantly and effectively defuse potential power struggles. For example, many students dread composing sentences and paragraphs. Spending sufficient time with prewriting activities such as brainstorming topics, making word walls of topic-related vocabulary, and completing graphic organizers might help. When it is time to actually spend time with the independent task of writing, however, the teacher can boost students' interest in the task by providing options. Many students will write more if allowed to tape chart paper to the wall and use colored markers. Some prefer to use different colors of construction paper. Others will forget their discomfort or dislike of writing a paragraph if allowed to use a word processor or old typewriter. Bingo and Jeopardy type games that reinforce academic content, role-plays, hands-on activities, and brief content-related

videos are also effective as interest boosters. A word of caution should be shared here. Students will complain of being bored or act uninterested to access preferred activities. The teacher should carefully monitor students' behaviors so they do not realize that a lesson plan is being modified. Do not announce that plans have changed because of bad behavior.

4. *Restructuring, regrouping.* Restructuring or regrouping is useful when the room arrangement or schedule is interfering with optimum student cooperation. Students might not have enough personal space around their desks. Students who do not get along might be assigned to the same instructional skill group. The schedule might require students to spend too much time with passive, noninteractive tasks before being given opportunities to move around and converse with others, or it might over-stimulate them with too many active, less structured tasks during a period of the day. Restructuring and regrouping can occur as soon as a problem arises or can be accomplished through more thorough planning after collecting data and reflecting on students' needs.

5. *Proximity control.* Sometimes the presence of an authority figure is all a person needs to become aware of a behavior and self-correct. Police officers who park within clear view of motorist are exercising proximity control. They do not flash their lights, sound their sirens, or call undue attention to themselves. They are simply present and within range to take additional measures if the need arises. Proximity control in the classroom works much the same way. The teacher moves closer to a student who is showing signs of distress or beginning to act inappropriately. The teacher does not comment on the behavior, touch the child, or speak directly to the child. The teacher is simply present and available if the need arises. Many children will refrain from misbehaving in a classroom that is constantly monitored in this fashion. Others will become aware of their behavior and self-correct as the teacher gets nearer to their desks. The child who acts inappropriately to get the teacher's attention will not benefit from proximity control because this strategy may actually reinforce the undesired behavior. Planned ignoring paired with attention to an incompatible behavior would be more appropriate and effective in this case.

6. *Antiseptic bouncing.* Some students are not aware of their increasing levels of anxiety, frustration, or need for physical or sensory stimulation. They often persist at a task or engage in a conversation with a peer that overwhelms their limited capacity for self-control. An alert teacher can defuse the situation by providing the child with a brief respite from the situation by asking the child to run an errand or help with a simple classroom chore. This can be a particularly useful strategy to use when one student is being teased by another student. The potential victim can be asked to take a note to a neighboring classroom or sort construction paper scraps in the art center by color while the teacher deals discreetly with the student who was initiating the teasing. This gives the potential victim a respectable avenue for escape from the situation and provides time for other corrective actions to be taken. For students with ADHD or anxiety disorders, the need for increased movement and a break from a tedious academic task can be built into the routine of the classroom through classroom jobs as well as materials

arrangement that requires frequent and controlled movement around the room. Examples include (a) assigning class jobs such as distributing books and papers, filing papers, collating papers, or cutting, stacking, and stapling scrap paper; (b) requiring students to move clothespins from a line on one side of the room to another across the room as they complete assignments; and (c) providing targeted students with an individual desk and a chair at a group table. The students with an individual desk and a chair at a group table can move back and forth between the two options as their needs dictate. Neither assigned seat is designated as a place of reward or punishment. Both places are simply available and used as the student's needs dictate throughout the day.

7. *Hurdle help.* Sometimes a student signals distress by tapping a pencil, sighing, or beginning to crumple a paper. Offering assistance and support before the student refuses to complete the task or makes threatening comments can be effective in avoiding a power struggle. If the student is already upset enough to make "You can't make me!" type statements, offering choices that boost the student's interest can be enough to defuse the situation. When offering choices related to consequences, be careful to state the positives first. Reminding a student who is already upset about a potential aversive consequence usually escalates the student's anger and anxiety. Start by reminding the student of positive consequences that will follow the completion of the task.

8. *Tension decontamination (humor).* The use of humor can be difficult to manage well in the beginning. A teacher who makes a joke about a potentially upsetting situation can easily be perceived as mocking or disrespectful to students who do not know and trust the person. Once students know and trust a teacher, however, humor can be quite effective in reducing tension and restoring everyone's willingness to cooperate. During an affective lesson on the role of thoughts and emotions in making choices about behavior, Brad began to get off task. We had been experimenting with different types of balls to determine which ones would bounce the highest when dropped from a height of 5 feet. The class decided that the material from which each ball was made determined how high it would bounce. They agreed that the balls had no control over their performance. When I asked why this was true, one young man said, "They only have air inside. They do not have brains." I agreed enthusiastically and asked the 7-, 8-, and 9-year-olds to raise their hands if they had brains.

Everyone raised his hand except Brad. I asked Brad if he had a brain. He said, "No." I asked what was in his head. He replied, "I don't have a brain, I have a squirrel." Brad liked to entertain the class and get them off topic, so I quickly asked, "Well, Brad, does your squirrel have a brain?" Brad and the others in the class laughed. He agreed that the squirrel did have a brain, and we went on to discuss how our ability to think and feel emotions affected the choices we made about our behavior. Stopping the lesson to reprimand Brad would have likely resulted in Brad encouraging others to name animals in their heads and a performance of Brad's interpretation of squirrel-like behavior. Brad enjoyed the joke he started and rejoined the discussion appropriately with a quick, humorous response to his potentially disruptive comment.

9. *Diversion*. When children are very young, skilled parents divert their attention to avoid tears. A noisy rattle is offered as a substitute for an electrical cord. A game of peekaboo is played while the parent packs the car to keep the baby from crying every time the parent's head disappears into the trunk. As children get older, diverting their attention takes more thought and skill, but it can still be a powerful strategy for avoiding or defusing conflict.

Roy was a fifth-grade student who had been diagnosed with paranoid schizophrenia. When Roy believed he was in danger, he became extremely violent. One afternoon, he ran out of the classroom after an argument with a classmate. I followed him into the office, where he had cornered the guidance counselor. She was sitting at a desk while Roy held a pair of scissors over her head. I knew that any loud noises or sudden movements could precipitate an attack on the guidance counselor, so I moved slowly toward Roy and talked in soothing tones about making a bird out of a piece of paper.

As I began to fold a piece of typing paper from the desk, Roy shifted his eyes from the guidance counselor to me. He continued to hold the scissors over her head but became distracted by my story about the bird. When it was finished, I showed him how to make the wings flap by pulling on the bird's tail. He nodded approval. At that point, I asked him if he wanted the bird. Again he nodded affirmatively. I said, "I'll trade you the scissors for the bird." Without a word, Roy handed me the scissors. I placed the bird in his hand and asked him to walk with me to the behavior specialist's office. He led the way without another incident. Attempting to control the situation in any other manner might have ended in serious injury to the guidance counselor, Roy, and myself.

A much less dramatic example from personal experience occurred when a third grader crumpled his paper into a ball during a science lesson. This was his way of signaling his anger and frustration. Cursing and throwing classroom items usually followed. On this particular day, however, I quickly thanked him for the crumpled ball of paper and used it in a demonstration of mass. He was so intrigued with the science demonstration that he refocused his attention without further intervention.

10. *Removal of seductive objects*. Seductive items include things that distract students and disrupt the classroom routine. Toys and broken equipment are at the top of the list in any classroom. Young, immature students, however, will be distracted by anything that isn't immediately required to complete a task. They will play with crayons, markers, erasers, bits of scrap paper, scissors, rulers, and other common school tools. Keep unnecessary supplies and instructional items in a cabinet when not in use. Provide students with limited choices initially and make more items available as the students' abilities to manage those items increases. Remove instructional supplies that will not be used and broken equipment from the room. Keep furniture and items that can be easily thrown to a minimum. Disallow toys and electronic games from home. If the school encourages students to bring such items from home for Fun Friday activities or Show and Tell, designate a secure file cabinet or storage cabinet for such items. Students should have access to those items only during designated periods of the day.

11. *Direct appeal*. With all the emphasis on functional behavioral assessment and positive behavior support plans, we sometimes forget to just ask the student to stop a problem behavior. Behaviors that are frequently exhibited will not come under control through direct appeal. A behavior that is relatively mild and rarely exhibited can often be brought under control simply by making the student aware of the behavior and its effects on others. A privately communicated, quiet, calm, and firm reprimand often attains the desired results without additional time or effort.

12. *Physical restraint*. Physical restraint should be used only as a last resort. Children who have been abused may re-experience the fear and anxiety they felt during an abuse situation. Others might not have histories of abuse but might feel additional anger and embarrassment over their lack of control. In addition, physical restraint can result in injury to the student or other staff members. Every attempt should be made to defuse a situation with verbal, nonaggressive de-escalation strategies. If restraint is determined to be the best option, remove the audience and call for support. Do not attempt to restrain a child without prior training. Do document the restraint, contact parents or guardians, and notify a supervisor.

■ PASSIVE AGGRESSIVE BEHAVIOR

Some students quietly refrain from following the teacher's directions without engaging in a direct confrontation. Others continually disrupt the classroom routine with requests and behaviors that are not problematic in and of themselves but occur too frequently and at inopportune times. These behaviors include but are not limited to tying shoelaces when it is time to line up to go to lunch, music, art, or physical education; sharpening pencils when it is time to begin whole-group instruction; doing the opposite of whatever is assigned; or quietly doing nothing. Some students will do their work and not turn it into the teacher, or finish part of the work and leave the rest incomplete even though they know what to do. These behaviors are different from simple attention-seeking behaviors because attention and other rewards do not reduce their frequency or intensity. Punishment has no effect either. Some students need to feel that they have control over each situation, and they exercise control through nonaggressive noncompliance. Some believe that the goal of passive aggressive behavior is to inspire anger in others. These students do not know how to express their own wants, needs, and angry feelings effectively and have little trust in the responsiveness of others to their wants, needs, and feelings. For these reasons, the usual rewards and punishments do not work.

Fisher, Osterhaus, Clothier, and Edwards (1994) outline 10 interventions to use when working with a student engaged in passive aggressive behaviors.

1. *Structure academic lessons and behavior management options to maximize the students' ability to make choices.* At the root of the passive aggressive behavior is a need to feel in control. These students often live with parents or caregivers who either are extremely intrusive and punitive,

are extremely permissive, or vacillate between the two extremes. These children cannot control the adults in their lives, so they resort to controlling their own responses. Increasing their opportunities to make informed choices can ease the tension and anxiety they feel.

2. *Establish high standards and communicate those standards calmly, clearly, and consistently to the student.* Continue to grade the student's work with the same criteria applied to the other students in the class. Provide feedback in a caring rather than a punitive way.

3. *Develop an empathetic understanding of these students and a warm relationship with them.* One of the hardest concepts to grasp when working with passive aggressive students is that they are suffering from feelings of failure and inadequacy in spite of their "You can't make me!" and "I don't care!" facades.

4. *Praise students sincerely for small steps forward.* Take care not to qualify the praise with a "but" statement such as "You're paragraph was well written. I appreciate the detail you included, but you could have done better on the spelling and punctuation." Omit from the praise any insinuation of pressure or disappointment.

5. *Do not use a reward system.* Passive aggressive students will probably sabotage the teacher's attempt at control by refusing to complete contingent tasks.

6. *Allow students to experience logical and natural consequences.* If they complete only 75% of their work, they earn a C. If they fail to complete classwork within a predetermined time, they will not have time for an earned activity.

7. *Do not withhold outside recess or physical education.* These students need the release of physical activity.

8. *Do not make an issue of homework.* Passive aggressive students will only increase the power struggles at home and at school. Allow them to make decisions about when to begin homework or how to make up missed assignments. If students persist in refusing to complete homework and homework is included in the grading system, then report the impact on their grade in matter of fact terms and leave the decisions to them.

9. *Interact with students in ways that do not require them to become defensive.* When students do not work, respond with a belief that they are not ready for the work instead of a remark that reflects that they could do the work if they tried. Telling passive aggressive students that you don't believe they are ready for the work often results in their insistence that they be given the assignment. They have a need to prove the teacher wrong.

10. *Actively teach anger management skills to these children. They are in as much need of help as a child who threatens and physically attacks others.* Anger management lessons taught in an empathetic and nonthreatening environment can be quite effective in helping them learn to make appropriate choices and express their wants, needs, and emotions more directly.

■ LEARNED BEHAVIOR VERSUS MANIFESTATIONS OF MENTAL ILLNESS

Sometimes nothing seems to work. Praise, rewards, reinforcers, tokens of all types, and the best research-based behavior management program available fails. On those days, a teacher can feel inadequate, discouraged, frustrated, and even enraged. One day early in my first year at a local elementary school where I taught primary-level students with severe emotional disorders, nothing worked. A child with an extensive sexual abuse history was screaming, running around the room, and making graphic sexual gestures. Another was climbing on bookcases and running across the tops of desks while singing songs about private body parts. A third was loudly accusing me of being unfair and threatening to have his dad call the police so they could come to school and kill me. A few other students were crawling under furniture to avoid academic tasks. The behavior specialist, administrators, classroom aide, and I ran from one crisis to the next. We finally got four of the eight students calmed down enough to take them outside to a picnic table while we attempted to deal with the other four. By the end of the day, I was not fit to be around other human beings. I called my husband to let him know where I was and checked into a hotel for the night.

Behavior modification, affective education, attention to the environment, and effective academic instruction will work most of the time for most of the students. There are days, however, when the best a teacher can do is to keep everyone safe. Why don't the best strategies research has to offer work 100% of the time? The answer to that question is simple, even if the solutions are not. Many of the challenging behaviors children exhibit are either age appropriate or learned. Age-appropriate and learned behaviors respond well to effective, research-based interventions. Some behaviors, however, are characteristic of serious mental illness and include physiological components not directly under the control of school personnel.

Psychiatrists, psychologists, neurologists, and other medical and mental health professionals continue to investigate the intertwined biological, cognitive, and social-emotional factors that affect behavior. When a child is in crisis, as a few of the students in the scenario described above were that particular day, it is hard to distinguish between deliberate acts of noncompliance and manifestations of mental illness. What should a teacher do?

The first rule is to maintain everyone's physical and psychological safety. Remove violent and aggressive students if possible. If it is not possible to remove the students who are physically aggressive, then find a safe place for those who are calmer and under control. When in doubt, continue to implement the usual behavior management system as consistently as possible. Even in the midst of the chaos, students will know that the supportive structure remains intact. This will assist in preventing unnecessarily disruptive behavior in the future.

Students with histories of trauma will need reassurance that they are safe. One young man of 8 who had been sodomized by a neighbor when he was 7 was directed to the cool-off carrel when he began to threaten others with physical harm. I held his hands and whispered in his ear that he was safe, that no one would hurt him, and that he needed to take slow, deep breaths. Leaving him alone in the carrel at that point would have increased his anxiety and the likelihood that he would attack other students. On days when the class is calm, he is able to benefit from the cool-off carrel without teacher assistance. Following the classroom management plan in addition to providing that student with supportive guidance maintained the physical and psychological safety required to assist him in calming down.

Students with the following disorders may need additional levels of support. The summary of characteristic behaviors is summarized from the *Diagnostic and Statistical Manual IV* (American Psychiatric Association, 1994).

Autism spectrum disorder: Autism spectrum disorders include a wide range of characteristics. In general, individuals with autism exhibit (a) impairments in areas of reciprocal social interactions and communication, (b) insistence on sameness in areas of daily routine, and (c) engagement in unusual behavior patterns. Behaviors can include one or more of the following:

1. Self-stimulation (rocking, hand-flapping)

2. Hypersensitivity to visual, tactile, or auditory stimulation

3. Self-injurious behavior

4. Sleep problems

5. Noncompliant behavior (tantrums)

6. Extreme fears of people or items not typically feared

About 75% to 80% of the children diagnosed with autism have a concurrent diagnosis of mental retardation. Those who develop functional speech and have an average or above average IQ exhibit difficulty with reciprocal social interactions and communication and related social functioning with peers and adults.

ADHD: Students with ADHD may appear to be driven. The behaviors can escalate to excessive climbing and running around the room. The children may also have great difficulty waiting for their turn in games and other activities, may interrupt others excessively, and may intrude on others. When the children are tired or not feeling well, the behaviors may escalate. Changes in medication (when medication is part of the treatment program) and changes in the classroom routine can also exacerbate symptoms.

Childhood disassociative disorders including post-traumatic stress disorder (PTSD): Students with disassociative disorders including PTSD experience a disruption in integrated mental functions such as memory, perception of the environment, and sense of identity. These students may go into a trance-like state during which they stare blankly, or they may begin to talk to or about "imaginary friends." During the period of disassociation, the student may react in an aggressive manner toward a perceived threat. These students need reassurance that they are safe, even when observable behaviors do not indicate that they can hear the speaker. It is important to talk quietly and calmly to them until they regain self-control and appropriate levels of engagement with the immediate environment.

Bipolar disorder: Students with bipolar disorder experience disruptions in mood and mood regulation that are characterized by alternating states of hypomania and depression. During hypomanic states, students may have a decreased need for sleep, have an inflated self-esteem, be more talkative than usual, rapidly change topics during conversation, excessively engage in pleasurable activities, and be highly distractible. During the depressive states, the student may sleep more than usual, exhibit disruptions in appetite, react irritably toward others, withdraw, express negative thoughts about self and life in general, experience no enjoyment in previously preferred activities, or increase acts of verbal and physical aggression.

Oppositional defiant disorder (ODD): Students with ODD exhibit a pattern of hostile and defiant behavior. They often lose their temper, argue with adults, deliberately annoy others, and blame others for their mistakes; they are easily annoyed by others and are often angry and spiteful or vengeful. As with students who have ADHD and conduct disorder, changes in classroom routine often exacerbate their inappropriate behaviors. Changes in adult supervision and peer group can also escalate negative responses.

Conduct disorder: Students with conduct disorder present a persistent and repetitive pattern of behaviors that violate societal norms. Inappropriate behaviors may include but are not limited to aggression toward people and animals (including forced sexual activity), destruction of property, theft, conning or lying to others, running away, and truancy. These students are particularly vulnerable to disruptions in the classroom routine as well as changes in the adult supervision or peers in a group.

Obsessive compulsive disorder (OCD): Students with OCD are preoccupied with orderliness, perfectionism, and control. They tend to be preoccupied with details, rules, lists, organization, and schedules. They may have difficulty completing academic tasks due to excessive time taken to organize materials before beginning, excessive erasing and rewriting of responses, and refusal to write anything that might possibly be incorrect. Rigidity and stubbornness characterize their interactions with adults and peers. Timed tests, unscheduled events that require a quick response, and power struggles with adults and peers are potential points of escalation.

Separation and attachment anxiety disorders: Students with anxiety disorders exhibit levels of anxiety and disruptions in daily life that are developmentally inappropriate. These children may worry excessively about the harm or potential loss of a loved one. This anxiety may interfere with sleep and leaving home to go to school or a social event; they may have repeated nightmares and refuse to be left alone even for very brief intervals. Changes in adult supervision and any perceived threat to safety (fire drills, storms, etc.) can increase the student's anxiety and behavioral symptoms.

Depression: Students with depression may sleep more than usual, exhibit disruptions in appetite, react irritably toward others, withdraw, express negative thoughts about self and life in general, experience no enjoyment in previously preferred activities, or increase acts of verbal and physical aggression. Unlike students with bipolar disorder, these students do not exhibit hypomania. They may, however, exhibit more severe manifestations of depression from one day to the next. Children with depression should be monitored carefully for suicidal thoughts (ideation) and plans. If a child expresses a desire to hurt or kill him- or herself, call parents and support personnel immediately. Do not leave the child alone. Never take threats lightly.

Anxiety, depression, and other internalizing disorders are often co-morbid with externalizing disorders characterized by verbal and physical aggression. Even with medication and careful monitoring by health and mental health professionals, students may become overwhelmed at times. Experiences that would not be overstimulating for children who have no previous traumas or mental illnesses may increase the vulnerable child's feelings of stress, frustration, fear, or anxiety. As stated previously, it is important to maintain the usual structure of the academic and behavioral program to whatever degree is possible for the students who are maintaining self-control as well as for the youth who are momentarily overwhelmed.

Be mindful, however, of the difference between deliberate noncompliance and manifestations of mental illness. Children who are overwhelmed by stress, frustration, anger, or anxiety needs to know that adults are present and responsive to their crisis. They should not be left unattended. They may be excluded from activities that they enjoy until they have regained self-control and are able to take responsibility for their actions, but this should not be done in a punitive way. It is appropriate for adults to empathize with the students while maintaining protective boundaries on activities in much the same way that an adult would empathize with a child who has the flu and cannot attend a scheduled field trip.

Responding to a child in crisis with anger, condemnation, threats, or predictions of future failure add to the child's sense that adults are not trustworthy, fair, and capable of offering support or protection and that they are deserving of vengeful reactions. Do not try to manage crisis situations alone. Call on the administrators, behavior specialist, guidance counselor, social worker, and other support personnel as well as parents and outside support agencies when prior parental permission has been granted. These moments are not the teacher's fault. These moments do require the teacher to respond calmly, quickly, professionally, and collaboratively.

In addition to taking care of the children's needs during times of crisis, be mindful of your own needs. I am rarely overwhelmed by the emotional outbursts of my students. When I am, however, I take my own mental health needs as seriously as those of the students. I find time alone to process the events of the day and make plans for the future. Talking with trusted colleagues, accessing the research on a particular issue, and talking with a clinical psychologist about my own emotional reactions to a situation are steps I have taken to deal effectively with difficult students and groups. Taking care of myself in general is an ongoing commitment. A balanced diet, regular exercise, recreation with family and friends, and outlets for creative, spiritual, and intellectual growth are essential.

■ CONCLUSION

Surviving the "You Can't Make Me!" moments requires proactive planning, attention to the emotional states of the students, and careful monitoring of adult's responses to students' needs. Effective teachers avoid power struggles by establishing a well-balanced schedule, actively teaching the desired behaviors, reinforcing students who comply, and responding predictably to noncompliance. A few students will require more intensive levels of support. Chapter 7 describes specialized interventions designed to support and teach students with more severe behavioral challenges.

7

Special Case Interventions

■ A NOTE TO GENERAL EDUCATION TEACHERS

The processes described in this chapter are often developed and implemented by support personnel and special education staff. General educators, however, are mandated by IDEA (2004) to be included in the development and implementation of Individualized Educational Plans (IEP), Functional Behavioral Assessment (FBAs), and Behavior Support Plans. Having team members who know how these processes are developed, implemented, monitored, and modified increases their efficiency and efficacy. General educators may also find the section entitled Methods for Integrating Individual Plans With the Group Plan, located near the end of this chapter, helpful when integrating a student with behavioral challenges into a general education setting.

■ INTRODUCTION

Special education teachers are taught to analyze a single student's behavior and to develop an intervention plan based on the analysis of that student's strengths and needs. Although this chapter addresses processes and interventions designed to facilitate appropriate behavior for individuals with more challenging problems, not every child with severe behavior problems needs an FBA or a Positive Behavior Support (PBS) plan. Individuals are apt to act in ways that bring undue attention to themselves and disrupt the classroom when the level of group development has not been considered and managed effectively. Phillip is an excellent example of a student who appeared to be in need of one-on-one assistance prior to the implementation of a classwide plan. His case is offered as a rationale for reexamining the stages of group development and classroom level interventions before assuming that a particular child is in need of an FBA and PBS plan.

Phillip entered a primary-level class for students with emotional and behavioral disorders (EBD); no classwide behavior management system was in place. He was being treated privately for ADHD and oppositional defiant disorder. He needed a high degree of structure; firm, caring supervision; and opportunities to learn socially acceptable skills for working with adults and peers. Instead, he entered a chaotic classroom. Five-year-old Phillip learned quickly that fighting was the group's preferred method for settling conflicts, that adults would give him more attention if he could convince them that he was a victim, and that escaping undesired tasks was easily accomplished by crying. During the 150 days he spent in the primary class as a kindergarten student, he was restrained by staff members or placed in secured seclusion more than 100 times. He was taken to the clinic for minor injuries more than 75 times. Administrators reported that he served some part of most school days in office detention.

A classwide plan was designed with the level of group functioning in mind at the beginning of his first-grade year. During the initial 90 days of that year, in the same class with the same peers, he was placed in secured seclusion only four times. (The four incidents requiring secured seclusion occurred on the same school day during the third week of school.) He went to the clinic once when he bumped his head on the wall after jumping over a model town he had built during an earned activity period during the 10th week of school. His only trip to the office to speak with administrators was to share his Student of the Week awards during Weeks 9 and 12.

Administrators had warned me about Phillip's aggressive and disruptive behaviors. They had advised me to begin an FBA as soon as school started. Instead of an FBA, however, I developed an inclusion plan so Phillip could participate in general education classes for part of the school day. Phillip needed clearly stated limits, contingent positive recognition, and a safe environment. He appeared to be the child who was most in need of an individualized behavior management plan. In reality, he was the youngest student in the primary class for students with EBD. He was the least able to cope with the lack of structure, cohesiveness, and safety that had characterized the classroom group the previous year. Two students eventually required FBAs and individualized PBS plans.

Phillip's case illustrates the importance of understanding group dynamics and the powerful effects of those dynamics on student behavior. Correctly identifying students with the most intensive need for individualized interventions saves time and other valuable resources. In addition, individualized plans are more likely to result in positive outcomes because the teacher and other staff members involved are not attempting to implement several plans simultaneously or overcome the overwhelmingly negative effects of an unstructured learning environment.

Researchers (Lewis, Sugai, & Colvin, 1998; Scott & Nelson, 1999) have discovered that even with a well-designed classroom-level behavior management system in operation, 1% to 7% of the students will need additional, intensive levels of support. The reauthorized Individuals With Disabilities Education Act (2004) mandates the development of an FBA with multiple data collection sources prior to the implementation of a PBS plan. Two young men in Phillip's class are representative of students who are in need of highly individualized behavioral assessment and intervention procedures.

Brad engaged in inappropriate discussions of body parts, bodily functions, and sexually charged content as often as 19 times in a 25-minute period. He sang little songs out loud, using graphic lyrics he composed himself, about licking private body parts; he turned typical classroom objects into phallic symbols and commented on other's work or actions with inappropriate references to elimination and/or sexuality; and on two occasions, he exposed himself. Jesse demanded immediate adult attention. When he did not get the attention he desired, he knocked over furniture, screamed, threw any object available, kicked, hit, scratched, and pulled hair.

Neither boy was responding to the classroom-level behavior management system. Both needed intensive, individualized intervention plans. In the next section, the FBA and PBS process is described in general terms followed by (a) a more detailed discussion of Jesse's and Brad's cases, (b) additional suggestions for intervention planning, (c) resources available, and (d) methods for integrating the individual plans into the overall classroom-level plan.

THE PROCESS ■

PBS is characterized by a data-driven problem-solving process that includes schoolwide, setting-specific, classroom, and individual levels of analysis and intervention (Lewis et al., 1998; Scott & Nelson, 1999). The steps for developing a PBS plan for an individual student are similar to the steps for developing schoolwide, setting-specific, and classroom levels of PBS. All levels of PBS include (a) the formation of a support team that has reached consensus about the need for developing a plan; (b) the identification of the problems that need to be addressed; (c) the collection of data related to identified problems; (d) the analysis of the data; (e) the development of a plan to address the problems; (f) the implementation of the plan; and (g) ongoing data collection, data analysis, and adjustment of the plan as the data reflect a need for changes (Lewis et al., 1998; Scott & Nelson, 1999). During the construction of an individual PBS plan, a well-developed FBA is often necessary (Foster-Johnson & Dunlap, 1993; Horner & Carr, 1997). Because behavior is purposeful, an understanding of the function of the behavior is often essential to the development of an effective PBS plan. Sometimes the function of a student's behavior is easy to ascertain. In those cases, the PBS team can construct a hypothesis about the function of the behavior based on data already available to the team and proceed with the development of a PBS plan. When the function of the behavior is not well defined, an FBA is conducted. Each step in the process is described below as a prelude to the discussion of two cases taken from prior experiences with Brad and Jesse, two former elementary-level students.

Step 1: Support Team Formation

The first step in the PBS process is to identify a support team to work directly with the child. This team will reach consensus on the need to develop a plan, the data that will be collected, the various interventions that will be implemented to address the student's needs, and the shared responsibility of each team member. The PBS team should be composed of the student's teacher, a parent or guardian, and any other support person with whom the child has regular contact. This may include any combination of the following: an administrator, guidance counselor, speech therapist, occupational therapist, physical therapist, behavior specialist, coach, and community agency representative. The PBS team should be large enough to (a) provide adequate information about the child's strengths and needs and (b) effectively implement the PBS plan. Care should be taken to ensure that essential individuals are included on the PBS team without making it so large that communication and the coordination of services become unmanageable.

Step 2: Problem Identification

Once a PBS team has been identified and consensus has been reached on the need for a PBS plan, the team must begin to identify the problem. A review of the student's school records should be conducted prior to the first PBS team meeting. (A form designed to aid in the organization of the review of school records can be found in Appendix A.) School records often contain valuable information about academic progress, discipline issues, health problems, psychological assessments, and social histories. Each member of the PBS team should be prepared to share past and present information relative to the student's strengths and needs.

Even with advanced preparation for the meeting and a shared commitment to assisting the child, however, various members of the PBS team may define a child's strengths and needs quite differently. The father may highly value his son's level of energy, physical strength, and agility. His primary concern may be related to academic failure. The classroom teacher, on the other hand, might believe that fighting, conflicts with peers, and frequent out-of-seat behaviors are the primary problems. Underneath the surface of the team's discussion, school personnel may actually blame the parents, and parents may view school personnel as uncaring or inadequate. Keeping the discussion focused on the shared commitment each team member has to facilitating the child's growth is essential. Forest and Lusthaus (1990); Pearpoint, O'Brian, and Forest (1993); Smith (1990); and Turnbull and Turnbull (1992) are among those who have developed person-centered planning processes for focusing teams on shared dreams and fears, the strengths and needs of the child, barriers, circles of support, long-term goals, short-term objectives, and other factors relevant to planning and intervention selection. A modified version of a Person-Centered Plan Template that combines Futures Planning (Mount, 1992) processes and the Planning Alternative Tomorrows with Hope (PATH) processes (Pearpoint et al., 1993), which was developed by the Florida Positive Behavior Support Project, can be downloaded at http://flpbs.fmhi.usf .edu/pbs_Person-Centered_Plan_ Template.pdf.

The completion of a person-centered plan is not necessary in all cases, but it can be quite helpful when team members have diverse opinions about the nature of a child's difficulties, when interactions among team members have been tense prior to the formation of the PBS team, or when team members come to the initial meeting with little or no background information. A complete person-centered plan that includes every frame can easily take 2 to 3 hours to complete. Most school-based teams do not have the luxury of spending that amount of time on the development of one student's profile. It is acceptable and advisable to select only the frames most pertinent to the student's history and needs of the team. Other time-saving techniques include: (a) determining the amount of time that should be allotted for each frame prior to the beginning of the meeting, (b) assigning a timekeeper to signal the team when the group has discussed a particular frame for the allotted time, and (c) completing only the frames that are most pertinent to the purpose of the meeting. The whole person-centered plan does not have to be completed in one sitting. The sections on dreams, fears, strengths, circles of support, and needs might be targeted for completion during the first meeting. These frames assist the team in establishing a level playing field from which to understand each other, the child, and the nature of the challenges ahead. This also facilitates a shared sense of responsibility, a common vocabulary, and an increased awareness and respect for the role each member of the team plays in the child's development.

It is essential to engage in some process for reaching consensus about the nature and needs of the student, even if a formal person-centered plan is not conducted. A modified plan can be limited to a 1-hour session. This is time well spent if it accomplishes the tasks of (a) acknowledging each team member's hopes and fears for the child without assigning blame, (b) facilitating a shared vision among all team members, (c) establishing a common language for communicating the child's strengths and needs, (d) highlighting information not previously available to all team members, and (e) developing a well-integrated approach to problem solving that includes key people in the child's life across multiple settings.

Sometimes a team is able to effectively problem-solve after engaging in this 1-hour person-centered planning meeting. The remaining four steps in the process, which are outlined in this chapter, can then be omitted altogether or collapsed into a brief and easily managed conclusion to the person-centered plan meeting that results in the development of a PBS plan. Follow-up communication among team members to check on the child's progress can then be conducted through e-mail, telephone calls, or regularly scheduled progress report sessions.

Jerry is an example of a child who initially appeared to be in need of a lengthy FBA and PBS plan but who responded well to the team's PBS plan after an initial meeting of the team. Jerry attended a general education class for students in the fourth grade for all subjects except written language. He was well liked by his peers and was considered a leader. He had a quick sense of humor, played guitar, sang, and loved all sports. Until the third grade, he struggled to identify letters of the alphabet and had difficulty connecting sounds to symbols when reading and writing. During the last academic year, however, he had suddenly made unprecedented growth and was now reading on a third grade level. His time in the resource room for students with specific learning disabilities (SLD) had been reduced from 90 minutes per day to 30 minutes per day. He had been assigned to a lower functioning reading group in his general education class, a group that was using the third grade general education textbook.

A PBS team had been assembled at the request of Jerry's teacher and mother. He had begun to get into fistfights on the playground, was sent to the office several times for throwing food in the cafeteria, and was refusing more and more often to attend the resource SLD class at his scheduled time. When parents and school officials attempted to talk with Jerry, he provided little information or insight. His most frequently repeated comment was "I'm not stupid!" During the person-centered planning meeting, the parents reported that Jerry's sister, Julie, is 15 months younger than Jerry and attends the second grade. Julie was recently placed in a third-grade book due to her accelerated reading level. Jerry had received all reading instruction in the SLD resource class prior to this year and was not as aware of the differences between his progress and his sister's progress in this area. Jerry had begun to refuse to read to his parents at home from the same book that his sister had. Jerry's classroom teacher then added that she had heard some of the students in her class refer to the SLD resource class as the "retard" class or the "slow learning for dummies" class. She had not heard anyone make fun of Jerry directly, but she had stopped a few of the students from teasing other children on several occasions.

The team decided that Jerry's behavior reflected his growing awareness of other students' perceptions of SLD, along with the realization that his younger sister had mastered his present level of functioning in reading. Without proceeding through the other steps in the FBA process, the team began to develop a plan. Parents requested that Jerry be served on a consultative basis for his SLD. The general education and special education teachers agreed that with his present level of achievement, his motivation, and the support he had at home from parents, he would benefit from ongoing but less obvious instructional interventions. In addition, the general education teacher offered to meet with the school's curriculum specialist to identify an alternative textbook for her fourth-grade students who were reading on a third-grade level. This would avoid the embarrassment Jerry felt over being assigned to the same book that his sister had.

The guidance counselor offered to initiate a series of lessons on diversity and disabilities with an emphasis on celebrities with SLD during her weekly visits to Jerry's classroom. She offered to allow Jerry and his parents to check out books about performers and sports heroes who had SLD from her resources. Some of these biographies were written at Jerry's reading level. The special education teacher asked to borrow a few to use in developing written language materials that Jerry and other classmates could use during lessons in the general education class.

The principal decided to invite Jerry to participate in the student court system that the school had established for dealing with nonviolent behavior problems. He believed that Jerry would benefit from discussions with other students by gaining some insight into his own behavior, by becoming more aware of cause and effect with regard to the decisions that he made, and by having a positive leadership role in school that extended beyond his own peer group.

Jerry responded immediately to the changes made at home and at school. He resumed his previously positive and achievement-oriented behaviors and handled minor conflicts without resorting to throwing food or fists.

Due to time constraints, other teams may not be able to take the time this team took to look at Jerry's situation from all perspectives. When members of a team attempt to address problems similar to Jerry's in isolation from other sources of information, erroneous assumptions are made that negatively impact the student. Jerry might have been assigned to an anger management class or a class for students who bully. This would not have addressed his frustration and embarrassment over his disability. Jerry might have been offered rewards for good behavior and punishments for noncompliant behavior. This would not have addressed his frustration and embarrassment over being assigned the same book his younger sister was assigned or being singled out to go to a different room for extra help.

It is important in the development of an FBA and a PBS plan to remember that each member of the team has valuable but incomplete information to share. Parents are the experts on what happens at home and in the community. The general education teacher is the expert about what happens in the classroom. The administrators or coaches are the experts on what happens in less structured environments like the bus circle, the cafeteria, and the playground. When developing an FBA and a PBS plan, it is essential to remember that the whole is more than the sum of its parts. We would not want a doctor to decide that we needed a particular type of medication or an invasive operation based on only one lab test or the examination of one symptom. The outcome of such an approach to our medical condition might be positive. The physician might beat the odds once in awhile with that approach. I, personally, would run from such a doctor. Likewise, when deciding how to proceed with complex behavioral issues, it is essential to attend to multiple settings, tasks, developmental issues, and a student's history. Again, it is a bit daunting to consider conducting a person-centered plan, given the time constraints under which schools operate; but bringing critical people together for an hour during the initial phase of a PBS process can save precious time for all the reasons provided earlier.

Step 3: Data Collection

Sometimes the meeting designed to build consensus and share background information does not result in a clear understanding of the nature and needs of a student's behavioral challenges. A review of a student's school records should have been conducted prior to the first PBS team meeting. Information from formal and informal academic testing, health records, discipline files, psychological reports, report cards, and social histories can be invaluable in assisting the team in understanding a child's strengths and needs. Even after a review of the student's records and a meeting to discuss other information PBS team members have, the behavior problems may not appear to follow a discernible pattern. The team may not have enough information to form a hypothesis about the function of the behavior.

Data must be collected to guide the team in understanding what the child is attempting to get and/or avoid. The team members should agree on one or two behaviors that they will observe over a period of 3 to 5 days. If the behavior is initially defined in general terms, for example, defiance or a tantrum, the team leader should further question members to clarify in behavioral terms exactly what the student does that is of concern. Defiance might be described as times when the student (a) refuses to follow an adult's directions, (b) verbalizes the intent to refuse to follow directions, or (c) screams, stomps feet, and walks away from an adult making a request. The behavior of concern needs to be clearly defined to facilitate data collection and communication.

Once the team agrees on the behavior or behaviors of concern, a variety of data collection strategies can be implemented. Antecedent, Behavior, and Consequences (ABC) Charts, scatter plots, structured interviews, and Likert scale–type assessments are useful in identifying patterns of behavior related to setting, tasks, time of day, materials, and function of the behavior. For students who are not able to participate in a structured interview, the Functional Analysis Screening Tool (FAST) developed by Iwata (1995) is quite helpful. The teacher, parent, and other personnel familiar with the child identify a behavior of concern, answer a series of questions in relation to the identified behavior, tally the responses, and consult a scale that identifies the function of a behavior. This assessment can be downloaded free of charge from Georgia's Behavioral Intervention Program Web site at www.pbsga.org/forms.htm. Additional forms designed for data collection and the implementation of interventions are also available on that Web site.

Specific behaviors can be measured in terms of frequency, duration, and intensity. Selecting the most appropriate method for measuring a behavior is important in the ongoing assessment of the PBS plan. If a student gets out of his or her seat for brief periods of time several times an hour, the team might decide to keep a record of the frequency of the behavior. If the out-of-seat behavior occurs infrequently but for longer periods of time, the team might decide to keep a record of the duration of the behavior. The intensity of a behavior is rarely measured in a school setting, but it would be possible, if the school had the tools required to measure the decibels of the sound a child made, for example. In some cases, the student throws items and destroys materials, draws disturbing pictures, or writes inappropriate words or phrases. Taking a sample of these behaviors by either taking a photograph or preserving samples is useful. Different forms designed for recording data can be examined in Figure 7.1 and in Appendix A. An additional resource, the *Facilitator's Guide, Positive Behavioral Support* (Hieneman et al., 1999), is available online at no charge at www.fmhi.usf.edu/cfs/cfspubs/psbsguide/facilitatorguidepbs.htm. It also contains helpful information and a variety of ready-to-use forms for facilitating the FBA and PBS plan processes.

When involved in data collection, select the most appropriate methods given the nature of the behavior under consideration. It is not desirable to collect more data than is necessary. Generally, a scatter plot is necessary only when the team is unable to identify a pattern of occurrence. If the behavior is predictably occurring at times of transition, at lunch, or during specific academic classes, the ABC chart is sufficient. As explained earlier, either the frequency, duration, or intensity of the behavior should be measured. It is rarely necessary or helpful to measure all dimensions of a behavior. Keep only enough data to assist in forming a hypothesis about the function of the behavior and to determine the efficacy of the PBS plan.

Step 4: Data Analysis

Once the data have been collected, the team will need to examine the data to determine the function of the behavior. Behavior is purposeful. The student is attempting to get or avoid a tangible object, an activity, the attention of peers, or the attention of adults. Sometimes the behavior has two functions. The student is, for example, attempting to avoid an academic task and get the attention of peers. An examination of Brad's and Jesse's data reveals the process that their PBS teams use to determine the functions of their behaviors. An ABC chart is helpful in this analysis because the consequences of the behavior provide clues about the function of the behavior. If students do not want to do a math worksheet, they may learn that calling the teacher an inappropriate name results in being sent to a time-out carrel where they escape the task. Part of the intervention for this behavior will include attention to the required tasks during math instruction. A punishment for calling the teacher names and a reward for completing the math assignment might be insufficient to change the behavior if the team also has academic assessment information that reveals significant learning problems in the area of math. A strategy

Figure 7.1   Sample Data Collection Forms

Individual Instructional Contingencies

Student's Name _____

Date _____

Evaluator(s) _____

Instructions:

1. Scan the components of instruction on the left side of the following table, labeled Individual Instructional Contingencies. Put an X next to instructional factors that have been determined to have positive or negative effects on the student's performance.

2. On the right side of the same table, record behaviors noted on anecdotals, scatter plots, interviews, student work, or other forms of documentation.

3. Next to the behaviors noted, record the source of the evidence. For some types of problems, an examination of the actual lesson content as recorded in the teacher's lesson plans might be required as part of the analysis process.

4. On the table labeled Instructional Themes, record themes noted from the four major components of instruction. Identify the behaviors and/or learning problems of concern. Write a hypothesis statement for each behavior or academic concept or skill identified. Develop an intervention for each hypothesis statement.

Anecdotal Records

Student _____   Observer _____

Targeted Behavior(s) _____

Time/Date	Setting	Antecedent	Behavior	Consequence

Suggested Charting Codes

Setting		People		Task	
CL Classroom	WG Whole Group	TR Teacher	SD Sit down	Sci Science
PG Playground	SG Small Group	PL Principal	Wkst Worksheet	LN Listen
PE Physical Education	IN Independent	AP Assistant Principal	RD Read	CL Color
CF Cafeteria	WP With Partner	BS Behavior Specialist	MTh Math	MP Manipulatives
HL Hall	AT At Desk	IA Instructional Aide	LA Language Arts	CP Computer
C/B Car/Bus Loading Area	OF On Floor	OS Other Student	SS Social Studies	SL Stand in Line

Individual Instructional Contingencies

Student's Name _____

Presentation	Behavior/Evidence
_____ **Pace** (Rate of speech and/or nonverbal cues)	
_____ **Modality** (Visual, auditory, tactile-kinesthetic, combination)	
_____ **Intensity** (Volume; visual characteristics: number, hues, size; texture)	
_____ **Materials** (Preferences related to modality, level of engagement)	
_____ **Task Variation** (Active/passive, simple/complex, long/short, nonpreferred/preferred)	
_____ **Topic/Content Area** (Relevant, meaningful)	
_____ **Difficulty Level** (Cognitive, social-emotional, motor)	
_____ **Length of Lesson**	
_____ **Partial Versus Whole-Task Training**	

Response	Behavior/Evidence
_____ **Pace** (Wait time, optimum rate for attention maintenance)	
_____ **Modality** (Visual, auditory, tactile-kinesthetic, combination)	
_____ **Intensity** (Volume, motor response, product quantity/quality)	
_____ **Materials** (Preferences related to modality, level of engagement)	
_____ **Task** (Active/passive, simple/complex, long/short, nonpreferred/preferred)	
_____ **Topic** (Relevant, meaningful)	
_____ **Difficulty Level** (Cognitive, social-emotional, motor)	
_____ **Error Analysis** _____ Skill(s) _____ Concept(s)	

Scheduling	Behavior/Evidence
_____ Time of day	
_____ Transitions	
_____ Sequence of activities	
_____ Interaction of activity sequence and length	

Setting	Behavior/Evidence
Space/Location _____ Carrel _____ Desk _____ Small room _____ Large room _____ Noninstructional area/inside _____ Noninstructional area/outside	
Grouping Configuration _____ Alone _____ One-on-one with an adult _____ Small group/adult support _____ Small group/peers _____ Large group/adult support _____ Large group/peer buddy _____ Large group/no individual support	

Instructional Themes

Presentation	Response	Scheduling	Setting

Target behavior(s)/academic concept(s): These rows need more space. Give each item at least 3-4 rows for writing information.

Hypothesis(es):

Intervention(s):

Scatter Plot

Student _____   Observer _____

Targeted Behavior(s) _____

Times/Setting/Activities/People	Dates

A. Write time, setting, and task-specific information in the left column and the observation date(s) on the column headings across the top.

B. Identify the behavior(s) to be observed. If more than one behavior is being charted, designate a letter or symbol for that behavior.

C. Place the letter or symbol for the behavior in the box that corresponds to the time/task row and the date column. If the target behavior does not occur, leave the box blank.

Suggested Charting Codes

Setting		People	Task	
CL Classroom	WG Whole Group	TR Teacher	SD Sit down	Sci Science
PG Playground	SG Small Group	PL Principal	Wkst Worksheet	LN Listen
PE Physical Education	IN Independent	AP Assistant Principal	RD Read	CL Color
CF Cafeteria	WP With Partner	BS Behavior Specialist	MTh Math	MP Manipulatives
HL Hall	AT At Desk	IA Instructional Aide	LA Language Arts	CP Computer
C/B Car/Bus Loading Area	OF On Floor	OS Other Student	SS Social Studies	SL Stand in Line

Point Card

Name _____ Day _____ Level _____ Date _____

Returned Signed Card [ ]   Bus Points [/]   Comments

Follow staff directions.

Remain in assigned area.

Complete assigned tasks.

Target behavior:

Balance [ ]

_____   _____   _____
Teacher's Signature   Student's Signature   Parent's Signature

Target Behavior Data Collection Sheet

Student's Name _____   Dates _____

Follow staff directions. _____

	M	T	W	Th	F	M	T	W	Th	F	M	T	W	Th	F	M	T	W	Th	F
100																				
90																				
80																				
70																				
60																				
50																				
40																				
30																				
20																				
10																				

Remain in assigned area. _____

	M	T	W	Th	F	M	T	W	Th	F	M	T	W	Th	F	M	T	W	Th	F
100																				
90																				
80																				
70																				
60																				
50																				
40																				
30																				
20																				
10																				

Complete assigned tasks. _____

	M	T	W	Th	F	M	T	W	Th	F	M	T	W	Th	F	M	T	W	Th	F
100																				
90																				
80																				
70																				
60																				
50																				
40																				
30																				
20																				
10																				

for integrating different sources of information about the function of a behavior is illustrated in Figure 7.2.

The analysis of behavioral data should result in a hypothesis statement that includes (a) the conditions under which the behavior occurs, (b) the behavior of concern, and (c) the function of the behavior. This statement defines the foundation of the PBS plan.

Step 5: Positive Behavior Support Plan Development

Once the function of a behavior has been identified, the team is ready to develop a PBS plan. The plan should include educative strategies, environmental interventions, methods and schedules of reinforcement, and a crisis plan if the behavior of concern includes potentially harmful or excessively disruptive behavior. Educative strategies include skill instruction in behaviors that are incompatible with the behavior of concern, cognitive behavioral training to address inaccurate beliefs or attributions, and academic accommodations or modifications, when needed, to decrease avoidance behaviors. Environmental interventions include schedule changes, seating options, the size or aesthetics of a space, lighting, temperature, and access to people or objects.

In addition to attending to multiple components of support for the student, the PBS plan should also include shared responsibility for implementing the plan. One person should not be expected to implement all parts of a plan. Jerry's team shared responsibility for intervention implementation across the guidance counselor, the general education teacher, the special education teacher, the administrator, the parents, and Jerry himself. When students are old enough, it is important to include them. They can and should be expected to take responsibility for their part in the acquisition of skills and other forms of accountability.

Step 6: Data Collection and Plan Revision

Once a plan has been designed and implemented, it is important to continue to collect data at predetermined intervals. This data will assist the PBS team in determining the effectiveness of the PBS plan. Initially, the student's behavior can be expected to increase. Over a period of 3 to 4 weeks, however, the team should begin to observe a decrease in problem behaviors. As problem behaviors diminish in frequency, duration, or intensity, the PBS team may need to adjust the PBS plan to respond more effectively to the student's strengths and needs. Some interventions may need to be faded. If the student does not respond favorably to the PBS plan, the team can use the data collected to assist in making decisions about further adjustments to the PBS plan. An examination of Jesse's FBA and PBS plan illustrates the components and benefits of using the PBS approach to problem solving and intervention development.

■ **JESSE**

Jesse's PBS team was composed of his grandmother, the behavior specialist, the special education teacher, the classroom instructional aide, and an

Figure 7.2   Jesse's Data

Scatter Plot

Student ___Jesse___

Observer ___Behavior Specialist___

Targeted Behavior(s):
① Verbal demands directed toward staff
② Physical aggression toward environment
③ Physical aggression toward staff

DATES

Times/Setting/Activities/People	9/16	9/17	9/18	9/19	9/20	9/23	9/24			
9:30/CL WG TV Announcements	①②③	①②③③	①	①	①②③	① ④	②			
9:50/CL SG Math	① ① ③ ②②③③	① ① ②	①		① ①	②②③				
10:30/CL IN MTh WkSht	①② ①② ③②	①② ①② ③	① ①	②	① ① ①	① ① ①				
11:00/CL SG Earned Activity	①② ②③ ③	① ① ② ① ①	②	③	①②③	①②② ①③				
11:20/CF Lunch	①①①① ②②③③	①①① ②②②③③	②	BS w/ class	BS w/ class	student went home	Suspended			
11:50/CL One-on-one RD	① ② ①②③③	① ② ①②③	③	④	①	②③③				
12:30 Escorted by a staff member to a special bus ～										

A. Write time, setting and task specific information in the left column and the observation date(s) on the column headings across the top.
B. Identify the behavior(s) to be observed. If more than one behavior is being charted, designate a letter or symbol for that behavior.
C. Place the letter or symbol for the behavior in the box that corresponds to the time/task row and the date column. If the target behavior does not occur, leave the box blank.

Suggested Charting Codes:

Setting		People		Task	
CL	Classroom	TR	Teacher	SD	Sit down
PG	Playground	PL	Principal	Wkst	Worksheet
PE	Physical Education	AP	Assistant Principal	RD	Read
CF	Cafeteria	BS	Behavior Specialist	MTh	Math
HL	Hall	IA	Instructional Aid	LA	Language Arts
C/B	Car/Bus Loading Area	OS	Other Student	SS	Social Studies

WG	Whole Group			Sci	Science
SG	Small Group			LN	Listen
IN	Independent			CL	Color
WP	With Partner			MP	Manipulatives
AT	At Desk			CP	Computer
OF	On Floor			SL	Stand in Line

(Continued)

Figure 7.2 (Continued)

Anecdotal Records

Student __Jesse__   Observer __Instructional Aide__

Targeted Behavior(s):
① Verbal demands of staff
② Aggression – environment
③ Aggression – staff

Time/Date	Setting	Antecedent	Behavior	Consequence
9:50/9/18	CL	SG Mth w/MP Adding sums to 12	High pitched voice followed by feigned crying "Help me." Repeats request calmly	Use your Big Boy voice
10:30/9/18	CL	IN Mth Wksht w/MP	→ Repeat of SG incident	Teacher smiles, pats Jesse too, & shows him how to make 2 sets
11:02/9/18	CF	Asks repeatedly for BS	Compliance followed by small snack (8 Peanut halves) w/ teacher request to raise hand then Throws food / knocks over garbage can ... BS comes	
9:50/9/19	CL	SG Mth w/MP	Whines/Demands 3xs. Throws 2 xs knock chair over. Hits teacher	
10:30/9/19	CL	IN Mth wksht w/MP	Whines. Throws	
11:02/9/19	CF	Asks repeatedly for BS	Throws food. Throws open milk carton	BS Called
9:50/9/20	CL	SG Mth w/MP	Whines/Demands 2xs	
10:30/9/20	CL	IN Mth wksht w/MP	Whines/Demands 5xs	
11:20/9/20	CF	BS sits nxt to Jesse	Jesse smiles, eats, + interacts w/ BS + OSs	BS, teacher, + cafeteria aid praise Jesse

Suggested Charting Codes:

Setting

CL	Classroom	WG	Whole Group
PG	Playground	SG	Small Group
PE	Physical Education	IN	Independent
CF	Cafeteria	WP	With Partner
HL	Hall	AT	At Desk
C/B	Car/Bus Loading Area	OF	On Floor

People

TR	Teacher	BS	Behavior Specialist
PL	Principal	IA	Instructional Aid
AP	Assistant Principal	OS	Other Student

Task

SD	Sit down	Sci	Science
Wkst	Worksheet	LN	Listen
RD	Read	CL	Color
MTh	Math	MP	Manipulatives
LA	Language Arts	CP	Computer
SS	Social Studies	SL	Stand in Line

administrator. At the initial meeting to discuss Jesse's behavior, all team members agreed that Jesse's need for adult attention and acts of physical aggression directed at staff and the environment were of greatest concern. During the person-centered planning process, team members learned a number of important facts about Jesse's past and current situation.

Eight-year-old Jesse had a history of sexual abuse, was abandoned by his mother and father, functioned cognitively in the low-average range of intelligence, exhibited mid to late kindergarten skills in reading and math, and was on several different types of medication. His sleeping tended to erratic. When he had not had enough sleep, he was more likely to become aggressive. The team's dreams for Jesse included academic achievement, the development of friendships with adults and peers, and meaningful participation in groups. The team's fears were that without intervention, Jesse would live his entire life in institutions.

Because Jesse's aggressive behavior at school was most frequently observed to occur when he was tired, when he wanted to escape an academic task, or when he wanted the behavior specialist's attention, the team did not need to go through all steps in the FBA process. The special education teacher regularly used a daily point card that served as a modified scatter plot and had included anecdotal information on the point cards that provided information about the antecedents and consequences of Jesse's behavior. The behavior specialist and administrator had discipline records that included ABC chart information that supported the teacher's observations. In addition, the grandmother shared that at home, Jesse engaged in similar behaviors whenever she tried to do anything alone. She was not able to sleep, bathe, or toilet without Jesse demanding to be present.

The PBS team organized all the information collected and developed a hypothesis. A sample of a chart that can be helpful in the organization and analysis of data is provided in Figure 7.3.

The hypothesis that the PBS team developed after analyzing data collected on Jesse's behavior was that when he was tired or did not want to complete a task, he would throw materials; knock over furniture; and hit, kick, or scratch staff in order to avoid the undesired task and gain access to the behavior specialist. Based on that hypothesis, the PBS team designed the following interventions:

Environment

Jesse was seated near the dry erase board used for instruction and was provided more space around his desk than other students. He was seated in close proximity to the teacher. Jesse was given only the materials he needed to complete the assigned task. He was not permitted to have a pencil box, books, or other items in his desk. The student who sat next to him was quiet, friendly, and not prone to behave in aggressive ways. Jesse was shown a corner of the room with a comfortable cot he could use if he felt too tired to participate.

Instruction

Instructional interventions included teaching Jesse to ask for what he wanted or needed; providing multiple, brief, and highly engaging academic

Figure 7.3   An Analysis of the Data: Hypothesis Development

Student's Name _____ Sources of Information _____

Given these conditions,	the student does this (describe behaviors):	to get or avoid this _____.
Physical state:		**To Get:**
		Attention
Home or community factors:		Tangible
		Sensory stimulation
The immediate task, subject, and/ or materials:		Control
		To Avoid:
The people in the environment:		Attention
		Tangible
The environmental conditions:		Sensory stimulation
		Control

tasks; and providing choices for materials used during some of the tasks. Jesse's target behavior on his daily point card was "Use words to ask for what you want or need." His academic assignments were designed to be similar to the ones his classmates were expected to complete, but they were modified to meet his instructional needs. Instead of giving him a large worksheet with addition facts to compute, he was given a half sheet with 10 facts, provided with a brief break, and given the second half of the sheet. When using counters, he would be given two small bowls in which to place the number of counters that corresponded to the number in the addition problem. This allowed him to more easily manipulate and organize the counters. Counters and other manipulatives were made of foam, paper, or cardboard to reduce the likelihood of injury if he used them inappropriately. He liked using highlighters, markers, and stickers, so those were incorporated into his daily assignment plan.

Reinforcement

Jesse had developed a positive and trusting relationship with the behavior specialist. Unfortunately, he had also learned that if he hit the teacher, the behavior specialist would come to remove him from the room. Jesse was inadvertently being reinforced for his inappropriate behavior. To change Jesse's behavior, the PBS team decided to intervene at several levels simultaneously.

1. The teacher and behavior specialist explained to Jesse that they were very happy that Jesse liked having special time with the behavior specialist. Jesse was told that he would have the privilege only when he made good choices and used his words to ask for what he wanted and needed.

2. Jesse responded well to being given attention every 3 minutes, so the teacher and instructional aide took turns going to his desk every 3 minutes to give him a high five, pat his shoulder, praise his work, or provide him with a small snack when his work was complete.

3. Jesse was provided with a ticket for using words to ask for what he wanted or needed. This ticket represented 1 minute with the behavior specialist. Jesse was also able to earn additional bonus tickets for completing tasks without becoming upset, remembering to follow classroom rules, and playing cooperatively with a classmate during earned time activities.

4. Jesse was allowed to use the cot anytime he asked. He knew, however, that access to earned time activities was contingent on completing academic tasks.

5. The behavior specialist joined Jesse's class in the cafeteria each day during the initial implementation of this plan. Jesse was allowed to cash in his tickets for time with the behavior specialist after eating his lunch.

Crisis Plan

During the initial phases of this PBS plan, Jesse attempted to access time with the behavior specialist by throwing items; knocking over furniture; and hitting, kicking, and scratching the teacher and instructional aide. When frequent praise and friendly reminders to use words did not help, the teacher and instructional aide restrained Jesse and provided him with a safe, secluded place to calm down. During this time, Jesse was not left alone. He was monitored, and his behaviors were recorded at 2-minute intervals. As soon as he was under control, he was asked to use his words to ask for what he wanted or needed. When he was able and willing to return to class, he was escorted to his desk to resume his assigned task.

Follow-Up

Over a short period of time, Jesse's need for staff attention at 3-minute intervals extended to 5- to 7-minute intervals. He engaged in aggressive behaviors less frequently. Prior to the implementation of the plan, Jesse had engaged in aggressive behaviors three to five times in a 4-hour reduced-schedule school day. After the implementation of the PBS plan, his aggressive behaviors occurred less than one time per day. In addition, Jesse began to make academic progress and looked forward to playing with other children during earned activity periods. His grandmother reported that he expressed positive feelings about coming to school and was proud of his new academic skills for the first time in his life.

Jesse's history and psychiatric issues present serious and lifelong challenges for treatment. A PBS plan will not cure the multiple cognitive, emotional, and physiological disabilities that Jesse has. A PBS plan will provide Jesse with the best that educators have to offer in terms of behavioral treatment, instruction, and an increased quality of life.

For folks who wonder if all the work is worth it for young people like Jesse, I would say without hesitation, "Yes!" Anything we can do to reduce the pain, suffering, and proclivity for aggression in the life of a child is worthy of our time and effort. The benefits for the child and for society at large are immeasurable.

■ BRAD

Brad's PBS team was composed of his mother, the special education teacher, the behavior specialist, the reading specialist, and an administrator. Brad lived with his mother and an older sister. His father wrote to him occasionally, but he did not live in the same state and rarely visited. Brad had a history of sexual abuse and had been diagnosed with ADHD. He took a psycho-stimulant for the ADHD. He often complained of being hungry, but he would refuse to eat when given anything other than candy or cookies. His doctor was concerned about keeping him on his medication if he continued to lose weight. A review of Brad's school records revealed that he had an average IQ and severe short-term processing deficits that impacted his progress in reading and math. He was in the third grade and read on a beginning first-grade level. In math, he functioned on a second-grade level. He was an avid consumer of natural science videos and demonstrated a talent for visual arts of all types. He was most focused and content when painting, drawing, constructing a complex geometric pattern from blocks, or modeling a figure from clay.

The PBS team was most concerned about Brad's constant references to topics related to either elimination or sex and his tendency to climb under furniture or into garbage cans. Regardless of the academic lesson or earned activity in which he was engaged, he would sing graphic songs, expose himself, draw pictures of people urinating or defecating, make breasts or penises out of crumpled paper or clay, or move his hips back and forth in an effort to act out sexually on another person's backside, a table, or a desk. Some days were better than others. On his most challenging days, he would make as many as 12 to 15 inappropriate comments and gestures in a 30- to 45-minute period. Brad clearly needed to learn alternative strategies for expressing feelings, wants, and needs. To most effectively support his growth, however, the team needed to identify when he engaged in these behaviors, when he refrained from engaging in these behaviors, and what the function of these behaviors was in different settings. The PBS team identified the ability to participate appropriately in a group, meet his needs in socially acceptable ways, and achieve academic success as their dreams for Brad. Their fears were that Brad would be removed from school, become a dropout, or be arrested as he got older if he did not learn more acceptable ways to behave. His circle of support at home was his mother, sister, grandmother, and doctor. His circle of support at school was his special education teacher, the reading specialist, the behavior specialist, and the administrator. Barriers to achieving success included his ADHD, processing deficits, and the effects of his prior sexual abuse. Potential sources of assistance included school personnel and resources, community-based counseling, parent support group, and participation in a community-based art education program with the assistance of a respite care mentor.

To determine a hypothesis about Brad's problem behaviors, the PBS team decided to collect additional data. Brad's mother and teacher completed a FAST (Iwata, 1995), the behavior specialist completed a scatter plot over a 5-day period that included frequency data, the teacher provided ABC charts for 3 of the 5 observation days, and the administrator reviewed Brad's prior discipline reports seeking any discernible patterns in the antecedents and consequences related his target behaviors. The team reconvened the next week to analyze the data.

Brad appeared to engage in problem behaviors when he was attempting to avoid an undesired academic task or attempting to gain the attention of an adult—particularly when he was angry. The anecdotal records revealed low rates of problem behaviors when he was actively engaged in tasks that required the manipulation of objects or other types of active participation and higher rates of problem behaviors when he was asked to complete worksheets. The PBS plan was developed to address Brad's comments and actions related to elimination and sex. Because crawling under furniture and into garbage cans was less frequent and occurred as a more extreme response that began with the other behaviors under consideration, the team decided to make environmental changes and not address those behaviors separately. Brad's target behavior was to express his wants and needs with school-appropriate language. The plan included the following:

Environment

1. Place the 30-gallon garbage can in the storage closet after breakfast and lunch to make it inaccessible to Brad.

2. Remove all items from his desk. Provide instructional and earned activity items on an as-needed basis.

3. Position his desk near the teacher and the dry erase board used for instruction.

4. Provide additional personal space around his desk.

5. Seat another student on only one side of him. That student should be one who is not easily distracted by inappropriate comments and actions.

Instruction

1. Offer choices for completion of academic tasks and materials whenever possible.

2. Provide instruction in groups of two to three students to ensure active participation and constant monitoring.

3. Use success-oriented strategies such as direct instruction, response card drills, and self-checking materials.

Introduce new concepts by using concrete examples and previously mastered material. Follow a progression of instruction that begins with concrete, easily manipulated objects, then moves to two-dimensional paper representations (photographs, charts, graphic organizers) and finally to abstract strategies (logic, formulas, mnemonic devices). When teaching fractions, for example, engage Brad in making a set of manipulatives by folding and cutting different colors of construction paper. The black piece can be kept whole. Red can be cut into two equal pieces, blue into four, green into six, and purple into eight. For the first few days of instruction, Brad can be asked to identify how many pieces of red equal a black, blue equal red, and so on. After Brad is comfortable with the manipulatives and easily understands that different combinations of pieces can equal the same area, the concepts of numerator, denominator, and equivalent fractions can be introduced without overwhelming him. As he masters the concepts, the paper fraction strips can be replaced by a two-dimensional bar chart illustrating equivalent fractions. Over time, the equivalent fraction chart can be removed as Brad's understanding of how to compute equivalent fractions mathematically is established.

1. Teach Brad to recognize when he is making inappropriate gestures and comments. Begin by providing a teacher-directed visual cue. On the dry erase board near his desk, place stars (representing bonus points) to the right of his name and friendly reminder lines to the left of his name when he talks about elimination or sex or makes an inappropriate sexual gesture.

2. Prompt Brad to identify and express his feelings, wants, and/or needs when he begins to show signs of distress. Sometimes his inappropriate behaviors were preceded by drawing pictures, tearing paper, and whining about not wanting to complete a task. Before Brad used inappropriate language, made inappropriate gestures, or climbed under furniture and into the garbage can, the special education teacher or instructional aide would prompt Brad to talk about his wants and needs.

3. Whole-group affective education lessons were developed to address three types of irrational thinking: demanding, copping out, and overgeneralizing. Brad engaged in recognizing these thinking patterns when watching brief cartoons, listening to teacher-selected stories, and examining his own responses to daily classroom tasks. He also learned to rephrase those thoughts in ways that helped him feel calmer and happier.

4. The behavior specialist, administrator, and school resource officer talked with Brad about appropriate times and ways to discuss sexual topics.

5. Brad's mother was given information about a counseling program in the community that addressed childhood sexual abuse. She and Brad attended sessions there.

6. Brad's mother was given information about a community-based art program for youth. Brad could not attend alone because of his behavioral issues. A mentor was located through the counseling center. The mentor went to the art lessons and enrichment activities with Brad on weekends.

Reinforcement

1. Brad earned bonus points throughout the school day for completing assignments, raising his hand and waiting to be recognized, remaining in his assigned area, and making appropriate comments.

2. If Brad made fewer inappropriate gestures and comments than was targeted for an identified period of time, he earned an additional 50 bonus points or a snack of his choice. Because his average baseline rate of inappropriate comments and gestures was 12 before lunch and 18 after lunch, the PBS team decided to reward Brad for making 10 or fewer inappropriate comments or gestures before lunch and 16 or fewer inappropriate comments or gestures after lunch. As Brad improved, the target number of inappropriate comments or gestures required to earn the reward decreased. In addition, he was eventually taught to self-monitor without the assistance of the teacher. Brad was able to use his bonus points to purchase a variety of activities and tangible items that included time and materials needed to complete art projects, small action-oriented toys, time to play computer games, and edible items such as granola bars, peanuts, and pudding. Note: Many teachers, administrators, and parents balk at the notion of rewarding a student who has made 10 inappropriate comments and gestures. They often want to see immediate compliance and total perfection before providing reinforcement. Unfortunately, a child who has been engaging in a behavior at high rates of frequency for a long period of time is not likely to stop the behavior entirely just because a plan has been established. Some essential rules for the PBS team to follow when designing a reward system include:

   a. Reward successive approximations to the goal. Think in terms of shaping behavior over time rather than making immediate changes.

   b. Move from adult-directed to student-directed strategies as the student's skills increase.

   c. Plan to fade the external supports (prompts and tangible or token rewards) in a systematic way over time.

   d. Provide a menu of reward options to facilitate the student's continued interest in the program. Students with ADHD often baffle parents and teachers because their interests can change so often. Don't expect an item of interest from one day or week to sustain the child over time.

   e. Provide options that are logical and well integrated with the overall plan. Having Brad use his talent for art to assist with instructional routines and engaging him in choices about instructional materials to be used in the completion of his assignments allowed him to use his strengths and meet his needs within the context of the overall instructional plan.

3. Brad was encouraged to share his art with the class and was assigned the task of illustrating academic concepts in math, science, and social studies for use on the bulletin board.

4. Brad's mother agreed to purchase art supplies and video games that he could use at home contingent on appropriate school behavior.

5. When academic tasks were completed, Brad was allowed to select from an array of earned activity options. His usual preferences were painting, modeling with clay, playing computer games, and making intricate designs with attribute blocks.

Crisis Plan

Brad occasionally needed to be removed from the class to regain self-control. If he exposed himself, he was removed from class immediately. When he began to make inappropriate comments and gestures, the teacher would prompt him to rephrase or self-correct. If he did not respond to teacher redirection, the use of the cool-off carrel, and a brief discussion with the behavior specialist, he was removed to a secluded room until he was able to comply with routine requests. During the time in the secluded room, he was not left alone. His behaviors were monitored and recorded every 2 minutes. When he had demonstrated the ability to comply for 5 to 15 minutes (depending on the severity of the behavior problems exhibited), he was returned to class. Any work not completed during the time away from class had to be completed before he could gain access to the earned activity period options. He did not earn bonus points or the 50 additional points during the period he was removed from class.

Follow-Up

Brad's progress was extremely slow initially. During the first 3 weeks of the implementation of the plan, his behavior problems actually increased. Some PBS team members wanted to abandon the PBS plan because of the spike in inappropriate behaviors. The behavior specialist and special education teacher urged the team to continue with the plan for a few more weeks. Over a period of 3 months, Brad's frequency of inappropriate comments and gestures decreased to 2 to 3 per week. He began to earn Turn-Around Student of the Week and Student of the Week awards in his class; his academic achievement levels and confidence in his own abilities improved dramatically—especially in reading; the garbage can was no longer put in the storage closet; and he began to eat some of his breakfast and lunch regularly.

Of particular interest was the improvement in behaviors that were not specifically targeted. One of the mistakes that folks make with students like Brad who have so many behavioral issues is to try to address everything of concern simultaneously. Refusing to eat, climbing under furniture, and climbing into the garbage can were problems, but they were not as central to meeting his primary need behaviorally, which was to learn to express his wants and needs within socially accepted limits. Brad believed that he was stupid. He had learned that he would be removed from academic tasks if he made inappropriate comments and gestures. He had also observed others making those types of comments and gestures to express anger. By understanding his problem behaviors as communication issues and an ineffective method for expressing anxiety and anger, rather than as discrete or separate acts of defiance, the PBS team was able to design a plan that protected Brad from emotionally overwhelming academic demands, supported his need to contribute meaningfully in the classroom and to have some sense of control over what happened to him there, and facilitated the acquisition of essential communication skills related to identifying and appropriately communicating wants and needs.

BEHAVIOR REDUCTION TECHNIQUES ■

Alberto and Troutman (1990, 2002) identified a hierarchy of behavior reduction techniques that represent a best practices approach to selecting alternatives for addressing behavior problems. In general, it is best to address as many problems as possible through the manipulation of environmental and task variables. Rather than reinforcing compliance and punishing noncompliance with regard to kicking over garbage cans, for example, it is easier and more effective just to remove the garbage cans until the student has learned alternative ways to meet needs. The first level of behavior reduction techniques involves the application of differential reinforcement. Reinforcing low rates of behavior, other behaviors, incompatible behaviors, or alternative behaviors takes the student's and staff's attention off the problem behavior and teaches the student that his or her needs and wants can be best met in other ways.

Differential Reinforcement

Sometimes differential reinforcement alone is insufficient. When a particular behavior has been working predictably and efficiently for a student, he or she is not likely to change the behavior—especially if the replacement behavior is more difficult to execute or does not as predictably have the desired result. In those cases, reinforcement for the problem behavior is terminated. This is called extinction. An example of this pairing of behavior reduction techniques is illustrated in a common classroom scenario. A boy tells jokes to make classmates laugh as a strategy for avoiding academic tasks. The teacher reinforces the student for on-task behaviors by providing him with Comedy Corner tickets to be redeemed at an appropriate and regularly scheduled talent show time in the weekly schedule. The student will be allowed to perform only if he has a targeted number of tickets. The teacher also convinces his classmates to ignore his jokes during work periods (removing the reinforcement of peer attention) through a classwide reward system. The student no longer has an audience during work periods and can more easily gain access to preferred activities and items through on-task behavior, so the off-task behavior decreases.

Extinction

Removal of desirable stimuli represents the next level of intervention designed to reduce problem behaviors. The first strategy is called response-cost. During a response-cost intervention, something the student likes, wants, and perhaps has earned is removed. The teacher might remove a

Figure 7.4 Brad's Data

Scatter Plot

Student _Brad_

Observer _Behavior Specialist_

Targeted Behavior(s) (1) Sexually inappropriate behavior: Exposing self, making pauses, talking about sexually explicit topics

(2) Escape behaviors: Climbs under and behind furniture / Climbing in garbage cans

DATES

Times/Setting/Activities/People	9/5	9/6	9/9	9/10	9/11	9/12	9/13
9:30/CL/WG TV Announcements	①	①	①	①			
9:50/CL SG Mth	①	①	②	①	①		
10:30/CL/IN Mth Wksht	②	②	②	②	②		
11:00/CL/SG Earned Activity	①	①	①	①	②		
11:20/CF/WG Lunch	①	②	②	②①	②		
11:50/CL/WG LN Restroom							
12:00/Music, Art/PE.	PE.	PE.	Music Art/PE.				
12:30/WG Affective Ed.	①	①	①				
1:00/CL/SG RD then CP	②	②	②	②			
2:00/CL/SG RD then IN Wksht	②	②	②	②			
2:30/PG/WG Recess	①	①	N. Recess				
3:00/CL/WG Sci or SS	②	②	②				
3:30/C/B Wait for bus	①	①	①				

A. Write time, setting and task specific information in the left column and the observation date(s) on the column headings across the top.

B. Identify the behavior(s) to be observed. If more than one behavior is being charted, designate a letter or symbol for that behavior.

C. Place the letter or symbol for the behavior in the box that corresponds to the time/task row and the date column. If the target behavior does not occur, leave the box blank.

Suggested Charting Codes:

Setting			People		Task		
CL	Classroom	WG	Whole Group	TR	Teacher	SD	Sit down	Sci	Science
PG	Playground	SG	Small Group	PL	Principal	Wkst	Worksheet	LN	Listen
PE	Physical Education	IN	Independent	AP	Assistant Principal	RD	Read	CL	Color
CF	Cafeteria	WP	With Partner	BS	Behavior Specialist	MTh	Math	MP	Manipulatives
HL	Hall	AT	At Desk	IA	Instructional Aid	LA	Language Arts	CP	Computer
C/B	Car/Bus Loading Area	OF	On Floor	OS	Other Student	SS	Social Studies	SL	Stand in Line

190

Anecdotal Records

Student _Brad_

Observer _Instructional Assistant_

Targeted Behavior(s):
1) Sexually explicit talk, exposing self, sexually explicit behavior
2) Climbing under + behind furniture + into garbage cans

Time/Date	Setting	Antecedent	Behavior	Consequence
9:50/9/9	CL	SG/MP Regrouping for sub. from 10s	Put 10s rod on private area + sang "lick my dick" song Repeated behavior	Teacher took manipulatives for 2 min-then returned them Manipulatives removed
10:30/9/9	CL	IN Wksht Subtraction w/ & w/o regroup	Sang "Lick my duck" song Repeat of behavior	Verbal redirection
2:00/9/9	CL	SG/ RD then IN Wksht	One incidence in response to illustration in book (titties)	5 incidents during independent wk period
3:00/9/9	CL	WG		
9:50/9/10	CL	SG/ Review of value of coins/ counting backward forward by 5 + 10s	Participated appropriately touching + counting coins	
10:30/9/10	CL	IN/ construct money chart	Quietly worked on chart	Teacher monitored + provided positive feedback
2:00/9/10	CL	SG/ teased by classmate	Told classmate to suck his duck Climbed in trash can + refused to get out	Teacher attempted verbal de-escalation Redirection Cool off BS
3:00/9/10	CL	WG/ Not allowed to go to recess first to lesson beginning Asked to watch Science demonstration on properties of air	"Lick my duck" song Draw pictures of nude Continued to escalate	Called BS Removal from room

Suggested Charting Codes:

Setting

CL	Classroom	WG Whole Group
PG	Playground	SG Small Group
PE	Physical Education	IN Independent
CF	Cafeteria	WP With Partner
HL	Hall	AT At Desk
C/B	Car/Bus Loading Area	OF On Floor

People

TR Teacher
PL Principal
AP Assistant Principal
BS Behavior Specialist
IA Instructional Aid
OS Other Student

Task

SD	Sit down	Sci	Science
Wkst	Worksheet	LN	Listen
RD	Read	CL	Color
MTh	Math	MP	Manipulatives
LA	Language Arts	CP	Computer
SS	Social Studies	SL	Stand in Line

ticket already earned for on-task behavior if the student tells jokes later in the work period. When teachers use token economy systems in which students earn points, tickets, play money, or some other form of classroom currency, it is common for the plan to include fines for certain behaviors. Teachers may charge points or money for the use of profanity, the destruction of property, or other undesired behaviors. I rarely use response-cost techniques with students who have EBD. Children have difficulty maintaining interest in a reward system if it can and will be taken away. Any use of response-cost should be carefully monitored to protect the reinforcement value of the stimuli being removed. Some suggestions for managing a response-cost intervention imbedded in a token economy system include:

1. Do not take away all of students' points, tokens, or money. Even if they have accrued a major debt, allow them to pay half of what they have at a time until they have taken care of their debt.

2. Offer students choices. If students throw an object, make a mess, or break something, I offer them the choice of making restitution by cleaning up the mess, repairing the object, or helping in some other way. Students can either pay points or work off the debt in "sweat" equity.

Time-Out

The other technique for removing desirable stimuli is called time-out for short, but stands for time-out from positive reinforcement. Adults and peer attention are powerful motivators for most children. Time-out from social environments and from preferred activities can be quite helpful in getting a student's attention and helping him or her learn more socially appropriate ways of behavior. Time-out is, unfortunately, too often overused, misused, and misunderstood. Most teachers enforce some type of time-out for noncompliance. If students want to be part of the classroom—if the activities, people with whom the students interact, and types as well as levels of sensory input are reinforcing—time-out from a desired environment will be helpful in shaping their behavior.

Time-out can occur at different levels. Nonseclusionary time-out occurs when a child remains in the classroom but is not able to earn reinforcers during a period of time. A form of nonseclusionary time-out occurs when a student is seated away from the rest of the group for a period of time. The student can see and hear but is not able to participate. If a student's behavior escalates and becomes too disruptive, exclusionary time-out might be implemented. Students would be removed to another room or placed in a carrel within the room that blocks visual observation. Students who become physically and/or verbally aggressive are sometimes taken to a time-out room for seclusionary time-out. These rooms should be used on a limited basis and within the legal guidelines of the district and state. Parent permission for their use as well as parent notification of each incidence should be documented in writing. At no time should a child be left alone. Constant monitoring during the use of seclusionary time-out as well as ongoing monitoring of the effectiveness of the intervention by the child's PBS team should be implemented.

What if the student hates being in the classroom, has no intention of learning to read, and dislikes the teacher? Time-out will actually reinforce undesired behavior. I have worked with students who so loved spending time alone that I offered them time in a seclusion room as a reward for appropriate participation in class. Threatening them with time-out for refusing to work or interact appropriately was like offering me an all expense-paid holiday to a tropical island. One particular young man named Joe liked being alone and escaping group activities so much that he was placed in a special school for students with severe EBD. He learned that if he cursed, threw books, or threatened people with physical harm, he would be secluded. He increasingly repeated inappropriate behaviors to get access to the seclusion room.

Joe appeared to be depressed when I met him the first time. He did not give eye contact or smile. He used as few words as possible when answering direct questions, never volunteered to talk, and pulled his shoulders down, communicating clearly that he did not want human contact. His records indicated that he had a higher than average IQ and was functioning on or above grade level in all subjects. When asked what he liked and was willing to work to earn, he said, "Nothing." The doodles on his notebook and assignments reflected an interest in drawing. He always carried a fine-tip marker in his pocket and frequently drew intricate pen and ink-style drawings. The "Getting to Know You" survey he completed indicated that he preferred to work alone.

Given his behavioral history at school, his level of academic achievement, and his talent for and interest in drawing, I developed a behavior plan for him that turned the usual punishment and reward system upside down for a while. Joe earned tickets for small increments (10 to 15 minutes) of appropriate classroom behavior. He could use those tickets for time in the seclusion room. In the beginning, he was able to earn 15 minutes in the seclusion room each time he had three tickets. He could save tickets to earn 30 minutes in the seclusion room. Tickets also bought him time with the art teacher, drawing paper, and art supplies. Instead of using a seclusion room for acting-out behavior, he was escorted to the behavior specialist's office when he refused to comply with routine instructional activities. Joe did not like going there. It was a small room that was often full of people and quite noisy. Our classroom was generally quiet. Each student had ample personal space around his or her desk. For most instructional activities, students had a choice of sitting at the group table or remaining at their individual desks.

Aversive Stimuli

The fourth level of behavior reduction techniques includes the presentation of aversive stimuli. Unconditioned aversive stimuli would include physical restraint or spankings. The Council for Children With Behavioral Disorders does not recommend corporal punishment. Some states still allow school personnel to punish students in this way. Restraint should be conducted only by trained professionals and only when verbal deescalation procedures are ineffective and the students' behavior presents a danger to themselves or others. Unconditioned aversive stimuli might include shouting or scolding a child. Conditioned and unconditioned aversive stimuli are not recommended and should be used with caution.

A list of ethical guidelines for selecting and implementing interventions is provided at the end of this chapter. In general, it is considered best practice to use the least invasive and most positive behavior correction technique that is also effective when addressing a student's behavioral problems. Overcorrection procedures represent one type of aversive stimuli, however, that can be useful for some students. Restitutional overcorrection requires the student to restore the environment only to its original condition prior to his inappropriate behavior. If a student dumps a garbage can, for example, he would be required to pick up the trash that fell from that container. Positive-practice overcorrection requires that the student engage in more of the appropriate behavior than would normally be required. A student who knocks over one chair, for example, might be required to unstuck and correctly place 10 chairs. Negative-practice overcorrection requires the student to repeat an undesired behavior multiple times. This might be implemented with a student who repeatedly engages in a particular behavior that might be less desirable if the student had an opportunity to engage in it past the point of interest.

This type of overcorrection is not often implemented, but it was successful with a kindergarten student who did not have flush toilets at home. He kept leaving the classroom to flush every toilet in the boys' restroom. Once the staff required him to flush every toilet repeatedly for an extended period of time, the activity lost its interest for him, and the problem behavior stopped.

■ ADDITIONAL INTERVENTIONS AND RESOURCES

Social Stories

Social stories were developed by Gray and Gerard (1993) to assist youth with autism who were having difficulty understanding specific social situations. Some students who have not been formally diagnosed as having an autism spectrum disorder nevertheless exhibit problems with receptive language and can benefit from the application of this instructional strategy. Social stories focus on a particular targeted behavior or behavioral sequence, such as making choices among activities offered when work is completed or taking turns with a preferred item such as the classroom computer. The social story presents the setting, the conflict, the people and objects involved, setting cues that aid the student in making positive choices, and a successful or satisfactory resolution. Each page of the social story is illustrated. The book is highly personalized, using the student's name as well as the names of specific people, items, and activities related to the targeted behavior. For younger children, photographs are often more effective than symbols or line drawings. The level of pictorial representation should be matched closely to the student's level of understanding and need.

Social Autopsies

Social autopsies were developed by Richard Lavoie (1994) as a method for teaching a student to analyze and evaluate a series of behaviors that resulted in a problem for the child. Once the child understands the chain of events that resulted in the problem, the child can then make a plan for self-correction. Adults sometimes assume that if a child knows the rules and chooses to violate one or more of the rules, the resulting aversive consequence is understood as the logical next step in the chain of events. Good choices result in positive consequences. Bad choices result in aversive consequences. That is the end of the discussion. The case is closed.

Unfortunately, navigating social situations is not that easy to understand. The classroom rules state clearly that students are to remain in their assigned areas; complete their assigned tasks; and keep their hands, feet, and other objects to themselves. Those rules and the resulting consequences for compliance and noncompliance are well understood within a few weeks of school, with appropriate levels of contingent teacher response. What if something happens that is not clearly covered by a classroom rule? Students with limited behavioral repertoires and little prior adult support in problem solving are left to fend for themselves. This often results in less than acceptable behavior.

George's dilemma illustrates the limits of rule setting and the need for a problem-solving model. George desperately wanted to have friends. He had had a rocky school career and had been home-schooled for almost a year due to extremely aggressive and disruptive behavior that was modeled in a home highly charged with domestic violence and aggravated by severe ADHD. George understood that he was not allowed to hit, kick, spit on, or knock down classmates. He had made tremendous progress during the first 3 months of third grade in learning to remove himself to a cool-off area when he felt tense and in using words (quiet, school-appropriate words) to express his wants and needs. He and his parents were quite proud of his new found self-control.

On one particular day, however, George was playing cards with a classmate. The classmate began to make moves that George interpreted as cheating. George expressed his irritation appropriately. The other student explained that he had been taught to play by the alternative rules. Both young men asked for clarification. I helped them come to an agreement about the rules. The game proceeded. Within a few minutes, however, a loud smack rang across the room. The other student had slapped George across the face for accusing him of cheating. Before I could get to the table, George had the student in a headlock. George knew that he was not to hit, kick, slap, or knock down other students. He did what he thought was best in the situation. He did not attempt to hurt the student who had slapped him; he just restrained him until adult assistance arrived.

Unfortunately, the other student reported that George had strangled him, that he could not breathe, and that he felt as if he was going to die. I was close enough to the boys to see that George had not applied pressure to the other student's throat, so George escaped serious disciplinary action by administration. We did, however, need to have a talk about what happened, how the problem could have been avoided, and what to do in the future if he had another disagreement over a game or any other classroom task. The student who slapped George in the face was certainly out of line. He spent time in in-school suspension and engaged in a social autopsy as well. I want to focus on George because (a) he did attempt to make a good choice given a difficult situation; (b) he had a history of violent and aggressive behavior toward peers; and (c) he represents the type of child who is too often blamed because of past offenses, or given minimal attention because of his apparent self-control during the conflict.

When conducting a social autopsy, the first step is to identify the problem. Students often have difficulty correctly identifying the problem. The problem in George's situation began with a conflict over the rules of a card game. When the other student didn't comply with the agreed upon rules, George assumed that the child was attempting to cheat. What in reality had happened was that the other student acted without thinking based on the rules he had been taught previously. If George had simply reminded the student of the new rules or asked for clarification, the other student probably would have apologized and followed the new rules. Once he was accused of cheating, he felt he had to defend himself and acted out inappropriately. George did a great job of exhibiting self-control by not hitting the other student after being slapped in the face. Restraining the other student might not have been the best choice given the setting, the availability of adult support, and the probability that the other student would increase his attempts to hurt George. As we talked through the problem, George agreed that he could have made other choices. In the future, he decided that he would ask the other student for rule clarification instead of accusing him of cheating. He also decided that he would shout, "Stop!" and move toward a teacher if anyone tried to hit him. Figure 7.5 outlines the steps for conducting a social autopsy and George's plan.

Later that day, I took time to talk with both boys together about their plans for handling future conflicts. They were not permitted to play together for the remainder of that day, but they did play cards again during an earned activity period the next day. Both boys followed their plans, were rewarded with praise and positive adult attention, and felt proud of their newfound friendship. Sometimes adults forbid students with a history of fighting to play together. We do children a great disservice when we limit their access to opportunities for growth. This does not allow the students to learn from their mistakes, implement their plans, and practice more prosocial behavior under the guidance and support of adults. We would not deny students who failed a spelling test the opportunity to learn the words missed. Likewise, we must not deny students who make social and behavioral mistakes the opportunity to learn new skills.

Figure 7.5   Steps for Conducting a Social Autopsy (as defined by Lavoie, 1994)

1. Identify the problem.

2. Brainstorm responses that others might typically exhibit in a similar situation.

3. Interpret the meaning of those responses.

4. Develop a plan for responding to the hypothetical responses.

5. Determine criteria for self-evaluating the next time a similar incident occurs.

General Cognitive-Behavioral Curricula

The goal of addressing behavior through a systematic instructional process is to teach students to effectively self-monitor, self-evaluate, and self-regulate their thoughts, emotions, and behaviors. Sometimes a student's behavior is a simple response to an unexpected, short-term, or easily manipulated environmental variable. A child refuses to remain on task during small-group instruction because he or she hates the feel of chalk dust, for example, and is provided with a dry erase lap board as an accommodation.

Sometimes children have not been taught a particular skill such as raising their hand and waiting to be recognized before speaking. The teacher explains the reason for acquiring the skill, defines the context for applying the skill, identifies peers who model the skill, and prompts students by raising her hand and placing her pointer finger over her lips when students forget to use the skill. Students are provided with opportunities to speak when they apply the skill and are ignored when they forget to apply the skill. In a short time, students master the skill, and nothing further needs to be done.

Sometimes students have a skill but find another behavior more efficient. They might grab materials out of other students' hands instead of asking for them. Once again, the teacher implements a brief instructional process that highlights the rationale for using the desired skill as well as the efficiency of simply asking compared to the conflicts and additional punitive consequences that occur when students grab. With consistent attention to the positive behavior, students quickly learn to ask instead of grab. Nothing more needs to be done.

Some children, however, have individual traits and may have also experienced challenges at home or in the community that make the acquisition of social skills more difficult. These children need instruction in identifying the interrelated effects of physiological reactions, emotions, thoughts, behaviors, and consequences. Cognitive behavioral curricula address all five components of overt behaviors and provide information as well as skill instruction on effectively integrating thinking, feeling, and behaving. In addition to the cognitive-behavioral curricula suggested in Chapter 4 for use with the whole class, the following materials and resources may be of assistance when addressing the needs of individuals with specific and more intensive behavioral challenges. Some of the resources listed below are designed to be used directly with youth. Others provide invaluable information and intervention suggestions for parents and educators.

1. *Think Good—Feel Good: A Cognitive Behavior Therapy Workbook for Children and Young People* (Stallard, 2002). This book provides a review of the cognitive-behavioral research, suggestions for addressing the needs of children under the age of 12, interactive lesson plans with reproducible worksheets, and additional online resources and support. The author, Paul Stallard, is an experienced clinical psychologist who has conducted extensive research in the application of cognitive-behavioral techniques in the treatment of childhood posttraumatic stress disorder.

2. *The Explosive Child* (Greene, 2001). This book is written for parents and educators about the nature and needs of youth who are easily

frustrated, chronically inflexible, and prone to temper outbursts characterized by physical or verbal aggression. The author describes the differences and similarities of youth with ADHD, bipolar disorder, or oppositional defiant disorder and those with a still-unnamed disorder he refers to as inflexible-explosive disorder. This book provides parents and educators with an understanding of the physiological and neurological processes as well as the language-processing deficits that children and youth with this behavioral profile exhibit. This book offers concrete guidelines for working with the child to strengthen communication skills and develop a repertoire of socially acceptable coping skills.

3. *Putting on the Brakes: Young People's Guide to Understanding Attention Deficit Hyperactivity Disorder* (Quinn & Stern, 2001) and *The "Putting on the Brakes" Activity Book* (Quinn & Stern, 1993). These companion books are useful in teaching students with ADHD about their disorder and how to manage the challenges while taking full advantage of the benefits of this condition.

4. *Shelley, the Hyperactive Turtle* (Moss, 1989). This wonderful story can be used in explaining ADHD to younger children.

5. *The ADD Answer: How to Help Your Child Now* (Lawlis, 2004). This is a resource for parents and educators who are working with children who have ADHD. Like some of the others mentioned in this section, this book is not a curriculum, but it is a valuable resource for those interested in facilitating academic and behavioral growth in the life of a child with ADHD.

6. *It's Nobody's Fault: New Help and Hope for Difficult Children* (Koplewicz, 1996). This book is written primarily for parents and educators. Dr. Koplewicz explains the neurological and biochemical components of disorders such as ADHD, obsessive compulsive disorder, conduct disorder, phobias, social anxiety, and others. He provides additional information on medications, treatment, parenting, and school-based interventions.

7. *The Difficult Child* (Turecki, 2000). This book is useful in analyzing a child's behavior to distinguish between learned behavior problems and characteristics of temperament that are biologically determined. Dr. Turecki guides the reader through the research on temperament, describes processes for correctly categorizing behaviors as learned or biologically determined, and helps establish effective plans for managing each type of behavior.

8. *A Mind at a Time* (Levine, 2002). This book addresses learning and behavior problems through the perspective of a physician concerned with neurological development. Many of our youth with more extreme behavioral and learning problems have neurological strengths and deficits that are poorly understood and rarely addressed in the typical school environment. This book offers classroom-based examples of differences among learners and strategies for addressing those differences.

9. *Youth Suicide: What the Educator Should Know* (Guetzloe, 1989). This is one of the most comprehensive books on childhood and adolescent depression and suicide available to educators. The guidelines for working

with children and youth who exhibit signs of depression are essential for educators to understand and apply.

Aggression Replacement Training

Arnold Goldstein (1988) developed a systematic approach to teaching students to recognize and manage aggression. Many students are not aware of the physiological warning signs that they are becoming increasingly upset until they lash out verbally or physically. Goldstein's structured approach includes assisting youth to recognize their personal triggers, identify the accompanying physiological signs of distress, and develop the strategies and social skills necessary for avoiding the escalation of a conflict situation.

Curriculum written specifically for children who are 8 to 14 years old includes helpful illustrations, interactive questionnaires, role-plays, and games that facilitate students' understanding and skill mastery. Terry Trower's (1995) *Self Control Patrol Workbook* translates the research on anger management into a child-friendly format. A game by the same name that was developed by Dr. Playwell (a.k.a. Dr. Larry Shapiro) can be purchased through Childswork, Childsplay at www.childswork.com or by calling 1 (800) 962-1141. This company publishes a large assortment of books, games, and affective lesson-support materials that can be used with individuals, small groups, and large groups. Free registration to several newsletters related to classroom and school-based mental health issues is also available at the above-mentioned Web site. Some of the materials that Childswork, Childsplay publishes are exclusively developed for trained mental health professionals and would not be appropriate for classroom use without the support and guidance of a licensed mental health provider. Contact the company and your local supervisor or administrator if you have any doubts about using a particular curriculum or game in the classroom.

Another publisher that specializes in curriculum for children at the elementary level is the Grace Contrino Abrams Peace Education Foundation, Incorporated at P.O. Box 181153, Miami Beach, Florida 33119. Fran Schmidt, Alice Friedman, and Jean Marvel (e.g., 1992) have written books and workbooks at the primary and intermediate levels on the topics of conflict resolution and peer mediation. These materials can also be used with individuals, small groups, and large groups.

In addition to materials that have been specifically developed to teach anger management, real-aloud stories and literature commonly incorporated into the reading and language arts curriculum can be used to illustrate concepts and skills essential to effective anger management. *Aesop's Fables* (adapted by L. Kincaid, 1997) and *The Children's Book of Virtues* (Bennett, 1995) are among the materials I use to facilitate deeper understandings and generate discussions. Children are often able to recognize the ineffective thoughts and behaviors as well as the effective coping strategies of a character in a story. This initial recognition in a nonthreatening, hypothetical context increases their awareness, integrates the emotional content with a broader context, and increases the likelihood that the students will make connections between the anger management lessons and classroom-based experiences.

Social Skills Instruction

Social skills curricula, like anger management curricula, can be individualized, implemented in small groups, or applied to the whole group. Many schools have adopted a character education curriculum that includes lessons on classroom rules, school rules, and the social skills related to the values adopted under the umbrella of a PBS plan or character education initiative. Students from diverse backgrounds may define concepts such as respect and honesty differently than the adults with whom they work. The children may have been raised in a culture that values different character traits as well. A behavior defined as cheating in one culture might be viewed as a spirit of cooperation and respect in another culture. To more completely address the needs of the whole class, especially in the initial stages of developing a classroom culture, refer to the information in Chapters 3 and 4. To address the social skills instruction needs of individual students or small subgroups of students within a large-group setting, consider the following:

1. Students may lack social skills due to insufficient training (skill deficit), or they may fail to use social skills due to insufficient motivation (performance deficit). If a student does not have a skill, instruction is necessary. If a student has a skill but does not use it, reinforcement for using the desired skill is necessary. Remember that behavior serves a function and is typically governed, to one degree or another, by a law of efficiency—the desired skill should not be any harder to perform than the undesired behavior and should result in a more powerful and more predictable reward.

2. Small immediate rewards are more powerful than long-term, distant punishers. Threats to implement a punishment and predictions of future failure are typically ineffective. Praise, pats on the back, smiles, and other social reinforcers should follow the desired behavior constantly in the beginning and intermittently as the skill is mastered. If tangible rewards such as tokens or food are used, pair them with social reinforcers and fade the tangible rewards slowly over time after the student is predictably applying the desired skill.

3. Do not expect a social skills curricula, anger management curricula, or general cognitive-behavioral curricula to work quickly or in isolation of the overall classroom management system and academic instructional plan. Targeted skills for individuals and the whole group must be applied and reinforced throughout the school day.

4. Modeling is an important instructional strategy. Students with EBD do not, however, tend to automatically model appropriate peer behavior. If having positive peer models were enough, no programs for these students would be necessary. To maximize the potential for positive modeling in any environment, (a) attend to the students who are exhibiting the desired behavior first and with the most enthusiasm; (b) ensure that all adults in the environment consistently and predictably model desired behaviors at all times; (c) explicitly define the social skills required for jobs and responsibilities that students value and make the mastery of those

social skills a prerequisite to earning a job or responsibility; (d) systematically recognize students' movement toward mastery; (e) provide visual (pictures as well as words) cues that remind students of the desired skills and their movement toward mastery; and (f) consistently reinforce the efficiency of the skill through discussion, the hierarchy of consequences, the formal curriculum, and recognition of peer and adult models.

Social skills curricula, like anger management curricula, should include child-friendly illustrations, explanations, role-play activities, games, and other support materials designed to facilitate students' understandings of the purposes of social skills, the setting characteristics that govern the application of a particular skill, the steps necessary for executing the skill, and strategies for self-evaluating.

McGinnis and Goldstein (1999) developed a structured learning approach to social skills acquisition titled *Skillstreaming the Elementary School Child*, which includes a developmental hierarchy of skills with their critical components or steps sequentially identified. Skills begin with instruction on how to listen and progress through more complex social skills such as conflict resolution. Support materials contain homework assignment formats to facilitate generalization of skills, structured student journal formats to facilitate reflection and internalization of content, individual and whole-group assessments, and progress charts for recording individual as well as whole-group skill mastery.

Another book I have found useful is *Social Skills Activities for Special Children* (Mannix, 1993). The activities in the book are divided into three broad sections on accepting rules and authority figures, relating to peers, and developing positive social skills. Sample parent letters are provided for each section, and the activities are well structured to maximize student learning and involvement. The book *Skillstreaming the Elementary School Child* (McGinnis & Goldstein, 1999) would be quite useful as a supplement. Other commercially available curricula can be found at At-Risk Resources, www.at-risk.com or 1 (800) 99-YOUTH.

Kid Tools

Kid Tools is a free, downloadable online resource through the University of Missouri, at www.kidtools.missouri.edu/, which was developed by a grant program entitled, Kid Tools Support System (1993). The program includes ready-made, modifiable templates for behavioral contracts, self-monitoring, data collection, and cognitive-behavioral plans. A teacher resource section within the program explains how teachers can engage students in the implementation of the tools within the program at an external level (under teacher direction), in shared fashion (with the student and the teacher collaboratively engaged), or at an internal level (under the student's direction). The program is equipped with primary-level and intermediate-level options. Audible directions are available by clicking on the childlike character that appears on each screen. For younger children, options within the program for developing a behavior contract, a self-monitoring form, or some other behavior management strategy can be accessed by dragging an icon to the desired space on the screen.

Teachers who have taught children to use this program have reported that the children moved more quickly than expected from an external, teacher-directed focus to an internal, student-directed focus because of the high degree of motivation the children had with regard to using the *Kid Tools* (Kid Tools Support System, 1993). This program is well designed for classroom use. A companion tool, *Kid Skills,* focuses on metacognitive strategies essential for academic achievement. Both programs can be downloaded for either Macintosh or PC digital formats.

■ METHODS FOR INTEGRATING INDIVIDUAL PLANS WITH THE GROUP PLAN

In one primary class that I taught, several students with behavioral disorders thought it was funny to tease a child with autism by making sudden movements in his direction. Tyler would feel threatened and begin flapping his arms and squawking like an injured duck. The boys would fall out of their desks laughing at his discomfort. Fortunately, other students in the class were careful not to frighten Tyler. They would walk slowly toward him, announce their arrival if they came from behind, and talk in soothing tones. I began to compliment those students and offer snacks that both Tyler and the other students enjoyed when I saw them working together appropriately. The two students with behavioral disorders quickly began to imitate the students who were being helpful with Tyler. In the beginning, they worked only to earn positive attention from me and the snack that sometimes accompanied the praise. Over time, however, they learned to enjoy helping Tyler without constant adult support or the use of tangible rewards.

Integrating an individual's PBS plan into the overall classroom instructional and behavior management systems is easier if the teacher has already established instructional and behavior management routines that simultaneously allow for individual differences within a structure and predictable pattern of operation that sustains and facilitates growth in all children. All children like predictable schedules. All children need a balance of active and passive activities. All children benefit from the introduction of a variety of concrete, pictorial, and abstract strategies when learning new content or reviewing previously learned concepts and skills. All children need to know what is negotiable and what is nonnegotiable. All children benefit from visual cues and prompts. All children enjoy the power of making age-appropriate choices.

When behavior management is integrated into the overall operation of the classroom and conceptualized in terms of the concepts and skills to be learned, practiced, and reviewed regardless of whether those concepts and skills are primarily related to academic achievement or appropriate social-emotional behavior, integrating an individual's plan into the overall classroom plan is easier to accomplish. Some general guidelines that facilitate the integration of individual plans into the overall classroom management and discipline plan include:

1. Provide visual cues and prompts to assist all students in remembering the rules and expectations.

2. Provide a menu of options from which students can select preferred reinforcers or rewards.

3. Schedule regular review sessions for reteaching and reinforcing behavior skills.

4. Establish a culture of acceptance for differences by celebrating individual strengths and responding compassionately and respectfully to individual needs for support.

5. Provide seating options within the structure of the classroom that reflect the nature of the task and the need of the person engaged in the task. A student with ADHD, for example, may have a hard time focusing during independent work periods if required to sit at a group table. Making seating options available to everyone instead of singling out the student with ADHD reduces the stigma of suggesting that a student move to a more private work station during parts of the day.

6. Provide options within the structure of the classroom for choices of materials and support resources. Students who need to listen to a tape recorder or have earphones when working at the computer so that they can hear part or all of a lesson will accept this accommodation more readily if all students have been encouraged to use the tools most appropriate for their needs.

7. Clearly define negotiable and nonnegotiable requirements for class participation. Do not violate the nonnegotiable requirements when developing an individual's PBS plan.

8. Make a desired reinforcer selected for an individual on a PBS plan available to all other students. Explain that the requirements for earning the reinforcer will vary based on the strengths and needs of each individual.

9. Remember that students' questions about an individual's PBS plan reflect their need to be reassured that they will be treated fairly. If a particular student's needs are extreme, the other students are generally more relieved that the adults are addressing the problems than worried over potentially unfair treatment. Protecting the overall integrity of the classroom behavior support plan, however, is important. Make adjustments either to the classwide plan or to the individual PBS plan to ensure consistency and predictability. One year, for example, I had a child who only responded to edible rewards. He came into the class after we had established a rule about having one snack period in the morning and one in the afternoon. Rather than having all the students angry with the new student and with me or losing control of the whole group because of the new student's need for edible reinforcers, I explained that in honor of the new student, we would be having more frequent, but smaller snacks for a period of time. As the new student's skill mastery allowed for longer intervals between snacks, we returned to our original snack schedule.

10. Teach students to understand behavior and social-emotional issues in terms of skills and thought processes that correspond to increasing levels of responsibility and privilege. Explain that as their skills increase, their responsibilities also increase, along with choices and freedoms that were not available to them at an earlier level of development. One teacher

established a clear link between responsible behavior and privileges by providing each student with a book of coupons at the beginning of the school year. Each coupon represented a level of social-emotional mastery that corresponded to a specific set of choices. Trustworthiness was defined as being honest even when mistakes were made, and following school rules even when a teacher was not present. The corresponding choices and privileges included being a hall monitor, being able to take messages from the classroom to other parts of the school, and being eligible to be a peer buddy to a new classmate during a period of orientation. Establishing such a system from the beginning allows for individualization of behavior support plans by making new responsibilities and privileges targeted for one student available for others as well.

■ THE ETHICS OF INTERVENTION SELECTION AND IMPLEMENTATION

The field of education devoted to teaching students with EBD is relatively new. Scientific foundations are rapidly changing as new technologies allow researchers to observe the brain and its functioning during everyday tasks. Conditions once thought to be under the complete control of the individual are now known to have a biological basis.

Koplewicz (1996), Levine (2002), and Turecki (2000) are among the researchers who caution parents, educators, other professionals, and the general public against assuming that one intervention or professional or theoretical approach represents all one needs to know to effect a cure. Given the diversity of research foundations, skills, and options for interventions currently available, it is imperative that those of us within the education field consider ethical guidelines when working with youth and their families.

The Council for Children With Behavioral Disorders (as cited in Scheuermann & Evans, 1997) published a statement in support of ethical treatment for students with EBD. This statement asserts that above all other considerations, professionals in this field should "do no harm." This mandate to do no harm includes: (a) engaging in assessment processes that are culturally and linguistically appropriate; (b) protecting the confidentiality of information about children, their families, their medical diagnosis, and all other personal data; (c) maintaining a person-centered orientation to planning and intervention; (d) providing state-of-the-art positive behavior support and academic instruction; and (e) collaborating with other professionals and community agencies to maximize the integrity and fidelity of a child's treatment plan. There is no place in this ethical orientation for corporal punishment, abuse of any kind, or neglect. To fail to provide appropriate levels of service for a child who is clearly in need is to commit educational neglect or, in more extreme cases, abuse.

Green (1996) suggests that practitioners develop a habit of healthy skepticism. If an intervention sounds too good to be true, it is probably ineffective at best. In addition, Green suggests that practitioners ask many questions about the research foundations on which a particular intervention program has been based and the efficacy of the program itself as evidenced by empirical studies. In addition to Green's suggestions, Scheuerman and Evans (1997) suggest that practitioners ask themselves if the procedure or assessment appears to be reasonable, given the research and best practice information available at the time; then they should proceed with caution and, when in doubt, wait.

CONCLUSION ■

Federal law (IDEA, 2004) mandates that school personnel address the needs of students with behavioral challenges through the development of an FBA and an individualized PBS plan. Special educators, administrators, support personnel, and general educators share responsibility with parents and the child in the process of increasing the student's likelihood of success. PBS plans include attention to the environment, academic instruction, affective education, reinforcement, crisis planning (when needed), and follow-up. Fewer children require the highly specialized assessments and intervention plans described in this chapter when school-wide, setting-specific, and classroom-level PBS processes have been implemented. For the 1% to 7% who do require the processes described in this chapter, however, the PBS team's time and effort are most efficiently and effectively used when each person on the team knows his or her role and contributes reliably to the ultimate goal—facilitating the growth of a child.

Some children require ongoing support for a number of years. Educators, support personnel, parents, and the children themselves can grow weary. A sense of helplessness and hopelessness can erode even the most highly motivated. Chapter 8 addresses the research on resilience and reasserts the message that giving up is simply not an option.

8

Resilience

INTRODUCTION ■

After several years of working in a segregated center for students with emotional and behavioral disorders (EBD), I returned to general education environments with the belief that what had worked for the most challenging students would certainly work in less restrictive settings. My naïveté and optimistic expectations failed to prepare me for the resistance many educators had to learning about, developing, and implementing effective behavioral and academic programming. Let's face it. Educators have more on their plates than anyone in their right minds would expect of individual professionals: No Child Left Behind, Positive Behavior Support, the Individuals With Disabilities Education Act, increased mandates for collaboration, additional demands for testing, and the pressure for all teachers to be highly qualified to teach all types of students—those with English as a second language, those with disabilities that range from mild learning disabilities to severe emotional disturbances, those from low socioeconomic backgrounds, those from diverse cultural backgrounds, and those with gifts and talents, not to mention the decreasing numbers of so-called normally developing children. So, what makes me think we need more information, well-designed behavior management plans, and success-oriented academic materials and strategies? Those cornerstones of our work are the foundations on which our children thrive and we, as their teachers, survive.

While working as an assistant professor at a college in Georgia, I was contacted by an assistant principal at a local elementary school. The school was located in a low socioeconomic neighborhood. The majority of students lived in poverty. Many did not live with biological parents. Teachers sent students to the office on disciplinary referrals at a rate of 12 to 20 per day. State officials were threatening to put the school on probation due to the students' declining academic achievement levels in reading and math. Fewer than 25% of the students scored on or above grade level on nationally normed tests.

The assistant principal was desperate. She knew that the children in that elementary school were capable of behaving and learning. She also knew that the staff was on the verge of giving up. They had been trained in educational strategies and behavior management techniques, but they did not believe that their training was relevant to the needs of the youth with whom they worked. Cooperative discipline and cooperative learning were not going to work with children who believed that all conflicts should be settled with profanity and physical aggression. Reader's theater and writing workshops sounded wonderful. Unfortunately, the students lacked enough self-confidence even to begin such enriching activities. The teachers firmly believed that home situations had to be corrected before effective teaching and learning could begin.

Because no magic wand was available to change the poverty that engulfed the neighborhood, the assistant principal began to talk about the research on resilience. Together, we developed a carefully scaffolded approach to helping the teachers overcome their own learned helplessness with regard to reaching and teaching this challenging population of young people. That assistant principal very wisely addressed her teachers' deepest fears and most self-defeating thought processes before moving forward with additional training in behavior management or academic instruction. Over a 2-year period, the school went from abysmal failure to award-winning levels of success.

The first step in that process was helping teachers understand the powerful influences they have on youth each day. During our first workshop, the teachers were asked to identify famous people from brief biographical sketches. How many of the resilient souls described below can you identify?

Guess Who

_____1. When I was in the first grade, I had trouble keeping up with the rest of the class. Kids started calling me a dummy. I felt so awful that I started trying to find ways to avoid going to school. My mom told me that the only way to overcome a problem was to face it. I started going to special classes. Mom got me a tutor. With a great deal of effort, I graduated from high school and was granted a scholarship to the University of

Nebraska. I went on to be a five-time Pro Bowl defensive end for the Kansas City Chiefs.

_____ 2. Even as a small child, I wanted to be famous. Perhaps this is because my mother had told me that she could have been somebody if she had not gotten pregnant with me. I lived in an orphanage and with foster parents until I was 3 years old. My mother married eight times. My dad was arrested for drugs and writing bad checks. He was a morphine addict. I was defiant, had low self-esteem, and had a poor attitude. Teachers thought that I was just uncooperative. I found out that I have a learning disability when my daughter began to have trouble in school. We both took some tests. Now I know that I didn't learn to read until I was 18 because of the learning disability. I am not bad or stupid. I just didn't learn things the same way that my friends did. You probably would recognize me for being a singer, actress, and Oscar winner.

_____ 3. I was adopted at birth. My adoptive father was an abusive alcoholic. He hurt and frightened me often. To make matters worse, I had a serious stuttering problem and a learning disability called dyslexia. Because of my dark skin, other kids made fun of me and called me names. By the age of 12, I was so depressed that I began using drugs and attempted suicide. Fortunately, I am very good at swimming and diving. I won my first gold medal in the Olympics in 1984. You can still see me on TV when I make commentaries on special diving competitions.

_____ 4. My dad left my mom before I was born. She moved to Mississippi and gave me to my grandparents. I learned about honest work from my grandfather, who was a farmer. I learned about the power of words from my grandmother. At age 5, I moved to Michigan. By then, I had developed a stuttering problem. I quit talking to anyone other than my best friend, Chubbie, a one-eyed crow, and Shep, the family dog, by the time I was 8. I was afraid that I would be rejected by my family, teachers, and peers if I talked. When I was 15, a teacher thought I had plagiarized a poem. To prove that I had really written it myself, he demanded that I recite it on the spot in front of the class. Everyone was amazed that I had such a rich and moving presentation style. Mr. Crouch, my teacher, urged me to join the debate team. After that, my confidence really began to soar. You know me as the voice of Darth Vadar and Mufasa.

_____ 5. My dad left my mom, brother, and myself when I was young. My mother was a strong person who always encouraged me to strive for my highest level of achievement. Mom and I didn't know that I had a learning disability. By the time I got to high school, things were just too difficult for me. I dropped out of school. I also got involved with drugs such as marijuana and LSD. By the time I was 17, I knew that I needed help. I checked myself into a rehabilitation center. Before I finally got the opportunity to show the world what I could do, I had more rough times. For a while, I lived on welfare. Because of what I know, I do as much as I can for single mothers, drug-addicted youth, those with AIDS, and others in need. I have been nominated for the Academy Award and have received a Golden Globe and Image Award. I was also named the Humanitarian of the Year in 1989 by the Starlight Foundation.

_____ 6. I was born into a large family. When I was young, I was frequently bothered by blurred vision. I required intensive tutoring to get through school and never did really learn to spell. One psychologist described me as an able boy who had established a reputation for thoughtlessness, sloppiness, and inefficiency. I had several false starts in careers before I finally found success. I fought in a war, became a hero, and am best known for having been a President of the United States.

_____ 7. I have Down syndrome. The doctors told my mom and dad that I would never walk, talk, or feed myself. I have achieved many more things than anyone ever imagined possible. I can read at an elementary level, do some math, swim, and hold a job. With the loving support of my family, I followed my dream to become an actor. You have seen me on TV. I also helped author a book and serve as a spokesperson for the Ronald McDonald McJobs Program.

■ RESEARCH ON RESILIENCE

Researchers in the field of resilience have identified risks and assets within individuals, families, and communities that impact the growth and development of youth (Garmezy, 1994; Werner & Smith, 1982). Youth who present academic and behavioral challenges that put them at risk for school failure may encounter one or more of the risk and protective factors listed in Figure 8.1. Use this figure to identify the risk and protective factors of one or more of the famous people featured in the biographical sketches.

Youth who are at risk often exhibit challenging behaviors characterized by combinations of the following attributes: (a) high rates of absenteeism, (b) frequent acts of defiance toward those in authority, (c) poor peer relationships, and (d) inadequate academic achievement (Dugan, 1989; Maguin & Loeber, 1996; Werner, 1996). Risk factors within the student, the family, and the school or community at large that contribute to behavior and academic problems may present an overwhelming constellation of challenges to the youth and those charged with facilitating the youth's growth and success. Researchers have discovered, however, that all risk factors do not have to be eliminated for an individual to self-right. Strengthening the protective factors and reframing potential risk factors as opportunities or challenges rather than problems can often promote success (Garmezy, Masten, & Tellegren, 1984).

During their school years, the people described in the *Guess Who?* section would not have been expected to achieve great things. Many people believed that they were beyond hope. The people who believed that these youth had strengths worth cultivating helped to turn the direction of their lives from mediocrity or destruction to fulfillment and success. Neil Smith's mother did not let him accept his difficulties with learning as an excuse to stop working. Cher had a talent for singing and met a mentor in Sonny who helped her develop that talent. Greg Louganis suffered tremendously at the hands of an abusive adopted parent but was a gifted athlete who eventually earned the recognition and support of coaches, peers, and the general public. James Earl Jones, Whoopi Goldberg, John F. Kennedy, and Chris Burke each in his or

Figure 8.1   Risk and Protective Factors

	Risk Factors	Protective Factors
Individual	Poor impulse control (Garmezy, 1985)	Internal locus of control (Lazarus, 1991; Murphy & Moriarity, 1986; Werner & Smith, 1982)
	Attributions of helplessness (Bernard, 1990; DiGuiseppe & Bernard, 1990; Werner & Smith, 1982)	Sense of humor (Masten, 1994)
	External locus of control (Lazarus, 1991; Murphy & Moriarity, 1986)	School success (Rutter & Quinton, 1984)
Family	Academic failure (Werner & Smith, 1982)	Easy temperament/Able to recruit friends and adult assistance (Garmezy, 1985; Murphy & Moriarity, 1986; Rutter, 1979)
	Relationships with peers who are engaged with antisocial behavior, drugs, or alcohol (Masten, 1994)	Relationships with supportive peers & adults (Marchant et al., 2001)
	Poverty (Werner, 1989)	Parents/caregivers who value an education (Comer, 1988; Marchant et al., 2001)
	One or both parents/caregivers addicted to drugs or alcohol (Berlin & Davis, 1989)	Parents/caregivers who are able and willing to access resources (Sorenson, 1993; Werner, 1989)
		Parents/caregivers who provide healthy limits & age-appropriate supervision (Werner, 1989)
	Single parent/caregiver home (Emery & Forehand, 1994)	At least one adult who has a warm, loving relationship with the child (Werner & Smith, 1982)
		Warm, cohesive family structure (Garmezy, 1985)
Community	Few school resources (Freiberg, 1994; Marchant, Paulson, & Rothlisberg, 2001; Peng, 1994)	Schools with high academic and behavioral standards (Freiberg, 1994; Peng, 1994)
	Unresponsive school personnel (Marchant et al., 2001)	School & teacher responsiveness (Marchant et al., 2001)
	Few opportunities for developing a system of support (Giovannoni & Billingsley, 1970; Hunter & Kilstrom, 1979)	Network of family and community involvement including church attendance (Giovannoni & Billingsley, 1970; Hunter & Kilstrom, 1979)
	Inadequate health care (Garmezy, 1985; Sorenson, 1993)	Adequate health care, housing, food, and transportation resources (Garmezy, 1985)

her own way overcame the odds. Some had supportive family members. Others relied on teachers. Their gifts to the world are varied, but all exemplify what researchers in the field of resilience have discovered.

1. Risk and protective factors reside within the individual, the family, and the community (which includes the school) (Garmezy, 1994; Werner & Smith, 1982).

2. Risk factors do not have to be removed or remediated for an individual to succeed (Garmezy et al., 1984).

3. Teaching a person to compensate for or cope efficiently with a weakness is often sufficient (Garmezy et al., 1984).

4. Identifying and fully developing an individual's strengths and protective factors is essential (Garmezy et al., 1984).

Moderating the risks and strengthening the protective factors is effective in facilitating resilience (Garmezy et al., 1984). Youth who are able to accept responsibility for their present and future well-being by (a) recognizing and changing ineffective thinking processes, (b) communicating wants and needs positively, (c) accepting healthy limits, (d) problem solving, and (e) setting realistic goals can overcome the challenges inherent in their environments. Youth who have at least one adult in their lives who (a) provides warmth and love, (b) communicates high expectations, (c) accesses resources in the community when the need arises, (d) establishes healthy boundaries, and (e) is able to set realistic goals experience an additional level of support that has been found to be effective during the self-righting process.

■ FACILITATING RESILIENCE IN SCHOOLS

Ryan's Story

Ryan was brought to my attention at a school staffing meeting several years ago. His teacher, the guidance counselors, and the school administrators had asked me to attend and offer suggestions. Ryan was in the second grade, was struggling in reading, and had not qualified for special education services after a year of testing, observations, and interventions. His aggressive behavior, however, appeared to be escalating. None of the children in class would sit next to him because he would kick or slap them at random intervals with no apparent provocation. The week before the staffing meeting, he had intentionally slammed another child's head into the bathroom door and thrown a book at the teacher.

The teacher had kept anecdotal records of his aggressive behavior and had completed a teacher questionnaire that indicated the function of Ryan's behavior to be attention seeking and power or control. He was also beginning to avoid reading tasks by crying, crawling under furniture, refusing to speak, or throwing items and threatening the teacher with physical harm. Information from the mother included reports of aggression toward her and a younger sibling, a pattern of noncompliance at home, and inconsistent parental responses to Ryan's violent behavior ranging from passive acceptance to harsh, impulsive retribution. Ryan clearly needed professional support.

The school-based team implemented the following positive behavior support plan:

1. Teach Ryan to use words to express his emotions rather than his feet and fists.
   A. Provide him with anger management training through a guidance counselor-directed group.

   B. Give him a red laminated card to use to signal anger. When Ryan presents the card, he will be allowed to sit in a predetermined place to cool down. He will be encouraged to draw or write about his emotions in a journal. When the teacher has time later in the day, she will talk with him about his drawings and/or writings. He will take the journal to his group anger management meetings and discuss it with the guidance counselor if necessary.

   C. Ryan will earn tickets, points, or some other token reinforcer when he follows the procedure described in B. He will be allowed special one-on-one time with a preferred adult when he has earned a predetermined number of tickets.

   D. If Ryan is able to handle his emotions without using the cool-off area, he will earn bonus tickets. Bonus tickets will gain him access to a menu of reinforcers such as (a) a positive call home to his mother, (b) positive time in the office helping with shredding or some other task, (c) positive time with a custodian, (d) additional physical education time, and so on.

   E. After a period of success, the menu of options will include the opportunity to invite a peer to join him for reward time to help him reestablish positive peer relationships, establish a sense of positive power with peers, and shift his interest in attention from adults to peers.

2. Remove Ryan from all positive stimulation when he hits or kicks. He should have office detention with no opportunities for engaging in fun activities or positive conversations. He might even be expected to pay for aggression with one or two tickets. Take care not to allow him to have a negative number of tickets or constantly return to zero tickets. If he experiences no success, he will not be motivated to continue.

3. Request that a social worker visit the home to discuss a home-based application of the school plan. Mother needs to be taught to disallow the aggression and to reinforce positive behavior.

4. Ask Ryan to attend a peer-tutoring training session with the curriculum specialist. Assign Ryan to be a peer tutor to a first grade student who needs practice reading sight words and simple stories.

5. Allow Ryan to read independent level stories into a tape recorder to share with the student he is tutoring.

6. Provide Ryan with computer games that strengthen his sight word vocabulary and fluency.

The plan outlined above provided Ryan with supportive structures and immediate feedback regarding his expression of want and needs. He learned to control aggressive behavior and looked forward to time with the custodian he selected as the person with whom he wanted to spend positive time. This man had a gruff exterior but expressed enormous love for children. He showed Ryan how to make simple repairs to doors, desks, and chairs. Ryan liked learning to use tools and took great pride in his new skills. He was often called upon to raise or lower a student desk, adjust the legs of a chair, or identify the reason for the squeaks made by rusty hinges on outside doors. Ryan also expressed sadness for the first-grade student who was struggling with reading skills. He was particularly careful to encourage the student and began writing simple stories to add to the collection of tapes, flashcards, and books he shared weekly with the child he tutored.

Unfortunately, problems continued at home. The social worker reported that his mother just wasn't able to implement the suggested behavior plan. Ryan did, however, improve in his reading ability as well as in his ability to form relationships with adults and peers. He never did qualify for special education services and progressed over the period of a school year to the point that he no longer required intensive behavioral and academic support. School personnel did, however, continue to offer supportive mentoring and opportunities for Ryan to have an active and positive role in his classroom group.

The Ryans of this world and the educators who firmly and compassionately reach out to them are my heroes—not the rock stars, movie stars, or sports figures our youth so often want to emulate. In spite of their talents, the love and support of significant people in their lives, and the opportunities in their communities for success, these young people could have given in and given up. They could have told themselves that the struggle wasn't worth it—that the stakes were too high and the rewards too inconsequential. They could have focused on the pain, inequities, and dysfunction within and around them. Instead, they decided one step at a time to move forward.

We must believe in ourselves and in our children to uncover, discover, and nurture the heroes that are already there.

Think of a young person with whom you work who is struggling. Complete Figures 8.2 and 8.3 with regard to that youth. In the section labeled "Targeted Youth," write details about how the risk and protective factors are exhibited.

After investigating a student's risk and protective factors, begin to identify opportunities for strengthening the student's protective factors and moderating the effects of the risk factors. Remember that it is not necessary to eliminate risk factors. Sometimes the most effective strategies focus entirely on accentuating the positive opportunities for growth in a student's life. Brendtro, Brokenleg, and Van Bokern (1990) developed a model for organizing and understanding the self-righting process called the Circle of Courage. Young people require a balancing of their needs for achievement, attachment, autonomy (the ability to make developmentally appropriate choices), and altruism or service. Those at risk are experiencing difficulty in one or more of those areas of need.

Opportunities for meeting needs in the area of achievement are difficult for youth with learning problems to access. Children are particularly vulnerable to inadequate opportunities for attachment. They must attach to an

Figure 8.2   Risk Factors and Potential Roadblocks

Risk Factors	Targeted Youth
Learning problems	
Problems with manners	
Poor peer relationships	
Poor relationships with adults	
Lack of persistence	
Poor impulse control	
Learned helplessness	
Controlled by others	
Few interests	
Few coping strategies	
Difficult temperament	
Other:	

Figure 8.3   Assets and Protective Factors

Protective Factors	Targeted Youth
Wide range of interests	
Easy temperament	
Academic achievement	
Ability to learn	
Sense of morality	
Sense of initiative	
Ability to distance self from harm	
Skills/talents	
Positive peer relationships	
Positive relationships with adults	
Sense of humor	
Problem-solving skills	
Ability to set goals and work to achieve them	
Physical health	
Able to attract positive attention	
Resourceful	
Willing to access support	
Many coping strategies	
Other:	

adult before learning can be maximized. Many children with challenging behaviors do not experience positive relationships with adults in the school environment. Like Ryan, their disruptive and aggressive behaviors tend to escalate until one or more school-based personnel are able to develop the corrective relationships with them that they need.

Restraints on autonomy—opportunities to make age-appropriate choices—are often the first limitation put on children with behavioral problems. The more the children act out, the more restrictive the adults' responses to their behavior become. The children increase their efforts to resist the control imposed on them, and the stage is set for continual and escalating power struggles. Defusing the spiraling conflict cycle requires a commitment to teaching youth to control themselves rather than issuing a mandate for compliance to overwhelming external controls. Behavior management programs that emphasize skill mastery and responsible decision making are in keeping with a culture of respect for the autonomy of the child and with Foundational Principle 1—The only person I can control is myself.

The fourth need identified in the Circle of Courage, altruism, is the one least likely to be included in school programs. Service to others affords students with rich opportunities for learning, developing relationships with others, exploring career options, and feeling a sense of power and self-worth that comes from giving of themselves in a meaningful way. Ryan, for example, met his need for altruism through the tutoring of a younger child. He strengthened his own decoding and sight word skills during those peer tutoring sessions. He also found it difficult to see himself as incapable while helping another.

In Figure 8.4, school-based opportunities for meeting the needs identified in the Circle of Courage (Brendtro et al., 1990) are listed as a point from which to begin the brainstorming process with regard to your own classroom, school, and community.

Figure 8.4   Circle of Courage (based on Brendtro, VonBockern, & Brokenleg, 1990)

Achievement

- Strategy instruction
- Curriculum modifications
- Precision teaching
- Direct instruction
- Cooperative learning
- Social-skills training
- Conflict resolution
- Portfolio development

Attachment

- Clubs
- Mentoring
- Athletics
- Peer buddies
- Student assistants
- Classroom grandparents
- Home and community projects

- Block scheduling
- Multiyear teaching
- Cooperative learning
- Curriculum development: relevant themes
- Effective behavior management

Autonomy

- Peer mediation
- Assignment options
- Self-advocacy training
- Age-appropriate choices

Altruism

- Peer mediation
- Classroom jobs
- Cross-age peer tutoring
- Service learning projects

Use the planning format in Figures 8.5 and 8.6 for the youth you identified earlier as you think about ways to strengthen opportunities for achievement, attachment, autonomy, and altruism, given the student's individual constellation of protective and risk factors.

Figure 8.5   Protective Factors and Opportunities for Success

Achievement	Attachment	Autonomy	Altruism

Figure 8.6   Risk Factors and Opportunities for Moderating Their Effects

Achievement	Attachment	Autonomy	Altruism

■ A PROFESSIONAL RESPONSE TO DIFFICULT PARENTS

Collaborative, supportive home-school alliances provide children with multiple protective factors simultaneously. Children are presented with clearly defined rules, expectations, and recognition for academic achievement and appropriate behavior. Unfortunately, parents of children with EBD often struggle to maintain a balance between their need to protect and advocate for their child and their need to work with school personnel. One of the challenges parents must overcome is the process of grief and acceptance that can occur when the children they have are not the easily managed children they expected to have.

Some parents are unsure about age-appropriate social-emotional, cognitive, and behavioral expectations. They either expect too much from their children and punish them for being unable to comply or expect too little and overindulge the children. These parents can benefit from information about age-appropriate expectations and basic principles of discipline (Appendix B provides a package of information to copy and give to parents). The parents who have not resolved their own feelings of anger, guilt, shame, or sadness may have difficulty responding effectively to educators' efforts to help.

Figure 8.7 describes behaviors that are typical of parents at specific stages of grief and acceptance and strategies that educators can implement to increase the likelihood of developing a collaborative relationship with them. It is important to continue to attempt to communicate with the parent about the student's strengths and potential for future success. Make telephone calls at least three times per semester, just to compliment the

Figure 8.7   Stages of Grief and Acceptance

Stage	Parent Behavior/Response	Professional Response
Shock, disbelief, and denial	Guilt or shame Deny or discount the severity of the symptoms of the disability Shop for a more acceptable diagnosis Completely refuse to accept any diagnosis *and* the necessary supports	Listen with acceptance Encourage the expression of emotions Assure parents that the emotions are normal Share the child's strengths with the parents When the parents are ready, direct them to appropriate resources and services
Anger and resentment	Express anger toward those who are trying to help Resent friends who have children who do not have disabilities Attempt to argue with professionals Attack professionals and blame them for not "fixing" the problem(s)	Practice reflective listening Encourage parents to express anger and resentment Refrain from arguing with parents Refrain from becoming defensive when attacked verbally
Bargaining	Believe that if they do what they are told, the disability will disappear Bargain with God—"I'll do _____ if you take this away" Be vulnerable to intervention scams, charlatans, and folk remedies	Practice active listening Show support Avoid forcing your viewpoint on the parents Avoid criticism Provide information that will assist them in selecting the best intervention or service
Depression and discouragement	Begin to accept reality and grieve over the loss of the child they expected Be unable to look at the child's potential and see only the child's deficits Isolate themselves and the child from family, friends, and the community Have little energy for or interest in interventions or services	Practice active and reflective listening Suggest resources (respite, parent support groups) Discuss counseling options Discuss the child's strengths Match the parent with another parent who has reached acceptance
Acceptance	Begin to see the child's strengths instead of focusing on his/her needs May begin to take a proactive approach to facilitating their child's growth	Continue to listen Praise progress Continue to accentuate the child's strengths Begin to relinquish the role of case management to the parents Support the parents' sense of empowerment Encourage them to reach out to other parents who are still grieving
Important points to remember	The severity of the disability as well as the cultural beliefs, familial support system, and professional support system available to the parents or guardians affects the initiation and progress of the stages. As the child reaches a chronological age associated with important developmental milestones and fails to master critical developmental skills, the parents may go through one or more of the stages again. As the family reaches important periods of transition, the parents may go through one or more of the stages again. The stages tend to be revisited and tend to follow a cyclical rather than a linear pattern.	

Note: As defined in O'Shea, D. J., O'Shea, L. J., Algozzine, R., & Hammitte, D. J. (2001). *Families and Teachers of Individuals With Disabilities*. Boston: Allyn & Bacon.

child. Send postcards with positive messages at least once each grading period. Remember that the parent is doing the best that he or she knows how to do—even if the parent's behavior is difficult to understand. Remember, also, that the parent will be less effective if he or she is continually angry with the child over school-related issues.

Occasionally, I have taught children whose parents were abusive in response to notification of the children's misbehavior or who reacted punitively when the children did not have perfect days. Those parents need education. The children need protection. In those cases, I sent only messages about positive behavior home with the children until the parents and I had developed a clear communication process and a mutually acceptable, collaborative discipline program.

■ A RATIONALE FOR STRENGTHENING PROGRAMS FOR CHILDREN WITH EMOTIONAL AND BEHAVIORAL DISORDERS

Children are vulnerable to the weaknesses in our school programs because they have fewer resources with which to make decisions and change the situations they encounter. The factors listed below represent a review of the risks embedded throughout this book, as well as opportunities for life-changing intervention in the lives of children.

1. Among the multiple risk factors that affect students with EBD, low achievement in reading (Coutinho, 1986) and poor general performance across academic content areas (Foley & Epstein, 1992; Forness, Kavale, Macmillan, & Duncan, 1996; Meadows, Neel, Scott, & Parker, 1994) contribute significantly to increased behavioral problems, entry into the juvenile justice system, high dropout rates (64% for youth with EBD), and post–high school functioning characterized by high rates of incarceration and dependence on social services (American Psychological Association, Commission on Violence, 1993; Nelson & Pearson, 1994; Walker et al., 1995).

2. Youth who exhibit antisocial, aggressive behavior can be reliably identified as early as 3 to 4 years of age. The more severe the antisocial behavior patterns, the more stable the behaviors tend to be over time. The stability of statistical measures for aggression exceeds those of IQ over the life span. If these antisocial behavior patterns are not corrected by 8 years of age, the behaviors will present long-term challenges to intervention (Short & Shapiro, 1993; Walker, Colvin, & Ramsey, 1995).

3. Youth who attend highly structured, segregated school programs designed to meet the academic and behavioral needs of students with EBD exhibit higher rates of behavioral success and academic achievement (Carlberg & Kavale, 1980; Jacobson, 1987; MacMillan, Gresham, & Forness, 1996; Sparks, 1980). Schneider and Byrne (1984) reported that youth with EBD who attended programs for severe emotional disorders for 1 to 2 years exhibited higher rates of academic and behavioral success. Elementary-age youth successfully left programs for severe emotional disorders at a rate of 47% and a mean stay of 2.5 years.

4. Explanatory style is established as early as age 7. Youth who have experienced crisis, trauma, repeated failures, and harsh, demeaning disciplinary actions are at risk for developing learned helplessness (Seligman, 1995). Early corrective experiences during the elementary years, as well as direct instruction in learned optimism beginning in Grades 4 and 5, can provide students with the cognitive skills necessary for reframing life experiences, learning from mistakes, and overcoming risk factors associated with learned helplessness, such as chronic underachievement, poor interpersonal relationships, depression, and health problems (Seligman, 1995).

5. Students in programs for severe emotional disorders require a wider range of as well as higher rates of support services at the elementary levels than at the middle school and high school levels (Rockwell, 1999). Younger students are more dependent on the immediate environment. This increases the likelihood that they and their families will need a wider range of support and more frequent access to social work services, speech and language therapy, occupational therapy, physical therapy, licensed mental health services, constant monitoring to ensure physical safety, respite care for families, family counseling, wrap-around services, monitoring of medication, and intensive behavioral interventions requiring a team-based approach.

6. Children with diverse learning needs who do not develop academic skills at the same rate as peers are often described as lazy, noncompliant, disorganized, or passive when presented with an academic task. Researchers have discovered, however, that the challenges these students must overcome are more complex than surface behaviors alone might indicate. In addition, the complexity of the learning challenges creates a cumulative effect on achievement as students move from one grade level to the next (Baenen, Glenwick, Stephens, Neuhaus, & Mowrey, 1986; Collins, Dickson, Simmons, & Kameenui, 1995; Gresham, MacMillan, & Bocian, 1996; Meadows et al., 1994; Schneider & Byrne, 1984). An expanded list of characteristics common among learners with diverse needs, along with interventions found to be effective in research studies, includes the following:

    A. Low-achieving students lack sufficient knowledge of (a) self as a learner (Billingsley & Wildman, 1990; Palincsar et al., 1991); (b) task demands (Billingsley & Wildman, 1990; Palincsar et al., 1991); (c) how, when, and why to apply skills and strategies (Billingsley & Wildman, 1990); and (d) the resources needed to complete a task (Billingsley & Wildman, 1990).

    B. Low-achieving students require explicit instruction in skills and concepts. Their ability to learn incidental or tacit knowledge is poor (Chan et al., 1987; Rottman & Cross, 1990; Schunk & Rice, 1992).

    C. Low-achieving students require explicit instruction in generalization strategies. They do not make connections between skills and concepts within one content area or between skills and concepts across content areas without direct, teacher-mediated instruction (Chan et al., 1987; Schunk & Rice, 1992; Simmonds, 1990).

    D. Low-achieving students often lack background experiences with content-related prerequisite skills and concepts (Weisberg, 1988).

E. Low-achieving students require explicit instruction to link prior knowledge with current content (Weisberg, 1988).

F. Low-achieving students benefit from instruction in self-monitoring. They often make poor use of time and other resources because they don't know what they don't know (Malone & Mastropieri, 1992; Schunk & Rice, 1992).

G. Low achievers attempt to avoid feelings of failure by engaging in one or more of the following behaviors: (a) withdrawing, (b) feigning interest, (c) shifting blame to an external agent, (d) selectively forgetting assignments or completing the wrong assignment, (e) procrastinating, (f) cheating, and (g) lowering expectations of self (Paris et al., 1991).

H. Low-achieving students often generalize a sense of failure in one area to a low perception of competence across all academic tasks. They exhibit a sense of low perceived competency in spite of average or high ability (Johnston & Winograd, 1985; Paris et al., 1991).

I. Low-achieving students benefit academically from attribution training. In studies that included academic strategy instruction without direct instruction in the covert cognitive components associated with learned helplessness, students did not exhibit increased academic achievement levels to the same degree as those who had instruction in academic strategies and attribution training (Schunk & Rice, 1992).

As the list above indicates, interventions for children with challenging behaviors must be multifaceted and well integrated. Rewards and punishments alone are woefully inadequate as interventions for the child who has learning, social, emotional, and behavioral problems. Protective structures, direct instruction in academic as well as social skills, attribution training, and opportunities for attachment, achievement, autonomy, and altruism represent the minimal response necessary for facilitating success.

■ FACILITATING EDUCATORS' RESILIENCE

The 1% to 7% of the student population that presents extraordinary levels of challenge can overwhelm even the most dedicated educator. Those who maintain high levels of enthusiasm and productivity over the course of their 20- to 30-year careers have been found to exhibit high rates of self-efficacy (Allinder, 1993). Self-efficacy includes a belief in one's general ability to teach and a belief in one's ability to teach the group of students currently assigned (Allinder, 1993). Unfortunately, teacher education programs rarely have enough time in their curriculum to fully address human growth and development, atypical development, cognitive processes, the full range of exceptionalities, ways to effectively teach students with each type of disorder, and classroom management. A belief in one's general ability to teach increases with time and attention to instructional and behavioral strategy development. Chapters 1 through 5 offer multiple concepts and strategies educators can use to increase their expertise in general. In addition to information offered in those chapters, the suggested readings, and the Web sites provided, educators can join various professional development organizations, attend conference presentations on self-selected topics, and take advantage of Web-based training offered from colleges, universities, and other sources.

To increase a sense of competence with a specific group of students, the information in Chapters 6, 7, and 8 is helpful. Some who required inordinate amounts of time and attention prior to the implementation of strategies described in the first five chapters will blend in with the crowd once environmental and group-oriented strategies are established. Other students may still demand more than their share of the staff's time and attention. Knowing when and how to intervene with students who have more intensive needs reduces stress and facilitates teacher self-efficacy.

When you are faced with particularly difficult students, however, don't try to take care of their needs alone. Every school should have a formal referral process that teachers can use to access the assistance of a guidance counselor, social worker, administrator, or student study team. Informal assistance should also be sought and accepted. Teachers who know the student or family well can be rich resources of information. Support staff in the cafeteria or office may know the child and family as well. Use professional judgment when discussing a student with another colleague or support staff member, but encourage a team approach to understanding and supporting the student. The following research-based attitudes and competencies in the area of behavior management have been found to be associated with teacher efficacy and longevity.

CHARACTERISTICS OF EFFECTIVE BEHAVIOR MANAGERS ■

1. Respect their own strengths and weaknesses as much as those of their students

2. Exhibit empathy and high self-efficacy (Allinder, 1993)

3. Respond calmly and assertively to disruptions (Lavoie, 1996)

4. Demonstrate an awareness of and respect for cultural differences (Kea, 1998)

5. Use what they know about developmental milestones and needs effectively

6. Demonstrate a working understanding of how learning occurs (Alberto & Troutman, 1990, 2002) by:
   a. Clearly communicating rules, goals, and expectations
   b. Establishing procedures for efficiently addressing routine tasks that minimize distractions and opportunities for off-task behavior
   c. Consistently and predictably responding to behaviors
   d. Maintaining a ratio of three positives to every corrective act when dealing with student behavior

7. Discriminate between issues of responsibility and problem ownership. Effective behavior managers do all in their power to prevent a problem but do not take responsibility for the student's behavior by becoming overemotional. They feel empathy toward the student's situation and at the same time allow the student to learn from his or her actions.

8. Analyze (Hewett & Taylor, 1980) the following:
   a. Their own behaviors
   b. Environmental factors
   c. Curriculum and instruction
   d. Students' needs

9. Reframe productively (Katz, 1997; Wolin & Wolin, 1993)
   a. Problem = A challenge that strengthens and motivates growth
   b. Crisis = An opportunity for learning
   c. Disciplinary issue = A prescription for dynamic change at the individual as well as the systems level

10. Effective behavior managers:
    a. Do not publicly embarrass students
    b. Do respect nonverbal cues to refrain from confrontation
    c. Do avoid power struggles with clear communication, consistent responses, and presentation of choices
    d. Do maintain professional responses even during conflict
    e. Do get and keep students' attention
    f. Do look for small movements toward a positive change (successive approximations) instead of expecting immediate and complete compliance or mastery
    g. Do notice and celebrate success!

When not at school or a professional development activity, take time for yourself. I conducted a survey of teachers who worked with students with EBD as part of my master's degree program. I wanted to find out how they coped with the stress of teaching students at high risk. Their self-reports included (a) drinking alcoholic beverages, (b) overeating, (c) talking with colleagues, (d) talking with friends or family members, (e) exercising, and (f) engaging in hobbies. The teachers who had taught high-risk students for 10 or more years reported that they drank alcohol and overate early in their careers; but after the first 2 to 3 years they learned to talk, exercise, and engage in a full life outside of school as a way to facilitate their own resilience.

They also reported that while their increased levels of competence did alleviate a significant level of stress felt in the beginning, the knowledge that what they did mattered—that students did benefit long-term from their positive learning experiences—actually created an ongoing sense of motivation for them. Few teachers of students with high-risk behaviors and challenges get to find out how the youth fared 5, 10, or 20 years later. Without feedback on the delayed positive outcomes that many middle and high school students exhibit in their late teens and early 20s, it is easy to wonder if all the drama and hard work is worth our effort.

CONCLUSION   ■

People like Marian Wright Edelman (1992) from Chapter 1, as well as the case of Ryan from this chapter, assure us that our efforts matter. That is why it is helpful to read the literature on resilience. Within the stories of real people are lessons about risk and challenge as well as protective factors and courage. Many people who have overcome the odds against them report that teachers, administrators, coaches, and school support personnel made the difference between giving up on themselves and giving life a chance.

In closing, I'd like to share one more story that illustrates the power of the positive actions we take on behalf of youth. Several years ago, a group of us were sitting on the floor of a lecture hall in a hotel during one of the Council for Exceptional Children conferences before heading to our rooms for the evening, sharing experiences we had had with our students. One high school teacher stopped us all in our tracks as she told us about a young lady in her school who was not in special education classes but who had a nasty attitude. Most of the students and teachers just tried to avoid her. This teacher, however, is very outgoing and persisted in saying hello to her every day as the girl passed her in the hall on the way to a class. Every day, the teacher's cheery attempt to engage the girl in conversation was met with a cold shoulder or rude, abrupt grunt.

Toward the end of the year, however, the girl approached the teacher and quietly asked if they could talk. The two of them ducked into this teacher's empty classroom. After a few tense moments, the girl said, "Do you remember the other day when you said hello to me?" The teacher wasn't sure which day the girl meant, but nodded yes. "Well, I had a gun in my purse that day. I was going to kill myself after school. When I got to my next class, I started thinking about how you always say nice things to me and try to talk to me. I decided that if you thought I was that important, maybe I shouldn't kill myself." No one knew that this girl was having suicidal thoughts. People just assumed that she was a difficult kid and left her alone as long as she didn't cause any trouble for anyone else.

We never know how powerfully our kindness may be perceived in the life of a young person. Those who have their needs met reliably and well in the world beyond the schoolhouse door may not even notice our efforts. The youth who struggle, however, carry our lessons of kindness throughout their lives. What we do matters, and how we do it matters even more.

NOTE   ■

The information about meeting the needs of students at risk is reprinted with the consent of the Council for Exceptional Children from Rockwell, S. (2006). *Tough to Reach, Tough to Teach: Students With Behavior Problems.* Arlington, VA: Council for Exceptional Children.

Appendix A

Forms

Appendix Contents

Individual Development

Developmental Profile

Group Development

How Am I Doing as a Student?
My Success Plan
Grade Graph by Subject
Student of the Week
Turn-Around Student of the Week
All About Me
All About Us!

Academic Instruction

Books I Have Read
Story Map
Word Problem Map
Rubric
Concept Development
Components of Skill Mastery

Behavior Management

Sample Classroom Procedures
Behavior Bingo
Think Sheet for Coping Style Instruction
Classroom Behavior Management Checklist
Classroom Discipline Plan

Data Collection

Individual Instructional Contingencies
Instructional Themes
Anecdotal Records
Scatter Plot
Point Card
Target Behavior Data Collection Sheet

Resilience

Risk Factors and Potential Roadblocks
Assets and Protective Factors
Protective Factors and Opportunities for
    Success
Risk Factors and Opportunities for Moderating
    Their Effects

Developmental Profile

Name _____   School Year _____

Assigned Grade _____   Teacher _____

Years	IQ	Social/ Behavioral		Math	Reading		Language Expressive/ Receptive		Motor Fine/Large
16									
15									
14									
13									
12									
11									
10									
9									
8									
7									
6									
K									
Pre K									

Notes: _____

_____

_____

_____

How Am I Doing as a Student?

• Arrive on time	1	2	3	4	5
• Bring materials	1	2	3	4	5
• Listen	1	2	3	4	5
• Follow directions	1	2	3	4	5
• Complete tasks	1	2	3	4	5
• Math	1	2	3	4	5
• Reading	1	2	3	4	5
• Spelling	1	2	3	4	5
• Language	1	2	3	4	5
• Science	1	2	3	4	5
• Social Studies	1	2	3	4	5

My Success Plan

Name _____   Date _____

What will I be learning this grading period?
What do I already know how to do well?
What do I need to learn?
How will I accomplish my goal?
How will I know if I have met my goal? What data will I collect?

How am I doing?

Dates I will review my progress and rate my level of achievement:

_____ 1 2 3 4 5   _____ 1 2 3 4 5

_____ 1 2 3 4 5   _____ 1 2 3 4 5

Parent Signature _____   **Teacher Signature** _____

Grade Graph by Subject

Student _____ Teacher _____ Grade _____ Dates _____

Subject:

Date:

A. Homework

B. Classwork

C. Test

D. Project

Average:

100	100
90	90
80	80
70	70
60	60
50	50
40	40
30	30
20	20
10	10

Student of the Week

Turn-Around

Student

of the

Week

All About Me

My name is _____

My favorite subject in school is _____

My favorite activities for fun at home are _____

_____

    Rate these activities. A "1" means that you don't care for the activity. A "3" means that it is ok with you. A "5" means that you really enjoy the activity. Circle the number that best represents your feelings.

1	3	5	Watching a video	1	3	5	Helping staff
1	3	5	Cooking	1	3	5	Tutoring
1	3	5	Playing outside	1	3	5	Field trips
1	3	3	Making a craft	1	3	5	Working alone
1	3	5	Playing inside games	1	3	5	Working with a partner

Name 3 people that you would like to have as a partner during group activities.

Name 3 items you would like to purchase from the classroom store.

All About Us!

Watch a video	1	2	3	4	5	6	7	8	9	10
Cook	1	2	3	4	5	6	7	8	9	10
Play outside	1	2	3	4	5	6	7	8	9	10
Make a craft	1	2	3	4	5	6	7	8	9	10
Play inside	1	2	3	4	5	6	7	8	9	10
Help staff	1	2	3	4	5	6	7	8	9	10
Tutor	1	2	3	4	5	6	7	8	9	10
Field trips	1	2	3	4	5	6	7	8	9	10
Work alone	1	2	3	4	5	6	7	8	9	10
Work with partner	1	2	3	4	5	6	7	8	9	10

Books I Have Read

Date	Title/Author	Pages	My Rating: 1 2 3 4 5

Books I Have Read   Page ___

Date	Title/Author	Pages	My Rating: 1 2 3 4 5

Story Map

Title: _____   **Author:** _____

Setting	
Characters	
Problem	
Action 1	
Action 2	
Action 3	
Solution	

Source: Rockwell, S. (2006). _Tough to Reach, Tough to Teach: Students With Behavior Problems_ (2nd ed.). Arlington, VA: Council for Exceptional Children. Used with permission.

Word Problem Map

What is the goal of the problem?	
Draw a picture to illustrate the problem.	
Select the necessary information.	
Decide operation(s).	
Compute: Add, subtract, multiply, and divide.	

Source: Rockwell, S. (2006). *Tough to Reach, Tough to Teach: Students With Behavior Problems* (2nd ed.). Arlington, VA: Council for Exceptional Children. Used with permission.

Rubric

Title: _____

4				
3				
2				
1				

Source: Rockwell, S. (2006). *Tough to Reach, Tough to Teach: Students With Behavior Problems* (2nd ed.). Arlington, VA: Council for Exceptional Children. Used with permission.

Concept Develpment

Concept

Definition & Critical Attributes

Examples

Non-Examples

Components of Skill Mastery

Skill

Application Cues

Examples

Non-Examples

Steps

Self-Check

Sample Classroom Procedures

Entering the Classroom in the Morning

1. Unpack your backpack.

2. Hang your backpack on your hook.

3. Sharpen your pencils.

4. Begin your handwriting assignment.

Preparing for Dismissal

1. Clean your area.

2. Copy homework assignments in your planner.

3. Put items needed for completing homework on your desk.

4. Wait for your row to be called.

5. Get your backpack from your hook.

6. Return to your seat and pack your backpack.

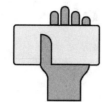

Getting a Restroom Pass

1. Wait until the teacher has finished giving directions.

2. Write your name on the board.

3. Take one of the Restroom Passes from the hook.

4. Go to the restroom.

5. Hang the restroom pass on the hook when you return.

6. Erase your name and return to your assigned task.

Behavior BINGO

Source: Rockwell, S. (2006). *Tough to Reach, Tough to Teach: Students With Behavior Problems* (2nd ed.). Arlington, VA: Council for Exceptional Children. Used with permission.

Behavior BINGO

STOP	Think	Act	Review
Good Choice	Bad Choice	1	2
3	4	5	Ask questions
Sit up	Lean forward	Nod	Track the speaker

Source: Rockwell, S. (2006). *Tough to Reach, Tough to Teach: Students With Behavior Problems* (2nd ed.). Arlington, VA: Council for Exceptional Children. Used with permission.

Think Sheet for Coping Style Instruction

 *Think Sheet*

What was the problem? _____

How did I feel?   Mad   Sad   Glad   Afraid

How did I act?

Shark   Donkey   Ostrich   Teddy Bear   Owl

What would the Owl think? _____

_____

What would the Owl do? _____

_____

What did you do the next time?_____

_____

How will you reward youself? _____

_____

Classroom Behavior Management Checklist

Instructions: Place a check in the blank next to each item that represents a characteristic of your classroom setting, processes, and plans. Insert other information requested in the spaces provided.

Physical Setting

__ Are the walls, floors, and furniture clean and in good repair?

__ Is the furniture adjusted to the proper size for the students?

__ Are bulletin boards and other visual aids at an appropriate height?

__ Are rules, routines, and procedures posted in a manner that is easy to see?

__ Are rules, routines, and procedures posted in a manner that all can read or understand?

__ Are unnecessary and distracting items removed from view and reach?

__ Are materials organized and easily accessible?

__ Do students have secure and adequate spaces for personal storage?

__ Is the furniture arranged to meet instructional goals for grouping?

__ Are areas of the room activity specific?

__ Are the lighting and room temperature appropriate?

__ Is the room an appropriate size for the number of students and the activities planned?

__ Are there choices for student seating arrangements (small group, independent)?

__ Is there space for prominent display of student work?

__ Are items on the bulletin boards and wall academically focused and updated regularly?

__ Is the room attractive and inviting?

__ Has furniture been placed to decrease traffic flow challenges?

__ Have pencil sharpeners and trash cans been placed to decrease student distraction?

Scheduling

__ Is the schedule of activities posted and reviewed regularly?

__ Are independent tasks for students to complete when entering the room posted and accessible?

__ Are transition and noninstructional activities posted and reviewed regularly?

__ Are high and low preference activities alternated?

__ Are high and low interaction activities alternated?

__ Are critical activities scheduled at the most optimum time of the day?

__ Are choices for acceptable activities posted for students who complete an activity early?

__ Are the materials for acceptable activities accessible?

__ Is there a method for reevaluating the schedule regularly?

__ Is there a method for posting changes to the schedule?

Instructional Planning

__ Are lesson objectives developed based on students' functioning levels?

__ Are assignments relevant and meaningful to students?

__ Are materials that students will be expected to use independently selected based on the students' academic achievement levels (reading and math)?

__ Are lesson plans designed to provide options based on student preferences and needs?

__ Are timelines adequate for the tasks planned?

__ Are classroom materials, equipment, and space allotments adequate for the tasks?

__ Do plans include methods for communicating the big ideas in lessons and units?

Source: Rockwell, S. (2006). *Tough to Reach, Tough to Teach: Students With Behavior Problems* (2nd ed.). Arlington, VA: Council for Exceptional Children. Used with permission.

___ Are methods included for assisting students in relating new objectives to previously mastered material?

___ Are learning strategies that help students organize, remember, and use information included in the plans?

___ Are strategies for assisting students in learning new skills and concepts designed to allow for the gradual removal of support as students reach higher levels of mastery?

___ Are connections among the concepts taught in different subject areas directly identified for students?

___ Are review and reinforcement activities planned frequently to allow students to gain fluency with individual skills and retain content cumulatively over time?

Instructional Delivery

___ Are task directions clear and brief?

___ Are oral directions paired with pictures, icons, or written words that students can read?

___ Is the pace of instruction appropriate for the needs of all students?

___ Is sufficient time allotted for demonstration and explanation?

___ Is the time allotted for a specific activity adjusted to meet the needs of all students?

___ Do students have known choices for appropriate activities if they complete a task early?

___ Are nonpunitive provisions made for students who need more time?

___ Are the methods for introducing new content selected with regard for the needs of the students (e.g., manipulatives, audio-visual aids)?

___ Are student checks for understanding conducted frequently?

___ Are strategies used to direct students' attention to important details?

___ Are students grouped according to their instructional needs?

___ Is sufficient time provided for guided practice?

___ Is specific academic praise provided during guided practice?

___ Is corrective feedback provided promptly and positively during guided practice?

___ Is sufficient time provided for independent practice?

___ Is specific academic praise provided during independent practice?

___ Is corrective feedback provided promptly and positively during independent practice?

___ Is the most appropriate instructional strategy (e.g., direct instruction, cooperative learning) used given the content and mastery levels of the students?

Of the instructional tasks listed below, check those that result in the highest level of student engagement for the majority of students:

___ Highly structured independent work

___ Recall tasks (math facts, fill-in-the-blank)

___ Comprehension tasks (multiple choice)

___ Application tasks (problem solving)

___ Evaluation tasks (rating self, others, or items on a predetermined criteria)

___ Cooperative learning

___ Peer tutoring

___ Teacher-directed instruction

___ Computer-assisted instruction

Source: Rockwell, S. (2006). *Tough to Reach, Tough to Teach: Students With Behavior Problems* (2nd ed.). Arlington, VA: Council for Exceptional Children. Used with permission.

Classroom Discipline Plan

Delineation of Roles

List the behaviors that are handled in the classroom:

List the behaviors that are referred to an administrator:

How are behaviors that are referred to administrators documented?

Rules: Behaviors that are expected at all times

__ Are the rules clearly different from procedures that are used for accessing an item or activity?

__ Are rules positively stated?

__ Is the number of rules limited to no more than five?

__ Are the rules worded in observable and measurable terms?

__ Are the rules posted on a chart that is large enough for all to see?

__ Are the rules written in words that all can read and/or illustrated with graphics or icons?

__ Are rules taught and reviewed regularly?

Routines: Procedures for entering, exiting, and accessing an item, assistance, or activity

__ Are methods and times for sharpening pencils, collecting lunch money, and accessing a pass to the restroom clearly posted?

__ Are sufficient opportunities provided for these routines?

__ Are provisions for special needs made with regard to the routines?

__ Are plans for exceptions to the routines and procedures provided for students (e.g., What happens if someone breaks his/her pencil lead before the end of class?)?

__ Are the methods and times for routines aligned with the rules of the class?

__ Are the methods and times for routines aligned with the instructional needs of the class?

__ Are routines taught and reviewed regularly?

Provisions for Monitoring, Teaching, and Acknowledging Behavior

Which behaviors are monitored?

How is the data recorded?

What methods are used to teach desired behaviors and rules?

Source: Rockwell, S. (2006). *Tough to Reach, Tough to Teach: Students With Behavior Problems* (2nd ed.). Arlington, VA: Council for Exceptional Children. Used with permission.

What methods are used to reinforce students who model the desired behaviors?

____ Social reinforcer (praise)

____ Activities

____ Tangibles

____ Tokens/Points

____ How are items and activities selected?

____ Do students and parents have input in the selection of reinforcers?

____ What criteria are used for earning the reinforcers?

____ What criteria are used for using (spending) or obtaining the activities, tangibles, and/or tokens?

____ Is specific behavioral praise provided at a rate of four positives to every one corrective statement?

____ Is specific behavioral praise provided contingent on the demonstration of the desired behavior?

____ Are reinforcers (verbal, nonverbal, items, activities) available to all who earn them?

____ Are reinforcers varied and individualized?

____ Is the schedule of reinforcement varied to maximize effectiveness (constant while students are learning and intermittent after mastering a behavior)?

____ Is data on student performance displayed prominently?

____ Are reinforcement opportunities posted?

Consequences for Behaviors That Violate Classroom Rules

What specific behaviors would violate the classroom rules?

What consequences are used when a student violates a classroom rule?

____ Are the consequences for rule violation sequential?

____ Are the consequences for rule violation educative?

____ Are the consequences for rule violation preplanned and posted?

____ Are the consequences for rule violation explained and reviewed regularly?

____ Are consequences delivered in a calm, matter-of-fact manner?

____ Are students reminded of their choices in a calm, positive manner prior to an escalation in behavior?

____ Are consequences delivered consistently and in a timely manner?

What behavior management techniques and consequences are used in the classroom?

____ Planned ignoring (for what?)

____ Nonverbal warnings (gestures, icons, visual or auditory cues)

____ Verbal warnings

____ Proximity control (adult moves closer to the student without interacting directly)

____ Antiseptic bouncing (removing a student from a situation prior to problem escalation)

____ Humor

____ Direct appeal (just ask the student to stop)

Source: Rockwell, S. (2006). *Tough to Reach, Tough to Teach: Students With Behavior Problems* (2nd ed.). Arlington, VA: Council for Exceptional Children. Used with permission.

__ Restructure an activity/move a student's seat

__ Time-out

__ Referral

__ Loss of points and/or loss of access to materials, people, or activities

__ Parent contact

__ Office referral

__ Other (Explain) _____

What educative strategies are used in the classroom to teach students with skill deficits?

__ Behavior Bingo and other games designed to teach classroom rules

__ Think sheet (problem-solving format for self-reflection)

__ Social autopsy (discussion of the events leading to and including the problem with an emphasis on [a] increasing the student's awareness of social expectations and [b] helping the student generate solutions for future situations)

__ Social stories (stories written to specifically address a social situation and solutions for an individual)

__ Social skills lessons (with a curriculum that includes modeling, feedback, role play, and homework)

__ Conflict resolution training

__ Aggression replacement training

__ Problem-solving skills

__ Other (Explain)

Source: Rockwell, S. (2006). *Tough to Reach, Tough to Teach: Students With Behavior Problems* (2nd ed.). Arlington, VA: Council for Exceptional Children. Used with permission

Individual Instructional Contingencies

Student's Name _____

Date _____

Evaluator(s) _____

Instructions:

1. Scan the components of instruction on the left side of the following table. Put an X next to instructional factors that have been determined to have positive or negative effects on the student's performance.

2. On the right side of the table, record behaviors noted on anecdotals, scatter plots, interviews, student work, or other forms of documentation.

3. Next to the behaviors noted, record the source of the evidence. For some types of problems, an examination of the actual lesson content as recorded in the teacher's lesson plans might be required as part of the analysis process.

4. Under the heading, Instructional Themes, record themes noted from the four major components of instruction. Identify the behaviors and/or learning problems of concern. Write a hypothesis statement for each behavior or academic concept or skill identified. Develop an intervention for each hypothesis statement.

Individual Instructional Contingencies

Student's Name _____

Presentation	*Behavior/Evidence*
____ **Pace** (Rate of speech and/or nonverbal cues)	
____ **Modality** (Visual, auditory, tactile-kinesthetic, combination)	
____ **Intensity** (Volume; visual characteristics: number, hues, size; texture)	
____ **Materials** (Preferences related to modality, level of engagement)	
____ **Task variation** (Active/passive, simple/complex, long/short, non-preferred/preferred)	
____ **Topic/content area** (Relevant, meaningful)	
____ **Difficulty level** (Cognitive, social-emotional, motor)	
____ **Length of lesson**	
____ **Partial versus whole-task training**	
Response	*Behavior/Evidence*
____ **Pace** (Wait time, optimum rate for attention maintenance)	
____ **Modality** (Visual, auditory, tactile-kinesthetic, combination)	
____ **Intensity** (Volume, motor response, product quantity/quality)	
____ **Materials** (Preferences related to modality, level of engagement)	
____ **Task** (Active/passive, simple/complex, long/short, nonpreferred/preferred)	

____ **Topic** (Relevant, meaningful)	
____ **Difficulty level** (Cognitive, social-emotional, motor)	
____ **Error Analysis** __ Skill(s) __ Concept(s)	
Scheduling	*Behavior/Evidence*
____ Time of day	
____ Transitions	
____ Sequence of activities	
____ Interaction of activity sequence and length	
Setting	*Behavior/Evidence*
Space/location ____ Carrel ____ Desk ____ Small room ____ Large room ____ Noninstructional area/inside ____ Noninstructional area/outside	
Grouping configuration ____ Alone ____ One-on-one with an adult ____ Small group/adult support ____ Small group/peers ____ Large group/adult support ____ Large group/peer buddy ____ Large group/no individual support	

Instructional Themes

Presentation	*Response*	*Scheduling*	*Setting*
Target behavior(s)/Academic concept(s):			
Hypothesis(es):			
Intervention(s):			

Anecdotal Records

Student _____   Observer _____

Targeted Behavior(s) _____

Time/Date	Setting	Antecedent	Behavior	Consequence

Suggested Charting Codes:

Setting		People	Task	
CL Classroom	WG Whole Group	TR Teacher	SD Sit down	Sci Science
PG Playground	SG Small Group	PL Principal	Wkst Worksheet	LN Listen
PE Physical Education	IN Independent	AP Assistant Principal	RD Read	CL Color
CF Cafeteria	WP With Partner	BS Behavior Specialist	MTh Math	MP Manipulatives
HL Hall	AT At Desk	IA Instructional Aid	LA Language Arts	CP Computer
C/B Car/Bus Loading Area	OF On Floor	OS Other Student	SS Social Studies	SL Stand in Line

Scatter Plot

Student _____   Observer _____

Targeted Behavior(s) _____

Times/Setting/Activities/ People	Dates											

A. Write time, setting, and task-specific information in the left column and the observation date(s) on the column headings across the top.

B. Identify the behavior(s) to be observed. If more than one behavior is being charted, designate a letter or symbol for that behavior.

C. Place the letter or symbol for the behavior in the box that corresponds to the time/task row and the date column. If the target behavior does not occur, leave the box blank.

Suggested Charting Codes:

Setting		People	Task	
CL Classroom	WG Whole Group	TR Teacher	SD Sit down	Sci Science
PG Playground	SG Small Group	PL Principal	Wkst Worksheet	LN Listen
PE Physical Education	IN Independent	AP Assistant Principal	RD Read	CL Color
CF Cafeteria	WP With Partner	BS Behaviort Specialis	MTh Math	MP Manipulatives
HL Hall	AT At Desk	IA Instructional Aide	LA Language Arts	CP Computer
C/B Car/Bus Loading Area	OF On Floor	OS Other Student	SS Social Studies	SL Stand in Line

Point Card

Name _____ Day _____ Level _____ Date _____

Returned Signed Card [ ]   Bus Points [⟋]   Comments

Follow staff directions.						

Remain in assigned area.						

Complete assigned tasks.						

Target behavior:						

Balance [ ]

_____   _____   _____
Teacher's Signature   **Student's Signature**   **Parent's Signature**

Target Behavior Data Collection Sheet

Student's Name _____   Dates _____

Follow staff directions. _____

_____

Source: Rockwell, S. (2006). *Tough to Reach, Tough to Teach: Students With Behavior Problems* (2nd ed.). Arlington, VA: Council for Exceptional Children.

Target Behavior Data Collection Sheet

Student's Name _____   **Dates** _____

Follow staff directions _____

	M	T	W	Th	F	M	T	W	Th	F	M	T	W	Th	F	M	T	W	Th	F
100																				
90																				
80																				
70																				
60																				
50																				
40																				
30																				
20																				
10																				

Remain in assigned area. _____

	M	T	W	Th	F	M	T	W	Th	F	M	T	W	Th	F	M	T	W	Th	F
100																				
90																				
80																				
70																				
60																				
50																				
40																				
30																				
20																				
10																				

Complete assigned tasks. _____

	M	T	W	Th	F	M	T	W	Th	F	M	T	W	Th	F	M	T	W	Th	F
100																				
90																				
80																				
70																				
60																				
50																				
40																				
30																				
20																				
10																				

Source: Rockwell, S. (2006). *Tough to Reach, Tough to Teach: Students With Behavior Problems* (2nd ed.). Arlington, VA: Council for Exceptional Children. Used with permission.

Target Behavior Data Collection Sheet

Student's Name _____   Dates _____

Target Behavior _____

	M	T	W	Th	F	M	T	W	Th	F	M	T	W	Th	F	M	T	W	Th	F
100																				
90																				
80																				
70																				
60																				
50																				
40																				
30																				
20																				
10																				

Daily Total

	M	T	W	Th	F	M	T	W	Th	F	M	T	W	Th	F	M	T	W	Th	F
100																				
90																				
80																				
70																				
60																				
50																				
40																				
30																				
20																				
10																				

Classroom Incident Report (CIR) Serious Incident Report (SIR) Bus Referral (BR)

	M	T	W	Th	F	M	T	W	Th	F	M	T	W	Th	F	M	T	W	Th	F
BR																				
CIR																				
SIR																				
Day on Level																				

Behavior Observation Sequence Level _____

Source: Rockwell, S. (2006). *Tough to Reach, Tough to Teach: Students With Behavior Problems* (2nd ed.). Arlington, VA: Council for Exceptional Children. Used with permission.

Risk Factors and Potential Roadblocks

Risk Factors	*Targeted Youth*
Learning problems	
Problems with manners	
Poor peer relationships	
Poor relationships with adults	
Lack of persistence	
Poor impulse control	
Learned helplessness	
Controlled by others	
Few interests	
Few coping strategies	
Difficult temperament	
Other:	

Assets and Protective Factors

Protective Factors	Targeted Youth
Wide range of interests	
Easy temperament	
Academic achievement	
Ability to learn	
Sense of morality	
Sense of initiative	
Ability to distance self from harm	
Skills/talents	
Positive peer relationships	
Positive relationships with adults	
Sense of humor	
Problem-solving skills	
Ability to set goals and work to achieve them	
Physical health	
Able to attract positive attention	
Resourceful	
Willing to access support	
Many coping strategies	
Other:	

Protective Factors and
Opportunities for Success

Achievement	Attachment	Autonomy	Altruism

Risk Factors and Opportunities
for Moderating Their Effects

Achievement	Attachment	Autonomy	Altruism

Appendix B

Important Notes for Parents

Appendix Contents

Dear Parents,

Some children are easier to raise than others. One child might enjoy school, make friends, and manage the demands of the classroom without undue concern. Another child might experience problems in learning, getting along with classmates, or following class and school rules.

I have been an educator for more than 30 years and a mother for more than 25 years. One afternoon while I was helping another teacher serve punch and cookies to the parents of students who had earned honors during the previous grading period, the teacher whispered in my ear, "So, this is what the good kids' parents look like." She didn't know that one of my three children had a specific learning disability and that another was diagnosed with ADHD. The third child was progressing quite well, attended honors classes, and had no learning or behavior problems. The first two children, however, presented quite a challenge at home and at school. I knew my colleague had meant no harm with the comment, but I could not let it go without a comment of my own. Too often, children and their parents are blamed.

In response to my colleague, I pointed to myself and said, "I am the good student's mother, *and* I am the bad students' mother." I briefly described the challenges of raising children with disabilities. I explained that all three children were good children from my point of view. Having a disability or biological disorder did not cause me to love them less or see them as bad. The other teacher was surprised and later asked insightful questions about how to best meet the needs of students she taught who presented challenges.

Children with learning and behavior problems need to feel safe, welcomed, respected, and understood. They need to learn to accept mistakes as powerful learning tools rather than as proof that they are not good enough. They need to overcome challenges, feel proud of their accomplishments, and know that the adults in their lives value the effort as much as the mastery of a new skill. They need to know that we care about who they are as well as who they can become.

So that you and the teachers, administrators, support personnel, and others who are interested in the growth of your child can work most effectively together, each person on the team needs to share information. I hope that this booklet is useful to you as you continue the journey of discovery that parenting represents. You and your child may have many challenges ahead. Focus on the joy of each small victory. Reach out to those who are willing and able to help. And, embrace the strengths within yourself, your child, your family, and your community. Resources are listed at the back of this pamphlet if you desire additional information.

Peace to you and yours,
Sylvia Rockwell
(The good kids' Mom ☺)

SECTION I: AGE-APPROPRIATE EXPECTATIONS ■

Children develop skills in many areas as they grow. Most children are better at some tasks than others. Skills that are important for school success include (a) the ability to follow directions and make friends (social skills); (b) the ability to use scissors and write (fine motor skills); (c) the ability to understand what is said and respond (linguistic skills); and (d) the ability to learn academic content in a variety of areas such as math, reading, language arts, science, and social studies. During the primary years (Grades K–2), the school might also measure a child's gross motor skills and physical strength during physical education classes. To make good decisions about a child's strengths and needs, age-appropriate expectations in all skill areas must be understood.

Each school district and state establishes highest student expectations and standards for the children in their schools. These grade level expectations do not include everything a child at a particular grade level is expected to master, but they do provide a general guideline that parents can use to monitor their child's progress. Your child's teacher, guidance counselor, or administrator can provide a list of required skills at each grade level.

Children desperately want to please the adults they love. They want their parents, extended family members, teachers, and other adults in their lives to be proud of them. They feel bad when they are unable to live up to the expectations that parents and teachers have for them. Knowing what is expected of children at specific ages can be helpful in deciding how to best support your child's growth and achievement.

The next section addresses individual differences. All children have strengths and needs that are specific to them. The information about age-appropriate expectations can help guide you in developing a more complete plan of action for your child as you explore his or her unique strengths and needs as a learner.

SECTION II: YOUR CHILD'S ■
STRENGTHS AND NEEDS

Some children experience more difficulty in one area or another than other children. One child does well in math while another struggles with math. One child listens and follows directions without a problem. Another child wiggles, interrupts, and gets off task often. Sometimes a child has learned to behave in a particular way to get attention or gain access to a preferred activity. Sometimes a child is acting or learning differently than other children because of a chemical imbalance or processing difference in the brain. Some behavior and learning problems are easily addressed with a behavior or academic success plan.

When a child's behavior or learning problems are related to a lack of opportunity to learn, teachers and other school personnel are usually able to help a child and parent without extra tests and support services. When a child's behavior or learning problems are related to a difference in the way the brain and nervous system receive and use information, teachers, parents, and support personnel in the school district may need to work together to identify the student's strengths and needs as a learner and design a plan to best meet the child's needs. Neither the lack of opportunity to learn nor the difficulty in learning because of a difference in how the brain works is the parents' or child's fault.

Expectations at home are different from expectations at school. Children are not generally required to raise their hands and wait to be recognized before speaking at the dinner table. Most families do not require children to sit for long periods of time working on academic tasks. A child's high energy levels, for example, might be appreciated in a family that enjoys playing sports together but be less appreciated in a classroom. The identification of a child's strengths and needs is not an attempt to blame or shame. The identification of a child's strengths and needs is an attempt to discover how to best address the child's unique style of learning. The goal of the process is to develop a plan with the highest likelihood of success. The following anecdote is from my personal experience as the mother of a child with ADHD.

Temperament

My daughter, Kala (who is in her late twenties), is a beautiful, creative, talented young woman. No one who meets her now even suspects that her pediatrician referred to her as a "mother killer" when she was 2. She had a very difficult and demanding temperament. She lived life at the extremes. When she was happy, she laughed, ran, jumped, and entertained all who would give her audience. When she was angry, she screamed at the top of her lungs for incredibly long periods of time. These tantrums often included breaking and throwing items within her reach. In response to being asked to pick up her toys and come to dinner, she once pulled the curtain rods out of the wall, stripped the sheets from her bed, emptied her toy box on the floor, and threw all of her clothes from her closet. This took less than 5 minutes. I could hear her but had to secure her brother in his high chair before going to her room to stop her.

Kala exhibited higher than average activity levels and intensity for girls her age and was at the top of the chart for boys. Her self-control was low—especially when frustrated or angry. She also exhibited high levels of sensitivity to sensory input of any type and was terribly unpredictable in her patterns of sleep during her infancy. She also had allergies to pollen, wheat, citrus, milk, and tomatoes.

Fortunately, I had a wonderful pediatrician who met on a consultative basis with me during her preschool and early elementary school years. Together we developed and updated regularly a plan for her that included (a) environmental supports for biologically determined traits that she could not control, (b) educative strategies for teaching her necessary coping skills, and (c) behavioral interventions for managing behaviors that were under her control. Some teachers were willing to work with the doctor and me to extend the plan into the classroom, and other teachers were not. The years when she had teachers who were unwilling to understand her needs were difficult. By the time she was 11, she had learned to control her impulses, ask for what she needed, and function without a formal support plan at home and at school.

Chess and Thomas (1986) identified 10 traits of temperament. These traits are (1) activity level, (2) approach/withdrawal, (3) concentration or attention span and persistence, (4) intensity, (5) regularity, (6) responsiveness, (7) distractibility, (8) sensory threshold, (9) adaptability, and (10) predominant mood. The extent to which an individual trait or combination of traits presents a challenge to a child depends to some degree on the expectations of those with whom the child interacts. The physical education teacher may find a child who is active, quick to participate in activities, and intense a real asset to the soccer team. That same child might be the librarian's worst nightmare.

Developing a plan for a child with a difficult temperament requires investigation to determine which behaviors reflect biologically determined traits and which behaviors have been learned. Environmental accommodations and direct instruction in coping strategies are most effective when addressing traits of temperament. Learned behaviors may require instruction in rules and expected behaviors. For example, a child who reacts to new situations by withdrawing and refusing to participate would benefit from being told of changes in activities in advance and being given time to observe others before being asked to engage in novel tasks.

Providing notification and time to observe might provide children with enough support to allow them to participate satisfactorily. If they have learned, however, that crying will gain them access to preferred staff members and activities, being told of changes in advance and being given time to observe might not be effective. They may need to be taught through a behavior support plan that (a) they can access preferred people and activities only if they comply with the required task, (b) they can ask for advanced notification of changes and time to observe novel activities, (c) they will feel calmer and more able to participate if they ask for and gain access to the support they need, and (d) they are capable of handling these challenges.

Stanley Turecki (2000) has written a tremendous book for parents, *The Difficult Child*, which can also be applied in classrooms. In this book, he recommends that parents and teachers remain neutral when responding to a behavioral challenge. Take time to analyze the situation and determine whether the child needs support due to a biological trait that is beyond his or her control, instruction in age-appropriate rules and expectations, or some combination of the first two options. In addition, he cautions adults engaged with a difficult child to avoid punishing traits of temperament. Children establish a sense of learned helplessness or learned optimism by the age of 7 (Seligman, 1995). Punishing children for a trait or behavior they cannot control encourages the development of learned helplessness. If a punishment or consequence for a learned behavior is warranted, be brief, be firm, be calm, be consistent, and do not engage in negotiations.

Greenspan (1995) identified five distinct groups of children with difficult temperament profiles. Each group experiences different challenges in the school environment and will need different types of responses from school personnel. The five groups are labeled (1) highly sensitive, (2) self-absorbed, (3) defiant, (4) inattentive, and (5) active-aggressive. Of those five groups, only the active-aggressive group has been associated with an identifiable pattern of parenting. Parents of these children inconsistently respond to their children's needs. The children exhibit little or no empathy, have difficulty expressing their wants and needs, and act impulsively without thinking about the situation and the best choices for their behavior.

The highly sensitive group is easily embarrassed and experiences more changes in mood. The self-absorbed group prefers to daydream and does not engage easily with others. The defiant group is more often negative when responding to others, particularly when they cannot be in control. They prefer highly concrete, well-organized activities. The inattentive group has difficulty maintaining attention to any given task for the required amount of time. This behavior had negative impacts on learning and social interaction.

The research on temperament has taught us that (a) tough-to-manage children do not necessarily have a disorder—they might just have a difficult temperament that will respond to environmental supports, instruction in coping strategies, and a consistently enforced set of rules and consequences; (b) the assumption that a child is choosing to act inappropriately can have long-term detrimental consequences if the response to that assumption is focused primarily on punishment; and (c) even biologically determined traits can be modified (for the betterment or to the detriment of an individual) through a variety of planned and unplanned factors and experiences.

Processing Differences

Levine (2002) has studied the differences in how children access and use information. These differences in neurological processing are important for parents and teachers to understand when making decisions about academic instruction and behavior plan development. Each of these constructs or systems works independently to contribute to a child's overall development. Other systems or constructs are affected if one system is not working as well as it should. Levine identifies the following systems of neurodevelopmental development: (a) attention control, (b) memory, (c) language, (d) spatial ordering, (e) sequential ordering, (f) motor, (g) higher thinking, and (e) social thinking. Each system must be able to effectively (a) receive input, (b) store information, (c) use information during internal processing, and (d) provide output. In a school environment, failure of any system to perform one or more of the four functions listed above can cause learning and behavior problems. A child who knows an answer but can't express it is different from a child who knows an answer but refuses to express it. Both children might look very much alike in a classroom, but they may need very different types of support. Each child's needs should be evaluated prior to selecting an intervention. The classroom setting, the type of learning task, and the individual child's strengths and needs should be considered before selecting a particular intervention. For a more complete examination of Levine's neurodevelopmental constructs, see *One Mind at a Time* and a video titled *Developing Minds* (2002), a production of WBGH Boston, available at www.wgbh.org.

Your Child' Developmental Profile

Your child's strengths and needs can be documented and assessed in a variety of ways. Most schools look at student work, discipline file information, relevant medical information, and formal assessments before making decisions about how to best meet a student's needs.

Brian had been referred to the child study team because of concerns over his behavior. He frequently interrupted the class with inappropriate comments and drew pictures or made toys out of materials in his desk when he was supposed to complete independent work. An IQ test revealed that Brian had a superior ability to learn. In spite of a high over-all IQ score, however, Brian's math ability was within the expected range for his age, and his reading achievement scores were significantly below age and grade-level expectations. A speech and language screening revealed that Brian comprehended words, directions, and concepts that were well beyond age and grade-level expectations; but he had difficulty expressing his thoughts, feelings, wants, needs, and understandings verbally. He also exhibited difficulty with the pragmatics of speech— knowing when and how to enter a conversation; understanding the subtle nuances between types of words, tone of voice, volume, and rates of speech expected in different settings; and the need to follow the topic of conversation or request a change in topic during class discussions. Expressive language difficulties negatively affected his behavior in the classroom as well as his ability to complete independent assignments. In addition, he did not know all the sounds of the letters of the alphabet. This made learning to read and spell difficult. Brian's listening comprehension was tested by having him listen to a passage read aloud and answer oral questions by pointing to a picture located in an array of pictures that represented the answer to the question; his score was above grade level. His listening comprehension score was more typical of a 12-year-old than an 8-year-old. He needed intensive work in the areas of expressive language and sound-symbol associations for reading and spelling.

Previous attempts to help Brian learn more appropriate behavior had failed. The emphasis had been on rewarding desired behaviors and punishing unwanted behaviors without considering Brian's language-processing deficits. Additional reading instruction provided during first and second grade had also failed to strengthen Brian's skills in identifying sounds for letters of the alphabet. Brian's new plan was expanded to include (a) language therapy to address expressive language skills and the pragmatics of speech; (b) intensive computerized instruction designed to target recognition and recall of phonemes, their associated written symbols, and the blending of those symbols into words; (c) visual cues in the environment to prompt Brian's memory of classroom rules, academic content, and the daily schedule; (d) accommodations such as a phoneme strip attached to his desk that included picture cues to assist him in decoding and spelling unfamiliar words, an illustrated word bank, and a handheld electronic spell checker with read-aloud capacity and a headset; (d) a self-monitoring system to strengthen his attention to assigned tasks during independent work periods; (e) social skills instruction; (f) a study buddy to assist with reading and spelling tasks and social skill prompting; and (g) a reward system that included academic performance as well as compliance with classroom rules.

The entire class was trained in peer tutoring skills prior to the assignment of study buddies. Brian was paired with a student who was skilled in reading and spelling and who needed assistance with math. Brian's classmates admired his artistic abilities, so he was given the title of Class Illustrator. He helped design posters, murals, and three-dimensional displays aligned with science, social studies, and math content. Over the course of the year, Brian's reading achievement score increased by 24 months, his math achievement score increased by 18 months, and his classroom behavior no longer caused concerns for his parents and teachers.

If the child study team had simply assessed Brian's levels of academic and behavioral functioning without investigating processing strengths and deficits, the interventions selected to address his behavioral and academic needs might have been insufficiently intense or entirely inappropriate. Brian's behavior and academic problems were not due to a lack of motivation or understanding of expectations. His inappropriate comments were related to expressive language-processing deficits and incomplete knowledge of the implicit rules of conversation. Punishing him for noncompliance would not teach him how to interact. Rewarding him for appropriate behavior without directly teaching desired skills might have created undue levels of stress as Brian struggled to understand why he was rewarded one day and punished the next. Brian's strengths and needs illustrate the necessity of looking at the whole child, targeting skills for instruction, and developing an intervention plan.

As a parent, you can help your child and the teacher by being aware of what your child does well and what your child struggles to do at home and in the community. Keep school personnel informed of medical problems that might impact your child's ability to learn or behave within the expectations for his or her grade level. Communicate regularly with the teacher and other support personnel who work with your child. Being an informed and active parent is an ongoing process. The benefits for your child are invaluable and immeasurable. You are not only your child's first teacher but also your child's most effective advocate. The third section of this booklet outlines the purpose for a team approach to problem solving and provides information on how to most effectively access school resources.

■ SECTION III: SUPPORT TEAM PARTICIPATION

Teachers and other school personnel often ask parents to (a) attend conferences, (b) provide information about their child's growth and development, (c) help their child learn new skills at home, and (d) consider granting permission for testing or placement in a program designed to meet one or more of the child's needs. This can be confusing. Teachers might report that a child acts or learns differently in school than the parent has seen at home. School personnel might use terms that are unfamiliar. Knowing what is right for your child might require a team approach. You know your child better than others and want what is best for him or her. The professionals have training in specific areas related to your child's needs. Together more can be accomplished to help your child.

There are four ways that you can be of tremendous assistance: (1) supporting your child's learning at home, (2) communicating with the teacher and other school personnel, (3) accessing and using information about how your child learns, and (4) working with your child's school support team as an informed and active member.

Supporting Your Child's Learning at Home

One of the best ways to support your child's learning at home is to establish a regular schedule that includes time for healthy meals, play, homework, recreational reading, and sleep. Children who are too tired have a hard time concentrating in school. Children need 10 or more hours of sleep each night. Having a regular bedtime helps them regulate their cycles of activity and rest. A typical school night might include time for homework followed by dinner, 15 minutes of quiet reading, and a bath. Before settling down for the night, the family might play a game or watch a television show together. As part of the "going to bed" ritual, a parent or older brother or sister might read a storybook or chapter from a longer book to the younger children. The exact time that each activity takes is not as important as the predictable nature of the activities. Children like repetition and generally respond well to a structure and schedule that meets their needs.

Another way to support your child's learning at home is to have a specific place for doing homework. Some children sit at a desk in their rooms, some sit at the kitchen table, and others spread their work on the coffee table in the den. The best place for a child to do homework will vary from home to home. Regardless of the actual place, a few guidelines are in order.

1. Make sure the child has enough light.

2. Make paper, pencils, and other necessary items easily available.

3. Keep the television, video games, and other toys out of sight. If the child is distracted by hearing one or more of them, turn them down or off.

4. Remain near, but do not hover. Homework is the child's responsibility. Parents can and should assist if the child has a question, but do not fall into the habit of doing homework for the child. If an assignment is too hard or takes the child too long to complete, write a brief note to the teacher explaining the problem. Do not keep the child up hours past his or her bedtime to complete an assignment.

5. Be consistent in setting aside time for completing homework and in assigning the place for doing the homework.

Children who have opportunities to talk with their parents, friends, and extended family members about current events in the news, art, music, television shows, movies, sports, and other generally topics have an advantage. They learn more new words, have more background knowledge, and have more interests. These advantages help them understand new concepts easier. Parents are children's first teachers. Be aware that children are learning about themselves, others, and the world through each experience that they have. Celebrate and accentuate every opportunity to help them grow!

Communicating With the Teacher and Other School Personnel

If your child has a learning, behavior, or health problem, it is best to make an appointment with a new teacher as early in the year as possible. Teachers want each child to be successful and welcome helpful information from parents. Don't assume that a new teacher will know what your child needs.

If your child begins to have difficulty, call the teacher first. Sometimes parents want to call the principal or the school superintendent first. Unfortunately, this can cause unnecessary misunderstandings and prolong the resolution of the problem. If, after you talk with the teacher, the problem is not satisfactorily resolved, however, the next call should be to the assistant principal or principal. If you do not know the expected procedures to follow in your child's school district, the teacher or principal will be able to direct you. All parents and students have due process rights that are protected under federal, state, and local laws and policies. Expect that all members of the school support team care about and want to help your child. If you and the teacher or other school personnel disagree about how to best meet your child's needs, it is best to follow the procedures set forth in your district.

Accessing and Using Information About How Your Child Learns

Children vary in the ways that they access and use information. Some remember what they see more easily than what they hear. Some must touch and manipulate objects to understand a concept. Others hear something one time and remember it forever. Pay attention to the ways your child prefers to learn, play, and work. Ask your child whether he learns his spelling words more easily when he writes them, spells them out loud, or looks at them. Play games with him or her to find out which methods are most helpful. Tell your child's teacher about what you have observed. Talk with your child about what works best for him or her. Help your child structure study and homework tasks in ways that are most effective.

In addition to your observations, ask your child's teacher about his or her learning strengths, as well as strategies that are most appropriate for a child with those strengths. Your child's teacher might have additional information that could be of use to you at home.

Participating on Your Child's School Support Team

You are a valuable member of your child's school support team. You know more about your child's likes, dislikes, temperament, and development than anyone else on the team. Other team members know a great deal about your child's school behavior and learning patterns. As difficult as it might be to accept that your child is having difficulty with behavior and/or learning in the classroom, the good news is that many people can and will help you and your child with the challenges ahead.

You can be most helpful as a member of the support team if you do the following:

1. Come to scheduled meetings.

2. Bring information about your child's development (health, motor skills, social interaction, language development, and understanding of everyday expectations at home and in the community).

3. Ask questions about assessments, test, and strategies if something is unclear.

4. Ask questions about how you can best support the school's efforts at home.

5. Request that school personnel consider implementing strategies at school that have worked well at home (as long as the strategies are within the guidelines of school district policy).

6. Keep records at home on relevant behavior and academic achievement concerns.

7. Consider granting permission for assessment and program placement.

8. Request opportunities to observe programs, curriculum, and/or methods before granting permission.

9. Actively working to remain informed on your child's strengths, needs, and treatment options.

Parents are children's first teachers and their most important advocates. Your value to the school support team is immeasurable. Together you and the team can make an amazing difference in the quality of your child's learning and lifelong potential for achievement.

SECTION IV: ADDITIONAL RESOURCES ■

Temperament

Stanley Turecki, M.D., has written an invaluable book for parents of children with difficult temperaments called *The Difficult Child* (2000). He describes his own struggle to understand one of his children. This book is by a parent for parents. Everyone with a difficult-to-manage child would benefit from his experience and research.

Behavioral Challenges and Mental Illness

Medical research continues to uncover the neurological and biochemical conditions that cause children to be predisposed to developing mental illness. In *It's Nobody's Fault: New Hope and Help for Difficult Children* by Harold Koplewicz (1996), blame and shame are replaced by medical facts and straightforward suggestions for home and classroom application.

Dr. Frank Lawlis (2004) has written a book for parents of children with ADD and ADHD called *The ADD Answer: How to Help Your Child Now*. He provides clear explanations of a variety of treatment options.

Learning Differences

For a more complete examination of Levine's neurodevelopmental constructs, see *One Mind at a Time* (Levine, 2002) and a video titled *Developing Minds* (2002), a production of WBGH Boston, available at www.wgbh.org.

In addition to Levine's work for parents on differences in neurological development, Sally Smith (1991) has written a book called *Succeeding Against the Odds*. It contains specific information for parents and teachers on how to teach children with learning problems to take responsibility for and management of their learning.

Other information about learning differences can be found at www.ldonline.com. Helpful checklists, videos, and books are available at that Web site. Among the most useful to parents and teachers are the items developed by Richard Lavoie.

Additional Web Sites

Autism Society of America
www.autism-society.org

Children and Adults with Attention Deficit Disorder
www.chadd.org

American Academy of Child and Adolescent Psychiatry
(53 Fact Sheets titled *Facts for Families*)
www.aacap.org

The following resources have been specifically selected for you and your child's use at home. If you desire additional information, do not hesitate to call _____ at _____

Note to the Practitioner

The Additional Resources section of the Parent Supplement can and should be compiled of information and forms specific to the needs of the parent or parents for which the supplement is intended. If a child is exhibiting behavior problems, you might want to photocopy items from the Appendix specific to data collection or add forms of your own describing behavior management strategies that you would like parents to use at home. If the child has difficulties with academic tasks, photocopy appropriate figures from Chapters 2, 5, and 7. Supplement this information with classroom-specific lists, such as titles of grade-leveled books for recreational reading at home, targeted sight words, math facts, science concepts, social studies content, and/or study skill support strategies.

Your classroom management plan, homework policy, and any individualized plans for academic instruction and behavioral support should also be included in the booklet.

Parents are children's first teachers. Their role in the continued development and education of their children is essential. Maintaining ongoing communication with them is invaluable.

References

Adams, M. J. (1990). *Beginning to read: Thinking and learning about print.* Cambridge, MA: MIT Press.

Adler, C. R. (Ed.). (2001). *Put reading first: The research building blocks for teaching children to read.* Ann Arbor, MI: Center for the Improvement of Early Reading Achievement.

Ager, C. L., & Cole, C. L. (1991). A review of cognitive-behavioral interventions for children and adolescents with behavioral disorder. *Behavioral Disorders, 16,* 276–287.

Alberto, P. A., & Troutman, A. C. (1990). *Applied behavior analysis for teachers: Influencing student performance* (5th ed.). Columbus, OH: Charles E. Merrill.

Alberto, P. A., & Troutman, A. C. (2002). *Applied behavior analysis for teachers: Influencing student performance* (6th ed.). Englewood Cliffs, NJ: Prentice Hall.

Allinder, R. (1993). I think I can. I think I can. *Beyond Behavior, 4*(2), 29.

American Psychiatric Association. (1994). *Diagnostic and statistical manual of mental disorders* (4th ed.). Washington, DC: Author.

American Psychological Association, Commission on Violence. (1993). *Violence and youth: Psychology's response.* Washington, DC: Author.

Anderson, J. (1988). *Thinking, changing, rearranging.* Portland, OR: Metamorphosis Press.

Andrade, H. (2000). Using rubrics to promote thinking and learning. *Educational Leadership, 57*(5), 13–18.

Baenen, R. S., Glenwick, D. S., Stephens, M., Neuhaus, S. M., & Mowrey, J. D. (1986). Predictors of child and family outcomes in a psychoeducational day school program. *Behavioral Disorders, 11*(2), 272–279.

Baker, S. K., Simmons, D. C., & Kameenui, E. J. (1998). Vocabulary acquisition. In D. C. Simmons & E. J. Kameenui (Eds.), *What reading research tell us about children with learning needs* (pp. 183–218). Mahwah, NJ: Erlbaum.

Bandura, A. (1977). *Social learning theory.* Englewood Cliffs, NJ: Prentice Hall.

Bandura, A. (1978). The self-esteem in reciprocal determinism. *American Psychologist, 37,* 344–358.

Bandura, A. (1986). *Social foundations of thoughts and actions.* Englewood Cliffs, NJ: Prentice Hall.

Battista, M., & Brown, C. (1998, January). Using spreadsheets to promote algebraic thinking. *Teaching Children Mathematics,* pp. 470–478.

Becker, W. C. (1977). Teaching reading and language to the disadvantaged—What we have learned from field research. *Harvard Educational Review, 47,* 518–543.

Bennett, W. J. (Ed.). (1995). *The children's book of virtues.* New York: Simon & Schuster.

Berlin, R., & Davis, R. B. (1989). Children from alcoholic families: Vulnerability and resilience. In T. F. Dugan & R. Coles (Eds.), *The child in our times: Studies in the development of resiliency* (pp. 81–105). New York: Brunner/Mazel.

Bernard, M. (1990). Rational-emotive therapy with children and adolescents: Treatment strategies. *School Psychology Review, 19*(3), 294–303.

Bijou, S. (1995). *Behavior analysis of child development.* Reno, NV: Content Press.

Billingsley, B. S., & Wildman, T. M. (1990). Facilitating reading comprehension in learning disabled students: Metacognitive goals and instructional strategies. *Remedial and Special Education, 11*(2), 18–31.

Blatt, M., & Kohlberg, L. (1975). The effects of classroom moral discussion upon children's level of moral judgment. *Journal of Moral Education, 4,* 129–161.

Bloom, B. S. (1976). *Human characteristics and school learning.* New York: McGraw Hill.

Bloom, H. (1995). *The Lucifer principle: A scientific expedition into the forces of history.* New York: The Atlantic Monthly Press.

Borkowski, J. (1992). Metacognitive theory: A framework for teaching literacy, writing, and math skills. *Journal of Learning Disabilities, 25*(4), 253–257.

Brandenburg, N. A., Friedman, J. M., & Silver, S. E. (1990). The epidemiology of childhood psychiatric disorder: Prevalence findings from recent studies. *Journal of the American Academy of Child and Adolescent Psychiatry, 29,* 72–83.

Brendtro, L., Brokenleg, M., & VanBokern, S. (1990). *Reclaiming youth at risk: Our hope for the future.* Bloomington, IN: National Educational Service.

Butterworth, B. (1999). *What counts: How every brain is hardwired for math.* New York: Free Press.

Carlberg, C., & Kavale, K. (1980). The efficacy of special versus regular class placement for exceptional children: A meta-analysis. *The Journal of Special Education, 14*(3), 295–309.

Carnine, D., Kameenui, E., & Maggs, A. (1982). Components of analytic assistance: Statement saying, concept training, and strategy training. *Journal of Educational Research, 75*(6), 374–377.

Carr, E. G., Horner, R. H., Turnbull, A. P., Marquis, J., McLaughlin, D., McAtee, M. L., Smith, C. E., Ryan, K., Ruef, M. B., & Doolabah, A. (1999). *Positive behavior support as an approach for dealing with problem behavior in people with developmental disabilities.* Washington, DC: American Association on Mental Retardation.

Chan, L. K., Cole, P. G., & Barfett, S. (1987). Comprehension monitoring: Detection and identification of text inconsistencies by LD and normal students. *Learning Disability Quarterly, 10*(2), 114–124.

Chan, L. K., Cole, P. G., & Morris, J. N. (1990). Effects of instruction in the use of visual-imagery strategy on the reading-comprehension competence of disabled and average readers. *Learning Disability Quarterly, 13*(1), 2–11.

Chess, S., & Thomas, A. (1986). *Temperament in clinical practice.* New York: Guilford.

Collins, V., Dickson, S., Simmons, D., & Kameenui, E. (1995). *Metacognition and its relationship to reading comprehension: A synthesis of the research.* Eugene, OR: National Center for the Improvement of Tools for Educators. Available at http://idea.uoregon.edu/~bcite/documents/techprep/tech23.html

Comer, J. (1988). *Maggie's American dream.* New York: New American Library.

Cornaldi, C. (1990). Metacognitive control processes and memory deficits in poor comprehenders. *Learning Disability Quarterly, 13*(4), 245–255.

Coutinho, M. (1986). Reading achievement of students identified as behaviorally disordered at the secondary level. *Behavioral Disorders, 11*(3), 200–207.

Crain, W. (2000). *Theories of development: Concepts and applications* (4th ed.). Upper Saddle River, NJ: Prentice Hall.

Deno, S. L., & Fuchs, L. S. (1988). Developing curriculum-based measurement systems for data-based special education problem-solving. In E. L. Meyen, G. A. Vergason, & R. J. Whelan (Eds.), *Effective instructional strategies for exceptional children* (pp. 481–504). Denver, CO: Love.

Deschler, D., Ellis, E., & Lenz, K. (1996). *Teaching adolescents with learning disabilities* (2nd ed.). Denver, CO: Love.

DiGangi, S. A., & Magg, J. W. (1992). A component analysis of self-management training with behaviorally disordered youth. *Behavioral Disorders, 17,* 281–290.

DiGuiseppe, R., & Bernard, M. (1990). The application of rational-emotive theory and therapy to school-aged children. *School Psychology Review, 19*(3), 268–286.

Dixon, M. E. (1985). Metacognition: Buzz word of the eighties. *Contemporary Issues in Reading, 1*(1), 66–75.

Dixon, R. (1994). *Research synthesis in language arts: Curriculum guidelines for diverse learners* (Monograph for the National Center to Improve Tools for Educators). Eugene: University of Oregon.

Dixon, R., Carnine, D., & Kameenui, E. (1992). *Research synthesis in mathematics: Curriculum guidelines for diverse learners* (Monograph for the National Center to Improve the Tools of Educators). Eugene: University of Oregon.

Dixon, R., Carnine, D., Lee, D., Wallin, J., & Chard, D. (1998). *Report to the California state board of education: Review of high quality experimental math research.* Eugene, OR: National Center to Improve Tools for Educators.

Driekurs, R., Grumwald, B., & Pepper, F. (1982). *Maintaining sanity in the classroom.* New York: Harper & Row.

Dugan, T. F. (1989). Action and acting out: Variable in the development of resiliency in adolescence. In T. R. Dugan & R. Coles (Eds.), *The child in our times: Studies in the development of resiliency* (pp. 157–167). New York: Brunner/Mazel.

Edelman, M. W. (1992). *The measure of success: A letter to my children and yours.* Boston: Beacon.

Ehri, L. (1998). Grapheme-phoneme knowledge is essential for learning to read words in English. In J. Metsala & L. Ehri (Eds.), *Word recognition in beginning literacy* (pp. 3–40). Mahwah, NJ: Erlbaum.

Elkind, D. (2001). *The hurried child: Growing up too fast too soon* (3rd ed.). Cambridge, MA: Perseus.

Ellsworth, J. (1996). "PEPSI" A screening and programming tool for understanding the whole child. *Teaching Exceptional Children, 29*(2), 33–44.

Emery, R., & Forehand, R. (1994). Parental divorce & children's well being: A focus on resiliency. In R. J. Haggerty, N.Garmezy, M. Rutter, and L. R. Sherrod (Eds.). *Stress, Coping, and Development: Risk and Resilience in Children* (pp. 64–99). Cambridge, England: Cambridge Press.

Erikson, E. (1950). *Childhood and society.* New York: Norton.

Fantuzzo, J. W., Rohrbeck, C. A., & Azar, S. T. (1987). A component analysis of behavioral self-management interventions with elementary school students. *Child and Family Behavior Therapy, 9*(1/2), 33–43.

Fisher, D., Osterhaus, N., Clothier, P., & Edwards, L. (1994). Passive-aggressive children in the classroom: The child who won't do anything. *Beyond Behavior, 5*(2), 9–12.

Foley, R., & Epstein, M. (1992). Correlates of the academic achievement of adolescents with behavioral disorders. *Behavioral Disorders, 18*(1), 9–17.

Forehand, R., & McMahon, R. J. (1981). *Helping the noncompliant child: A clinician's guide to parent training.* New York: Guilford.

Forest, M., & Lusthaus, E. (1990). Everyone belongs with MAPS action planning system. *Teaching Exceptional Children, 22,* 32–35.

Forness, S., & Kavale, K. (2001). Defining emotional or behavioral disorders in school and related services. In J. Lloyd, E. Kameenui, & D. Chard (Eds.), *Issues in educating students with disabilities* (pp. 45–61). Mahwah, NJ: Erlbaum.

Forness, S., Kavale, K., MacMillan, D., & Duncan, B. (1996). Early detection and prevention of emotional or behavioral disorders: Developmental aspects of systems of care. *Behavioral Disorders, 21*(3), 226–240.

Foster-Johnson, L., & Dunlap, G. (1993). Using functional assessment to develop effective, individualized interventions for challenging behaviors. *Teaching Exceptional Children, 25,* 44–50.

Freiberg, H. J. (1994). Understanding resilience: Implications for inner-city schools and their near and far communities. In M. C. Wang & E. W. Gordon (Eds.),

Educational resilience in inner-city America: Challenges and prospects (pp. 151–166). Mahwah, NJ: Erlbaum.

Fuchs, L. S. (1995). *Connecting performance assessment to instruction: A comparison of behavioral assessment, mastery learning, curriculum-based measurement, and performance assessment* (ERIC Digest E 530). Reston, VA: ERIC Clearinghouse on Disabilities and Gifted Education.

Gardner, H. (1983). *Frames of mind: The theory of multiple intelligences.* New York: Basic Books.

Gardner, H. (1993). *Multiple intelligences: The theory in practice.* New York: Basic Books.

Garmezy, N. (1994). Reflections and commentary on risk, resilience, and development. In R. Haggerty, L. R. Sherrod, N. Garmezy, & M. Rutter (Eds.), *Stress, risk, and resilience in children and adolescents: Processes, mechanisms, and interventions.* New York: Cambridge University Press.

Garmezy, N., Masten, A., & Tellegren, A. (1984). The study of stress and competence in children: A building block for developmental psychopathology. *Child Development, 55,* 97–111.

Gesell, A., & Ilg, F. L. (1946). The child from five to ten. In A. Gesell & F. L. Ilg, *Child development.* New York: Harper & Row.

Giovannoni, J., & Billingsley, A. (1970). Child neglect among the poor: A study of parental adequacy in families of three ethnic groups. *Child Welfare, 49*(4), 196–204.

Glasser, W. (1998). *Choice theory.* New York: Harper Perennial.

Goldstein, A. (1988). *The prepare curriculum: Teaching prosocial competencies.* Champaign, IL: Research Press.

Gray, C., & Gerard, J. D. (1993). Social stories: Improving responses of students with autism with accurate social information. *Focus on Autistic Behavior, 8*(1), 1–10.

Green, G. (1996). Evaluating for treatments for autism. In C. Maurice, G. Green, & S. Luce (Eds.), *Behavioral interventions for young children with autism* (pp. 15–28). Austin, TX: Pro-Ed.

Greene, R. W. (2001). *The explosive child.* New York: HarperCollins.

Greenes, C., & Findell, C. (1998). *Algebra puzzles and problems, grade 7.* Mountain View, CA: Creative Publications.

Greenspan, S. (1995). *The challenging child: Understanding, raising, and enjoying the five "difficult" types of children.* Reading, MA: Addison-Wesley.

Gresham, F., MacMillan, D., & Bocian, K. (1996). "Behavioral earthquakes:" Low frequency events that differentiate students at-risk for behavioral disorders. *Behavioral Disorders, 21*(4), 277–292.

Grossen, B., & Lee, C. (1994). *Research synthesis in science: Curriculum guidelines for diverse learners* (Monograph for the National Center to Improve the Tools of Educators). Eugene: University of Oregon.

Guetzloe, E. C. (1989). *Youth suicide: What the educator should know.* Reston, VA: The Council for Exceptional Children.

Harris, S. L. (1995). Autism. In M. Hersen & R. T. Ammerman (Eds.), *Advanced abnormal child psychology* (pp. 305–317). Mahwah, NJ: Erlbaum.

Hart, B., & Risley, T. R. (1995). *Meaningful differences in the everyday experience of American children.* Baltimore, MD: Paul H. Brooks.

Healy, J. M. (1990). *Endangered minds: Why children don't think and what we can do about it.* New York: Rockefeller Center.

Hewett, F. M., & Taylor, F. D. (1980). *The emotionally disturbed child in the classroom: The orchestration of success* (2nd ed.). Boston: Allyn & Bacon.

Hieneman, M., Nolan, M., Presley, J., DeTuro, L., Gayler, W., & Dunlap, G. (1999). *Facilitator's guide, positive behavioral support.* Tallahassee: Florida Department of Education, Bureau of Instructional Support and Community Services.

Horner, R. H., & Carr, E. G. (1997). Behavioral support for students with severe disabilities: Functional assessment and comprehensive intervention. *Journal of Special Education, 31,* 84–104.

Hunter, R., & Kilstrom, N. (1979). Breaking the cycle in abusive families. *American Journal of Psychiatry, 136,* 1320–1322.

Hurford, D. P., Darrow, L. J., Edwards, T. L., Howerton, C. J., Mote, C., Schauf, J. D., & Coffey, P. (1993). An examination of phonemic processing abilities in children during their first grade year. *Journal of Learning Disabilities, 26*(3), 167–177.

Individuals with Disabilities Education Act of 1997, 20 U.S.C.A. Chapter 33, Sections 1400—1491 (Statute). Reauthorized 2004.

Iwata, B. A. (1995). *FAST: Functional Assessment Screening Tool.* Gainesville, FL: Florida Center on Self-Injury.

Jacobson, B. (1987). *Effects of structured positive school environment on future success of emotionally disturbed bright underachievers.* Austin: University of Texas.

Janoff-Bulman, R. (1993). *Shattered assumptions.* New York: Free Press.

Johns, B., & Carr, V. (2001). *Techniques for managing verbally and physically aggressive students.* Denver, CO: Love.

Johnson, J. (1988). *Use of groups in schools.* Lanham, MD: University Press of America.

Johnston, P., & Pearson, P. (1982). *Prior knowledge, connectivity, and the assessment of reading comprehension* (Technical Report 245). Urbana: University of Illinois, Center for Study of Reading.

Johnston, P., & Winograd, P. (1985). Passive failure in reading. *Journal of Reading Behavior, 17*(4), 279–301.

Kameenui, E., & Carnine, D. (1998). *Effective teaching strategies that accommodate diverse learners.* Upper Saddle River, NJ: Prentice Hall.

Kameenui, E., Simmons, D., Baker, S., Chard, D., Dickson, S., Gunn, B., Linn, S.-J., Smith, S., & Sprick, M. (1994). *Research synthesis in early reading and literacy: Curriculum guidelines for diverse learners* (Monograph for the National Center to Improve Tools for Educators). Eugene: University of Oregon.

Katz, M. (1997). *On playing a poor hand well: Insights from the lives of those who have overcome childhood risks and adversities.* New York: Norton.

Kauffman, J. (2001). *Characteristics of emotional and behavioral disorders of children and youth* (7th ed.). Upper Saddle River, NJ: Merrill Prentice Hall.

Kea, C. (1998). Focus on ethnic and minority concerns. In *Council for Children with Behavioral Disorders Newsletter.* Reston, VA: Council for Exceptional Children.

Kehle, T. J., Bray, M. A., Theodore, L. A., Jenson, W. R., & Clark, E. (2000). A multi-component intervention designed to reduce disruptive classroom behavior. *Psychology in the Schools, 37*(5), 475–481.

Kendall, P. C. (1991). *Child and adolescent therapy: Cognitive-behavioral procedures.* New York: Guilford.

Kerr, R. (1990). *Positively! Learning to manage negative emotions.* Portland, ME: J. Weston Walsh.

Kerr, (1997). *Positively! Learning to manage negative emotions* (2nd ed.). Portland, ME: J. Weston Walsh.

Kid Tools Support System. (1993). *Kid tools.* Columbia: University of Missouri.

Kieran, C., & Chalouh, L. (1993). Pre-algebra: The transition from arithmetic to algebra. In D. T. Owens (Ed.), *Research ideas for the classroom: Middle grades mathematics.* Reston, VA: National Council for Teachers of Mathematics.

Kincaid, L. (1997). *Aesop's fables.* Newmarket, England: Brimax Books.

Kohn, A. (1993). *Punished by rewards: The trouble with gold stars, incentive plans, a's, praise, and other bribes.* Boston: Houghton Mifflin.

Koplewicz, H. (1996). *It's nobody's fault: New help and hope for difficult children.* New York: Random House.

Kounin, J. (1970). *Discipline and group management in the classroom.* New York: Holt, Rinehart, & Winston.

Kriegler, S. (2002). *Just what is algebraic thinking?* Retrieved March 25, 2006, at http://www.math.ucla.edu/~kriegler/pub/algebrat.html.

Larson, K. A., & Gerber, M. M. (1987). Effects of social metacognitive training for enhancing overt behavior in learning disabled and low achieving delinquents. *Exceptional Children, 54,* 201–211.

Lavoie, R. (1994). *Learning disabilities and social skills: Last one picked, first one picked on.* Washington, DC: WETA-TV. Available at www.Idonline.org.

Lavoie, R. (1996). *When the chips are down.* Washington, DC: WETA-TV. Available at www.Idonline.org.

Lawlis, F. (2004). *The ADD answer: How to help your child now.* New York: Penguin Books.

Lazarus, R. (1991). Cognition and motivation in emotion. *American Psychologist, 46,* 352–367.

Levine, M. (2002). *A mind at a time.* New York: Simon & Schuster.

Lewis, T., Sugai, G., & Colvin, G. (1998). Reducing problem behavior through a school-wide system of effective behavioral support: Investigation of a school-wide social skills training program and contextual interventions. *The School of Psychology Review, 27*(3), 446-459.

Litow, L., & Pomroy, D. K. (1975). A brief review of classroom group-oriented contingencies. *Journal of Applied Behavior Analysis, 8,* 341–347.

Lyon, G. R. (1998). Why reading is not a natural process. *Educational Leadership, 55*(6), 14–18.

MacMillan, D., Gresham, F., & Forness, S. (1996). Full inclusion: An empirical perspective. *Behavioral Disorders, 21*(2), 145–159.

Maguin, E., & Loeber, R. (1996). Academic performance and delinquency. In M. Tonry (Ed.), *Crime and justice: A review of research.* Chicago: University of Chicago Press.

Malone, L., & Mastropieri, M. (1992). Reading comprehension instruction: Summarization and self-monitoring training for students with learning disabilities. *Exceptional Children, 58*(3), 270–279.

Mann, V. (1993). Phoneme awareness and future reading ability. *Journal of Learning Disabilities, 26*(4), 259–269.

Manning, B. H. (1988). Application of cognitive behavior modification: First and third graders' self-management of classroom behaviors. *American Educational Research Journal, 25,* 193–212.

Mannix, D. (1993). *Social skills activities for special children.* West Nyack, NY: The Center for Applied Research in Education.

Marchant, G., Paulson, S., & Rothlisberg, B. (2001). Relations of middle school students' perceptions of family and school contexts with academic achievement. *Psychology in the Schools, 38*(6), 505–519.

Maslow, A. (1962). *Motivation and personality.* New York: Harper & Row.

Masten, A. S. (1994). Resilience in individual development: Successful adaptation despite risk and adversity. In M. C. Wang & E. W. Gordon (Eds.), *Educational resilience in inner-city America* (pp. 3–26). Mahwah, NJ: Erlbaum.

McGinnis, E., & Goldstein, A. (1999). *Skillstreaming the elementary school child.* Champaign, IL: Research Press.

McLoughlin, J. A., & Lewis, R. B. (2001). *Assessing students with special needs* (5th ed.). Columbus, OH: Merrill Prentice Hall.

Meadows, N., Neel, R., Scott, C., & Parker, G. (1994). Academic performance, social competence, and mainstream accommodations: A look at mainstreamed and nonmainstreamed students with behavioral disorders. *Behavioral Disorders, 19*(3), 170–180.

Miller, S., Crawford, D., Harness, M., & Hollenbeck, K. (1994). *Research synthesis in social studies: Curriculum guidelines for diverse learners* (Monograph for the national center to improve tools for educators). Eugene: University of Oregon.

Morgan, S. R., & Reinhart, J. A. (1991). *Interventions for students with emotional disorders.* Austin, TX: Pro-Ed.

Morse, W. C. (1985). *The education and treatment of socioemotionally impaired children and youth.* Syracuse, NY: Syracuse University Press.

Moss, D. M. (1989). *Shelley, the hyperactive turtle.* Bethesda, MD: Woodbine House.

Mount, B. (1992). *Person-centered planning: Finding directions for change using personal futures planning.* New York: Graphics Futures.

Murphy, L., & Moriarity, A. (1986). *Vulnerability, coping, and growth.* New Haven, CT: Yale University Press.

National Council of Teachers of Mathematics. (1989). *Curriculum and evaluation standards for school mathematics.* Reston, VA: Author. (ERIC Document Reproduction Service No. ED 304336)

Nelson, C., & Pearson, C. (1994). Juvenile delinquency in the context of culture and community. In R. L. Peterson & S. Ishi-Jordan (Eds.), *Cultural and community contexts for emotional and behavioral disorders* (pp. 78–90). Boston: Brookline Press.

Nelson, J. R., Smith, D. J., Young, R. K., & Dodd, J. M. (1991). A review of self-management outcome research conducted with students who exhibit behavioral disorders. *Behavioral Disorders, 16,* 169–179.

Nichols, P. (1993). Some rewards, more punishment: A look at application of behaviorism. *Beyond Behavior, 5*(1), 4–13.

Nichols, P. (1998). Teaching thinking skills—A class act. *Beyond Behavior, 9*(1), 12–19.

Oneill, R. E., Horner, R. H., Albin, R. W., Sprague, J. R., Storey, K., & Newton, J. S. (1997). *Functional assessment and program development for problem behavior* (2nd ed.). Pacific Grove, CA: Brooks/Cole.

Palincsar, A. S., David, Y. M., Winn, J. A., & Stevens, D. D. (1991). Examining the context of strategy instruction. *Remedial and Special Education, 12*(3), 43–53.

Paris, S. G., & Oka, E. R. (1986). Self-regulated learning among exceptional children. *Exceptional Children, 53*(2), 103–108.

Paris, S., Wasik, B., & Turner, J. (1991). The development of strategic readers. In R. Barr, M. Kamil, P. Mosenthal, & P. Pearson (Eds.), *Handbook of reading research* (Vol. 2, pp. 609–640). New York: Longman.

Pearpoint, J., O'Brian, J., & Forest, M. (1993). PATH: *A workbook for planning possible futures.* Toronto: Inclusion Press.

Peng, S. (1994). Understanding resilient students: The use of national longitudinal databases. In. M. Wang & E. Gorden (Eds.), *Educational resilience in inner-city America* (pp. 73–84). Mahwah, NJ: Erlbaum.

Piaget, J. (1970). *The science of education and the psychology of the child.* New York: Orion Press.

Premack, D. (1959). Toward empirical behavior laws: I. Positive reinforcement. *Psychology Review, 66,* 219–233.

Pressley, M. (1979). Increasing children's self-control through cognitive interventions. *Review of Educational Research, 49,* 319–370.

Pressley, M., Borkowski, J., & Schneider, W. (1989). Good information processing: What it is and what education can do to promote it. *International Journal of Educational Research, 13,* 857–867.

Quinn, P., & Stern, J. (1993). *The "putting on the brakes" activity book for young people with ADHD.* Washington, DC: Magination Press.

Quinn, P., & Stern, J. (2001). *Putting on the brakes: Young people's guide to understanding attention deficit hyperactivity disorder.* Washington, DC: Maination Press.

Redl, F. (1966). *When we deal with children.* New York: Free Press.

Rhodes, G., Jenson, W. R., & Reavis, H. K. (1993). *The tough kid book: Practical classroom management strategies.* Longmont, CO: Sopris West.

Rockwell, S. (1993). *Tough to reach, tough to teach: Students with behavior problems.* Reston, VA: Council for Exceptional Children.

Rockwell, S. (1995). *Back off, cool down, try again: Teaching students how to control aggressive behavior.* Reston, VA: Council for Exceptional Children.

Rockwell, S. (1999). *Center placement for students with severe emotional disturbances: Factors that contribute to positive outcomes.* Doctoral dissertation, University of South Florida.

Rockwell, S. (2006). *Tough to reach, tough to teach: Students with behavior problems* (2nd ed.). Arlington, VA: Council for Exceptional Children.

Rockwell, S., Cuccio, S., Kirtley, B., & Smith, G. (1998). *Developing personal and interpersonal responsibility in children and youth with emotional/behavioral disorders.* Reston, VA: Council for Exceptional Children.

Rockwell, S., & Guetzloe, E. C. (1996). Group development for students with emotional and behavioral disorders. *Teaching Exceptional Children, 29*(1), 38–43.

Rosenshine, B. (1971). Objectively measured behavioral predictors of effectiveness in explaining. In I. O. Westbury & H. A. Bellack (Eds.), *Research classroom processes.* New York: Teachers College Press.

Rosenshine, B. (1986). Synthesis of research on explicit teaching. *Educational Leadership, 43*(7), 60–69.

Rottman, T. R., & Cross, D. R. (1990). Using informed strategies for learning to enhance the reading and thinking skills of children with learning disabilities. *Journal of Learning Disabilities, 23*(5), 270–278.

Rutter, M. (1979). Protective factors in children's responses to stress and disadvantage. In M. Whalen-Dent. (Ed.), *Primary prevention of psychopathology: Vol. 3: Promoting social competence and coping in children* (pp. 49–74). Hanover, NH: University Press of New England.

Rutter, M., & Quinton, D. (1984). Long-term follow-up of women institutionalized in childhood: Factors promoting good functioning in adult life. *British Journal of Developmental Psychology, 18,* 225–234.

Sasso, G., Conroy, M., Stichter, M., & Fox, J. (2001). Slowing down the bandwagon: The misapplication of functional assessment for students with emotional/behavioral disorders. *Behavioral Disorders, 26*(4), 282–296.

Scheuermann, B., & Evans, W. (1997). Hippocrates was right, do no harm: Ethics in the selection of interventions. *Beyond Behavior, 8*(3), 18–22.

Schmidt, F., Friedman, A., & Marvel, J. (1992). *Mediation for kids.* Miami Beach, FL: Grace Contrino Abrams Peace Education Foundation.

Schneider, B., & Byrne, B. (1984). Predictors of successful transition from self-contained special education to regular class settings. *Psychology in the Schools, 21,* 375–380.

Schunk, D., & Rice, J. (1992). Influence of reading comprehension strategy information on children's achievement outcomes. *Learning Disability Quarterly, 15*(4), 51–64.

Scott, R. M., & Nelson, C. M. (1999). Functional behavioral assessment: Implications for training and staff development. *Behavioral Disorders, 24,* 70–84.

Seligman, M. (1995). *The optimistic child.* New York: Harper Perennial.

Shinn, M. R., & Hubbard, D. D. (1993). Curriculum-based measurement: Basic procedures and outcomes. In E. L. Meyen, G. A. Vergason, & J. R. Whelan (Eds.), *Educating students with mild disabilities* (pp. 221–253). Denver, CO: Love.

Short, R., & Shapiro, S. (1993). Conduct disorders: A framework for understanding and intervention in schools and communities. *School Psychology Review, 22*(3), 362–375.

Simmonds, E. P. (1990). The effectiveness of two methods for teaching a constraint seeking questioning strategy to students with learning disabilities. *Journal of Learning Disabilities, 23*(4), 229–233.

Singer, J., & Salovey, P. (1993). *The remembered self: Emotion and memory in personality.* New York: Free Press.

Slater, L. (1996). *Welcome to my country: A therapist's memoir of madness.* New York: Anchor Books.

Smith, S. (1988). Teaching the fourth r—relationships. *Pointer, 32*(3), 23–33.

Smith, S. W. (1990). Individualized education programs (IEPs) in special education: From intent to acquiescence. *Exceptional Children, 57,* 6–14.

Smith, S. (1991). Succeeding against the odds: How the learning-disabled can realize their promise. New York: Penguin Putnam.

Smith, S., Siegel, E., O'Conner, A., & Thomas, S. (1994). Effects of cognitive-behavioral training on angry behavior and aggression of three elementary-aged students. *Behavioral Disorders, 19*(2), 126–135.

Sparks, R. (1980). *The behavior-learning problems program of the Cincinnati public schools: A follow-up study.* Cincinnati, OH: University of Cincinnati.

Sorenson, E. S. (1993). *Children's stress and coping: A family perspective.* New York: Guilford.

Stage, S. A., & Quiroz, D. R. (1997). A meta-analysis of interventions to decrease disruptive classroom behavior in public education settings. *School Psychology Review, 26,* 333–368.

Stallard, P. (2002). *Think good—feel good: A cognitive behavior therapy workbook for children and young people.* Hoboken, NJ: Wiley.

Stanovich, K. (1991). Word recognition: Changing perspectives. In R. Barr, M. Kamil, P. Mosenthal, & P. Pearson (Eds.), *Handbook of reading research* (Vol. 2, pp. 418–452). New York: Longman.

Sugai, G., Horner, R., Dunlap, G., Hieneman, M., Lewis, T., Nelson, C. M., Scott, T., Liaupsin, C., Sailor, W., Turnbull, A., Turnbull, R., Wickham, D., Ruef, M., Wilcox, B. (2000). Applying positive behavioral support and functional behavioral assessment in schools. *Journal of Positive Behavioral Interventions, 2,* 131–143.

Swanson, H. L. (1989). Strategy instruction: Overview of principles and procedures for effective use. *Learning Disability Quarterly, 12*(1), 3–14.

Terr, L. (1990). *Too scared to cry.* New York: Basic Books.

Torgesen, J., & Mathes, P. (1998). *What every teacher should know about phonological awareness.* Tallahassee: Florida Department of Education.

Trower, T. (1995). *Self-control patrol workbook.* Plainview, NY: Childswork, Childsplay.

Tuckman, B. W. (1965). Developmental sequences in small groups. *Psychological Bulletin, 63,* 384–399.

Tuckman, B. W., & Jensen, M. A. (1977). Stages of small group development revisited. *Group and Organization, 3,* 419–427.

Turecki, S. (1989). *The difficult child.* New York: Bantam Books.

Turecki, S. (2000). *The difficult child* (2nd ed.). New York: Bantam Books.

Turnbull, A. P., & Turnbull, A. R. (1990). *Families, professionals, and exceptionality: A special partnership.* New York: Merrill.

Turnbull, A., & Turnbull, R. (1992, Fall & Winter). Group action planning (GAP). *Families and Disability Newsletter,* pp. 1–13.

Usiskin, Z. (1997). Doing algebra in Grades K–4. *Teaching Children Mathematics, 3,* 346–356.

U.S. Department of Health and Human Services. (2001). *Report of the surgeon general's conference on children's mental health: A national action agenda.* Washington, DC: Author.

Vernon, A. (1989). *Thinking, feeling, behaving: An emotional education curriculum for children, grades 1–6.* Champaign, IL: Research Press.

Walker, H., Colvin, G., & Ramsey, E. (1995). *Antisocial behavior in school: Strategies and best practices.* Pacific Grove, CA: Brooks/Cole.

Wallace, G., Larsen, S., & Elksnin, L. (1992). *Educational assessment of learning problems: Testing for teaching* (2nd ed.). Boston: Allyn & Bacon.

Weisberg, R. (1988). 1900s: A change in focus of reading comprehension research: A review of reading/learning disabilities research based on an interactive model of reading. *Learning Disability Quarterly, 11*(2), 149–159.

Werner, E. (1989). High risk children in young adulthood: A longitudinal study from birth to 32 years. *American Journal of Orthopsychiatry, 59,* 72–81.

Werner, E. (1996). Risk and resilience in individuals with learning disabilities: Lessons learned form the Kauai longitudinal study. In S. Green (Project Director), *Timely issues in print series: The resilience factor* (pp. 86–92). Greenville, NC: East Carolina University Press.

Werner, E., & Smith, R. (1982). *Vulnerable but invincible: A longitudinal study of resilient children and youth.* New York: McGraw-Hill.

Williams, B., & Carnine, D. (1981). Relationship between range of examples and of instructions and attention in concept attainments. *Journal of Educational Research, 74*(3), 144–148.

Wolin, S. J., & Wolin, S. (1993). *The resilient self: How survivors of troubled families rise above adversity.* New York: Villard Books.

Wood, F. (1996). Life stories and behavior change. *Beyond Behavior, 7*(1), 8–14.

Wood, M. M., & Long, N. J. (1991). *Life space intervention: Talking with children and youth in crisis.* Austin, TX: Pro-Ed.

Wong, B. Y., & Wong, R. (1986). Study behaviors as a function of metacognitive knowledge about critical task variables: An investigation of above average, average, and learning disabled readers. *Learning Disabilities Research, 1*(2), 101–111.

Yell, M. L. (1993). Cognitive-behavior modification. In T. J. Zirpoli & K. J. Melloy (Eds.), *Behavior management: Applications for teachers and parents* (pp. 199–241). New York: MacMillan.

Zionts, P. (1996). *Teaching disturbed and disturbing students: An integrative approach* (2nd ed.). Austin, TX: Pro-Ed.

Index